Who Took My MONEY?

Why Slow Investors Lose and
Fast Money Wins!

Other Bestselling Books by
Robert T. Kiyosaki & Sharon L. Lechter

Rich Dad Poor Dad
What The Rich Teach Their Kids About Money That The Poor And Middle Class Do Not

Rich Dad's CASHFLOW Quadrant
Rich Dad's Guide To Financial Freedom

Rich Dad's Guide to Investing
What The Rich Invest In That The Poor And Middle Class Do Not

Rich Dad's Rich Kid Smart Kid
Give Your Child A Financial Head Start

Rich Dad's Retire Young Retire Rich
How To Get Rich Quickly And Stay Rich Forever

Rich Dad's Prophecy
Why The Biggest Stock Market Crash In History Is Still Coming...
And How You Can Prepare Yourself And Profit From It!

Rich Dad's Success Stories
Real Life Success Stories from Real Life People
Who Followed the Rich Dad Lessons

Rich Dad's Guide To Becoming Rich
Without Cutting Up Your Credit Cards
Turn "Bad Debt" into "Good Debt"

Rich Dad's Who Took My Money?
Why Slow Investors Lose and Fast Money Wins!

WHO TOOK MY MONEY?

Why Slow Investors Lose and
Fast Money Wins!

By Robert T. Kiyosaki with Sharon L. Lechter, C.P.A.
The Authors of *Rich Dad Poor Dad*

WARNER
BUSINESS
BOOKS™

NEW YORK   BOSTON

This publication is designed to provide competent and reliable information regarding the subject matter covered. However, it is sold with the understanding that the author and publisher are not engaged in rendering legal, financial, or other professional advice. Laws and practices often vary from state to state and if legal or other expert assistance is required, the services of a professional should be sought. The authors and publisher specifically disclaim any liability that is incurred from the use or application of the contents of this book.

Warner Business Books
Warner Books

Time Warner Book Group
1271 Avenue of the Americas, New York, NY 10020
Visit our Web site at www.twbookmark.com.

The Warner Business Books logo is a trademark of Warner Books.

Printed in the United States of America

First Printing: May 2004
10   9   8   7   6   5   4   3   2   1

Library of Congress Cataloging-in-Publication Data

Kiyosaki, Robert T.
    Rich dad's who took my money? : why slow investors lose and fast money wins / Robert T. Kiyosaki with Sharon L. Lechter.—1st Warner Books Printing
        p.   cm.
    ISBN 0-446-69182-8
    1. Investments.   2. Finance, Personal.   I. Lechter, Sharon L.   II. Title.

HG4521.K563   2004
332.6—dc22   2004000828

Contents

Authors' Note

This book is for the person who wants more control over their money and wants to beat the average returns of average investors. This book will not tell you exactly what to do . . . that is because what you do to become rich and how you do it is really up to you . . . yet this book will help guide you in understanding why some investors achieve much higher returns than the average investor, with less risk and less money, and in much less time.

Ninety percent of investors are average investors and should continue saving, investing in mutual funds and their 401(k) and retirement funds. The information in this book is for the 10 percent who want to educate themselves to become professional investors and increase their investment returns and accelerate the growth of their financial portfolios.

Thank you.

Robert T. Kiyosaki
Sharon L. Lechter

How You Can Turn $10,000 into $10 Million in Ten Years

"Americans' greatest fear is running out of money during retirement."

— *USA TODAY* survey

"The primary reason people struggle financially is because they take financial advice from poor people or salespeople."

— RICH DAD

In December of 2002, a local newspaper in Phoenix, Arizona, ran an article on my book *Rich Dad's Prophecy*, which had just been released in October of the same year. I was surprised to find the article fair and balanced. The reason I was surprised is because many financial journalists did not have many nice things to say about this book.

Although it was a fair and balanced article, the journalist closed with one offhand remark that disturbed me. What disturbed me was his comment about my 39 percent return on my last investment. I felt his comment insinuated that I was either lying or exaggerating about my returns.

Now, most of us dislike people who brag or exaggerate. I know I don't care for such people. My problem with his remark was that I was not bragging or exaggerating. In fact, I was doing exactly the opposite—I was actually understating my return. In other words, my return was not just a paper return. My cash-on-cash return was measured in real money in my pocket, and the return was much higher than 39 percent.

I allowed his comment to bother me for several days. Finally, I called and asked for an appointment so I could set the record straight. I told him that I did not expect him to write anything more about me or publish a retraction. All I asked was that I go to his office with my accountant, show him my records, and explain how the 39 percent was achieved. His reply was cordial and we set an appointment.

After my accountant and I explained to him how the 39 percent was achieved and why it was actually understated, his only comment was, "Well, the average investor cannot do what you do."

My reply to that comment was, "I never said they could."

He then said, "What you do is too risky."

My response to that statement was, "In the last few years, millions of investors have lost trillions of dollars, much of it from stocks and mutual funds, which you recommend. Many people who lost money investing for the long term in mutual funds will never be able to retire. Isn't that risky?"

"Well, that was because there was a lot of corporate corruption," he replied defensively.

"That is partially true. But how much of the losses are due to bad advice, advice from financial planners, stockbrokers, and financial journalists? If investing for the long term in mutual funds is such a great idea, why did so many people lose so much money?"

"I stand by my advice," was his reply. "I still say that investing for the long term and diversifying in a portfolio of mutual funds is the best plan for the average investor."

"I agree," I replied. "Your advice is the best advice for the average investor . . . but not for me."

My accountant, Tom, then chimed in and said, "With a slight shift in focus and the use of different assets, the average investor could achieve much higher returns with much less risk. Rather than sit and watch the market jump up and down, listening to financial gurus trying to predict the next hot stock to pick, using Robert's rich dad's plan, an investor doesn't have to panic each time the market drops, or worry about which sector is going to go up next. Not only does the investor achieve much higher returns, with less money and less risk, money comes in automatically, like magic. In fact, I often call this strategy of investing *magic money.*"

The idea of a 39 percent return—and now *magic money*—was a little too much for such a short meeting with this journalist. With the mention of "magic money," the meeting was over.

As I said, the journalist was cordial and open-minded. A few weeks later, he wrote another article about me, even though I did not ask for it. While the article was accurate, he did not mention how I achieved high returns or anything about magic money.

The most important thing I am grateful to him for is the inspiration to write this book . . . a book that is *not* for the average investor.

FAQ (Frequently Asked Questions)

After the meeting with the journalist, I decided to write this book. I decided it was time to explain rich dad's formula for turning a small investment into an ultra-high return. This book would also offer me an opportunity to answer some frequently asked questions . . . questions I often avoid answering . . . questions such as:

1. "I have $10,000. What should I invest it in?"
2. "What type of investment do you recommend?"
3. "How do I get started?"

The main reason I have hesitated answering such questions is because the truthful answer is, "It depends on you. What I *would* do is often different from what you *should* do."

Another reason I hesitate answering such questions is because when I have answered such questions, explaining to people exactly what I do and how I achieve high returns with less money and less risk, their responses are often:

1. "You can't do that here."
2. "I can't afford it."
3. "Isn't there an easier way?"

Why So Many People Lose

In my opinion, one of the reasons millions of people lost trillions of dollars between the years 2000 and 2003 is because they were looking for easy answers as to where to invest their money . . . and there were many people ready to supply the easy answers . . . easy answers such as:

1. "Save money."
2. "Invest for the long term and diversify."
3. "Cut up your credit cards and get out of debt."

This book is *not* written for people who want easy answers. If you like the overly simplified financial answers most people are willing to accept, then this book is probably not for you. My answers may seem too hard or too difficult for most people.

This book is written for those who want to take more control over their money and make a lot more money with their money. If this is of interest to you, then please read on.

The Worst Way to Get Rich

While the journalist was correct in saying that his advice was great for the average investor, the facts are that his advice is one of the hardest ways to get rich. People with a job who put money into a retirement plan such as a 401(k) filled with mutual funds are taking the slow bus through life—and it is a bus with a worn-out engine, which means it does not go fast and does not ever reach the peaks of financial returns. It is also a bus that has bad brakes, which makes going down hills frightening.

While putting money into a retirement plan for the long term might be a good idea for average investors, to me, it is a slow, risky, inefficient, highly taxed way to invest.

There Are Better Investments

When asked the question "What should I invest in?" I will show the following chart if I have it handy.

While showing the chart, I add, "There are three different asset classes, which are *businesses, real estate,* and *paper assets*. The following compares two of the three assets. The chart compares real estate against investing in the S&P 500 index, which is what most average investors should invest in. I'll let the chart do the talking. I believe it shows the difference between mountain peaks and hills.

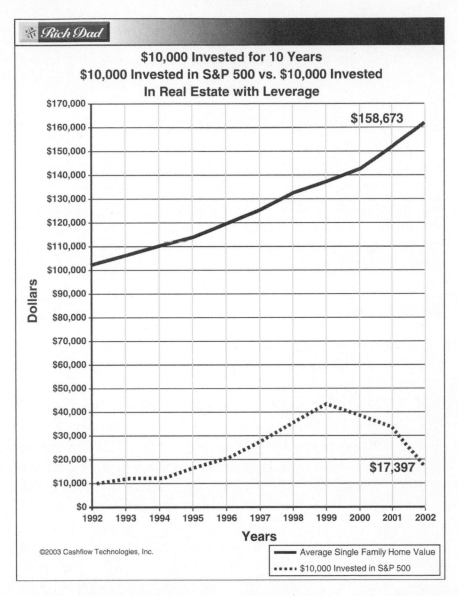

Explaining further I say, "A good simple investment is to put money into an S&P 500 index fund. For most mutual fund managers, the S&P 500 is their benchmark to beat; unfortunately, very few beat it."

That often brings up the question, "Why do you need a fund manager if few can beat the S&P? Why not just invest that money myself in the S&P?"

My reply is, "I ask the same question." Continuing, I say, "If you invest

$10,000 in real estate, you actually increase the basis of your investment using 90 percent leverage, in this case $90,000 of your banker's money. In the years between 1992 and 2002, your $10,000 in the S&P 500 would have increased to $17,397 and your $10,000 along with your banker's money would have gone up to nearly $158,673."

After people look at the chart for a while, the next question I often hear from them is, "Why don't more people invest in real estate?"

My reply is, "Because to invest in real estate, you have to be a better investor. Investing successfully in real estate not only requires more financial skills, investing in real estate is much more capital-intensive and management-intensive. Getting into paper assets such as mutual funds is much easier, less expensive, and requires very little management, which is why so many more people invest in them."

Average Returns

I point out, however, that the returns on the chart for real estate is a national average, and averages can be deceiving. In reality, returns on real estate were much higher in certain parts of the country and much lower in others. I explain: "The S&P 500 is an *international* market, while real estate is a *local* market. That means if you are a savvy real estate investor, you can often achieve even higher returns in real estate. Your $10,000 in the S&P 500 would achieve the same returns as everyone else received . . . while your $10,000 in real estate, during the same period, could be much higher than $158,673 or much lower. If you are a horrible real estate investor and property manager, you could lose the entire $10,000 you invested and possibly even more. If you are not good at real estate acquisition and management, you would be better off investing in the S&P 500. Success in real estate depends upon *you* as the investor. Success in the S&P depends upon the S&P 500 companies.

To the question "Can even higher gains than $158,673 be achieved from $10,000?" the answer is "Yes—but to achieve those returns, an investor often needs to use the power of a business." Of the three asset classes, a business is the most powerful of all assets, but it requires the most skill to start, build, and manage. For a person who is good at building a business and also good at investing in real estate, ultra-high returns are possible . . . returns that do not fit on the chart comparing the S&P against real estate. In other words, the returns are *off the chart.*

How to Achieve Ultra-High Returns

While some of the content of this book has been covered in other *Rich Dad* books, this book will go further into how ultra-high investment returns can be achieved than I have ever written about before. I will introduce the *accelerators* of money that my rich dad taught me about.

In this book you will find out why *diversifying* and *investing for the long term* is often not the best investment advice and why many people lose money in the market following that advice.

One of the best-kept secrets of successful investors is not *diversifying* but *integrating*. Rather than just investing in one asset, successful investors integrate two or three of the asset classes, and then *accelerate, leverage,* and *protect* the cash flowing through the assets. For example, Bill Gates became the richest man in the world by integrating the power of a business and the power of paper assets. He achieved the dream of many an entrepreneur, the dream of building a business and taking the business public through the stock market. In other words, he turned part of his business into paper, often known as "shares." If Bill Gates had not taken his company public, he would probably still be rich, but he might not have become the richest man in the world at such a young age. Simply put, it was the *integration* of two asset classes that *accelerated* his wealth. He did not become the richest man in the world from his salary as an employee of Microsoft and diversifying his salary into mutual funds.

Donald Trump achieves greater returns on his money by owning a business that invests in real estate. And Warren Buffett, the greatest investor in the world, achieves extremely high returns by owning a business that invests in other businesses.

Big Business Versus Small Business

This does not mean your business must be big or be in the business of real estate. The point is, an investor could own a small business and also invest in real estate. It is like having two professions, one profession for the person and one profession for their money, which I recommend. For example, the profession I am most known for is as an author. That is my profession. My money's profession is real estate. Again, the important point is *integration* of two or three asset classes rather than *diversification* within just one asset.

Even if you are a small business owner, you can take advantage of the same financial advantages as a big business. Just as a big business and the stock market made Bill Gates a multibillionaire, a small business and real estate and paper assets can make you a multimillionaire in less than ten years. The question is, *Can you become very good at investing in at least two different assets or asset classes?* If you can, financial magic can happen.

Synergy Versus Diversification

What you will learn about in this book is rich dad's formula for ultra-high returns. Rich dad taught his son and me to have strong advisors, and then to integrate and accelerate the power of these financial forces. These financial forces are:

1. Business
2. Real estate
3. Paper assets
4. Your banker's money
5. Tax laws
6. Corporate laws

Integrate means to combine and operate together. Diversify means to separate and operate apart.

If a person can integrate and accelerate all six of these forces, a person can achieve ultra-high returns, starting with very little money. If a person does an outstanding job—integrating all six of these forces—then magic money, or financial synergy, occurs.

What Is Synergy?

The word "synergy" is often defined as "the whole is greater than the sum of the parts." In simpler terms, it means $1 + 1 = 4 \ldots$ the sum, in this case 4, is greater than the parts, or the $1 + 1$.

Another example of synergy: Let's say you take a pumpkin seed and a pile of dirt. Dirt alone will not cause the seed to grow, even if you keep piling more and more dirt on top of the seed. If you add sunlight and water, in the proper combinations, to the pile of dirt, suddenly the seed begins to grow. It is the *synergy* among the dirt, sun, and water that causes the magic in the seed to occur. The same thing happens with money. With the right components, your money can grow like magic. If your money is only buried under a pile of diversified dirt, it may turn into a *mushroom* but it will not turn into *magic money.*

The Power of Synergy

This book is about how you can harness your money using the different financial forces and creating financial synergy . . . aka *magic money.*

Obviously, *this book is not for the average investor.* Repeating what the journalist said to me, when I explained how I attained a 39 percent return, "Well, the average investor cannot do what you do."

And repeating my reply to that comment, "I never said they could."

This book is for people who do not like turning their money over to strangers and then hoping and praying their money will still be there when they need it. This book is for the person who wants more control over his or her money and wants to beat the average returns of average investors. This book will not tell you exactly what to do—that is because what you do to become rich and how you do it is really up to you—yet this book will help guide you in understanding why some investors achieve much higher returns than the average investor, with less risk and less money, and in much less time.

Can You Make $10 Million Investing $10,000 in Mutual Funds?

Does this mean that after reading this book, you will be able to achieve similar results with your $10,000? Again the answer is, "It depends on you."

A more important question may be, "Do you think you can turn $10,000 into $10 million in ten years investing *only* in mutual funds?" The same question can be asked of someone who invests *only* in real estate. The answer in most cases is no. It is very difficult to achieve ultra-high returns from one asset class alone, which is what most people attempt to do. If they do invest in different asset classes, and integrate the power of the different asset accelerators, doing so will create investment synergy and make it possible to achieve ultra-high returns.

The Number One Fear of Americans

During a talk, a young woman raised her hand and asked, "Why are ultra-high returns so important? What about getting rich slowly? What is so important about money anyway? Isn't being happy more important?"

Every time I talk about money and getting rich, there is always someone in the audience with what I would call the cynical "money is not important" attitude. This time, being prepared, I smiled and handed out an article from *USA Today.* The newspaper had done a survey and discovered that *Americans' number one fear is running out of money.* Their number one fear was not cancer, crime, or nuclear war. The new number one fear is running out of money in their old age. The new fear is living a long life without money. Most people realize that Social Security and Medicare may not even be around to assist them in their old age.

Letting the young woman read the article to the group, I wrote on my flip chart, "The Game of Money." Under that title I wrote the following:

The Game of Money	
Age	**Game Period**
25 to 35	*1st Quarter*
35 to 45	*2nd Quarter*
———— Halftime ————	
45 to 55	*3rd Quarter*
55 to 65	*4th Quarter*
Overtime	
Out-of-Time	

After the young woman had finished reading the article, I said, "Did you know that by the year 2010, 78 million Americans will be sixty-five or older? One in three has no retirement plan."

"I've heard that," she replied. "But why do you call it a game?"

Taking a breath and pointing to the ages on the flip chart, I said, "A game is often broken into quarters. For example, a professional football game is played in fifteen-minute quarters. For many people, we leave school around twenty-five and plan on retiring at age sixty-five. That means the game of money we play is forty years long, which means that a quarter of the game is ten years in length. Sometime during those forty years, we hope to earn and set aside enough money to retire on. I was able to get out of the game shortly after the end of the second quarter, age forty-seven. My wife, Kim, was able to win her game by age thirty-seven, shortly after the end of the first quarter. Do you understand what I am saying about the game?"

The young lady nodded, still clinging to the USA Today article. "And if they do not have enough money and work beyond age sixty-five, that is what you call 'overtime.'"

"That's correct. That might actually be good, since working will probably keep them healthier. The difference is between *having* to work and *wanting* to work."

"And 'out of time' means you are alive but physically unable to work any longer."

Nodding, I said, "That's correct." I then asked, "Without telling me your age, would you be willing to tell me which quarter of the game of money you are in and if you are still in the game or have won the game?"

"I don't mind telling you how old I am. I am thirty-two years old, which puts me in the first quarter of what you call the game of money." Pausing awhile, she continued, "And no, I am nowhere near winning the game. I am deeply in debt with school loans, house payments, car payments, taxes, and just day-to-day living, which are taking up most of what I earn."

After a long silence, allowing her words to echo around the room, I said, "Thank you for your honesty. And if you were beginning the fourth quarter of life, let's say you were fifty-five, and you had just lost a lot of money in the stock market, could you afford to invest for the long term? Could you afford another market downturn? Could you afford to work and wait while your money earns less than 10 percent per year?"

"No," she replied.

"Now can you understand why having enough money is important, and why increasing your financial intelligence, and creating higher returns in less time with less risk are important?"

At that she nodded.

Wanting to reinforce my point, I asked, "Now can you understand why it makes little sense to bet your financial future on the ups and downs of a stock market? Now can you understand why it's not smart to turn your money over to strangers who are guessing as to which stocks will be hot and which stocks will be cold. Does it make sense to work hard and pay more and more in taxes the older you get, and then realize you have nothing to show for a life of hard work?"

"No," she said.

Knowing that she understood why taking control of her money for higher returns was important, I quietly added, "And do you understand why the greatest fear for Americans is to run out of money when they are old?"

"Yes," she said, her voice quivering. "My mom and dad are terrified they will have to move in with me in a few years. I'm afraid of that also. I love them dearly, but I am their only child. I have a husband and three kids. How can my husband and I afford our young family, my parents as they get older, our children's education, and our own retirement?"

Don't Be a Victim

Again the room was silent. I could tell that many other people were faced with similar financial challenges. "It's not the $10 million that is so important," I said softly. "It's about taking control of your own financial future. It's about you learning to play your own game of money rather than letting someone else take your money and play the game for you. I'm not talking about you getting rich quick, yet you could. It is about understanding why the rich are getting richer and what you need to do to not be a victim of the game of money. I don't want you to be a victim of the game and of those that run the game. By understanding the game, you can have more control and then can take greater responsibility over your money and your financial future."

It Is Not Too Late

"Can I win the game?" the young woman asked.

"Sure," I replied. "It begins with a change in attitude. After a change of attitude, write up a ten-year plan. I repeat: It's not about getting rich quick. It's about learning the game and playing the game. Once you learn the game, the game becomes more fun. As the years go on, most people say, 'Why didn't I do this earlier? This is a fun game.'"

"And if I do not change, I don't have much of a chance of winning . . . do I?"

"Well, I don't have a crystal ball, but with three young kids, aging parents, plus your and your husband's own financial needs, I would say the game is winning right now—not you. It's never too late to start . . . so start as early as possible. All I ask is don't wait until all your money and your energy are gone; or take bad financial advice and invest for the long term only to find out that the investments you put your hard-earned money in did not perform as well as you expected; or simply keep working harder and harder, hoping your money problems will go away, or even worse, knowing that you will never be able to stop working. Please do not be like the millions of people who wake up one day and ask, *Who took my money?*"

The young woman nodded and took her seat. I could see she had a lot of thinking to do. She had to decide to take control over her money or simply hand it over to people she hoped were financially smarter than she was. That is a choice only she can make.

And that is what this book is about. This book is about the game of money and your choice to either turn control of your money over to someone to play the game for you—or you choosing to take control of your money, your future, and the game.

As my rich dad said, "If you take control of your money, you take control of your life." He also said, "Give your money to strangers and your money will work for the strangers—before your money works for you."

Sharon's Notes

Robert has asked me to add notes at the end of each chapter from my perspective as both an accountant and a businessperson. I was raised in the traditional way of go to school and get good grades so you can get a good job.

My husband, Michael, and I have enjoyed successful professional lives together but the opportunities for success that were available to us twenty-five years ago when we started are not as readily available to people today. With the access to information today, it has never been easier, or more important, to take control of your own and your family's financial destiny. *Who Took My Money?* offers alternative investing strategies that you may want to consider.

My notes will either highlight Robert's comments or add additional content for your use.

This Book Is Divided into Two Parts

The first part of this book is about the synergy of advisors and different points of view. The reason a synergy of advisors is important is because your mind is your greatest asset. By having the input of many different advisors, good and bad, and synergizing their advice, we greatly enhance the power of our minds . . . our greatest asset. Most of us leave school thinking we have to do it all on our own. This book will show you the value of creating a team of experts to assist you.

One reason so many people lose their money or fail to attain ultra-high financial returns is because they receive their financial advice from financial institutions and salespeople . . . not from successful investors.

Of all your assets, your mind is your greatest, so you need the best advice possible.

The second part of this book is about the synergy of different assets and other financial forces. This part of the book shows you how to put together the power of a business, real estate, paper assets, tax laws, your banker's money, and the power of corporate structures to achieve ultra-high financial returns, with less risk and less money.

For now I will introduce the following chart, which highlights the difference between how people from the left side of the CASHFLOW Quadrant typically invest their money, and how those from the right side of the CASHFLOW Quadrant, the business owner and investor, invest their money. Another way to distinguish these investment habits is that those on the left side of the Quadrant typically park their money (save), while professional investors on the right side want to keep their money constantly accelerating and growing. Keep this chart in mind as you read this book.

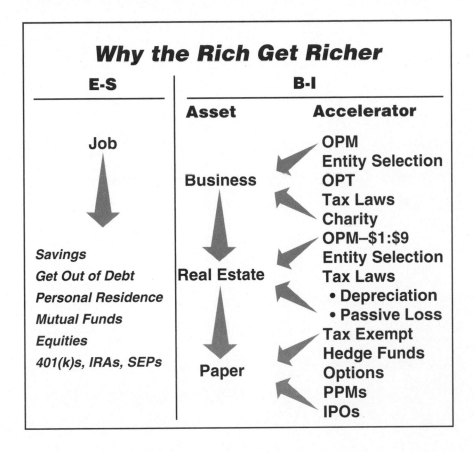

It was in developing this chart, near the end of writing this book, that Robert and I actually better understood our own methods of investment. It truly is the formula rich dad taught Robert and it is the formula Robert continues to use today.

The methods and vehicles used by rich dad, Robert, and other professional investors are analyzed and discussed. With a better understanding of the various asset classes and their related accelerators, you may discover new investment opportunities that can create a future of financial freedom for you and your family.

Part I

What Should
I Invest In?

"The better your investment education, the better
investment advice you will receive."

— RICH DAD

Chapter 1

Ask a Salesperson

"One of the first things you need to learn if you want to be a better investor is the difference between a sales pitch and sound investment advice."

— RICH DAD

"I have $10,000. What should I invest it in?" As mentioned in the introduction, for a number of years I really did not know how to answer this simple question. My early replies to this question were awkward, wordy, and rambling. The reason for my inability to answer such a simple question is simply because the appropriate answer is not that simple. We are all different. We come from different life paths, dreaming different dreams; emotionally we are wired differently, we have different financial backgrounds and different tolerances to financial risk. In other words, what *I* would do with $10,000 may not be what *you* should do with $10,000. In fact, what I did with $10,000 ten years ago is not what I would do with $10,000 today. As Einstein said, "It's all relative."

Finally, after being asked the same question enough times, I came up with an answer I believe is appropriate. Today, when asked the question, I reply, "If you do not know what to do with your money, put it in a bank, and do not tell anyone that you have money to invest." The reason I say this is because if *you* do not know what to do with your money, there are literally millions of people who do. When it comes to money, everyone has an opinion and advice on what to do with *your* money.

The Problem with Advice

The problem is that all advice is not good advice. Between March 2000 and March of 2003, millions of people lost $7 to $9 trillion in one of the biggest stock market crashes in history, many because they listened to the advice from so-called financial experts. The irony is, most of these financial experts are still handing out advice today and people are still listening to them.

During one of the worst stock market crashes in the history of the world, financial experts were advising people to keep their money in the market. Rather than sell, the experts told them to keep buying . . . and many people did keep buying, all the way down to the bottom.

There is an old saying that goes, "When taxi drivers are handing out stock tips, it's time to sell." Maybe that statement should be expanded to include financial advisors.

Voices of Sanity

During the insanity of the boom between 1995 and early 2000, two voices of sanity were Federal Reserve chairman Alan Greenspan and Warren Buffett, reportedly the world's greatest investor. Mr. Greenspan warned of *irrational exuberance* and Mr. Buffett simply stayed out of the stock market.

During the boom and the bust, Warren Buffett's name was often used in reference to smart investing. Financial advisors used his name as *the* authority figure as to why a person should get into the market. Financial advisors were saying, "Warren Buffett this and Warren Buffett that." When Warren Buffett's name was mentioned, people seemed to put more money into the market. What the advisors failed to tell their faithful investors was that Warren Buffett was *not* in the stock market.

In an interview in the November 11, 2002, edition of *Fortune* magazine, entitled "The Oracle of Everything," Mr. Buffett says, "I bought my first stock 60 years ago. Of those 60 years, 50 have been attractive to buy common stocks. In probably 10 years, I've not been able to find anything." One of the reasons he stopped buying stocks is simple. For those ten years, the period between 1992 and 2002, stocks were too expensive. I find it interesting that the world's greatest investor could not find anything to invest in, yet millions of first-time investors and their advisors did.

Criticizing the World's Greatest Investor

The article continues, noting that it was not too long ago, specifically at the height of the boom in early 2000, when many respected financial experts and publications began criticizing Mr. Buffett for *not* being in the market. One such expert, Harry Newton, publisher of *Technology Investor Magazine,* wrote, "Warren Buffett should say 'I'm sorry.' How did he miss the silicon, wireless, DSL, cable, and biotech revolutions?" A month later, the technology market collapsed, taking billions of dollars of investor money with it. Who should be saying "I'm sorry" today?

My Record

As a person who is often lumped into the group of so-called financial experts, it is important that you be aware of my record. In 2002, I received a phone call from a stockbroker in Baltimore, Maryland. He said, "I just finished reading your third book, *Rich Dad's Guide to Investing.* I congratulate you for predicting the crash of 2000. I wish I had told my clients to read that book before the market went down." Now, I do not believe I predicted the crash, I simply warned of it. But if you want to read the book, you can decide on the accuracy of my forecast.

The best testament to my record is not found in *my* record but in the records found in *Rich Dad's Success Stories,* the records of my readers. This is a book filled with personal stories of everyday people who did well financially, many between 2000 and 2003, the same period millions were losing trillions. So rather than touting my own financial success, which was pretty good during the market crash, my most important results are measured in the success of my readers. If you would like to check my record, please read *Rich Dad's Success Stories.*

Answer the Question

Good advice is crucial for financial success. There were many times I wish I did have the time to better answer the question "What should I do with $10,000" rather than just say, "Put it in a bank." After years of not answering the question "I have $10,000. What should I invest it in?" I have decided to answer the question in this book, *Who Took My Money?* The reason I decided to write this book in answer to the question is simply because *the question is a very important one.*

The Price of Bad Advice

In June of 2003, I was in a taxi heading for the airport. On the radio was a financial expert offering some investment advice, saying, "Now is the time to get back into the stock market."

"Why do you say that?" asked the radio host.

"Because all the lights are green," said the financial advisor. "This market is headed straight up." He then went on to his tirade of jargon and standard stock market talk that many of us have heard over and over again, before the crash, during the crash, and now after the crash.

Gazing out the window of the cab, I just tuned out the financial expert until the host took back control of the show. "Okay, let's open up the phone lines and let's hear from any callers who have questions for you."

The first caller to get through said, "I'm seventy-eight years old. My wife is seventy-five. In January of 2000 we thought we had a nice safe retirement portfolio. We had about one million dollars in mutual funds."

"That's great," said the host.

"Yes—but that was in January of 2000."

"How much do you have now?" asked the financial expert.

"Well that's the problem," the caller said. "In March of 2000, when the market began to crash, I called my financial planner for advice."

"And what did he say?" asked the radio host.

"He said about the same thing your guest is saying now. He said the market was just about to bounce back up . . . it was only a minor correction caused by a little profit taking. He never told us it was a market crash. In fact, he never told us that markets could go down or that mutual funds were not safe. Instead, he advised us to continue to invest for the long term, buy, hold, and diversify."

"So what did you do?" asked the host.

"We sat tight. We did as he told us to do. We held on and watched as the market kept falling. As the prices got lower, he even called to tell us to buy more while prices were low."

"So did you buy more?"

"We certainly did. But the stock market kept falling and we kept calling him. By August of 2002 he stopped taking our calls. We were later told that he had left the firm and we were turned over to someone else. Anyway, we got sick of opening the envelope from the investment firm. I couldn't stand seeing the money we worked all our lives for disappearing as the market crashed. We aren't working anymore and are wondering what we can do now."

"So how much money do you have left?" the host asked again.

"Well, after he stopped taking our calls, we took action and sold our mutual funds. My wife and I thought it was better to keep our money in cash. So after we cashed in our mutual funds, all we had left was about $350,000 and we put it in a CD at the bank."

"That's good," said the host. "At least you have some cash. "Three hundred fifty thousand dollars is nothing to sneeze at, you know."

"Well, the problem is, the certificate of deposit is only paying 1 percent interest per year. One percent of $350,000 is only $3,500 per year. Even with Social Security and Medicare, it's tough to live on that money. I'm afraid we might have to start eating into our savings, and if we do that, we'll be in even worse shape financially. What do you advise?"

"Do you have a home?" asked the financial advisor.

"Yes we do," said the caller. "But please don't ask us to sell it. That's all we have left. Besides, it's only worth about $120,000 and we have a mortgage of $80,000 on it. The reason we have a large mortgage is because when interest rates dropped, we refinanced and took out some extra money from the equity in our home."

"And what did you do with money from your home?" asked the radio host.

"It's gone. We lived on it. That's why I'm calling for some advice."

"Well, what advice would you give to this couple?" the host asked the financial planner.

"Well first of all, you shouldn't have sold your shares," said the financial expert. "As I said the market is coming back."

"But it kept going down for years," said the caller. "It's very frightening to lose so much when you're our age."

"Yes, yes, I know," said the expert. "But listen to me now. You should always invest for the long term. Buy and hold on. Keep diversified. Markets do go down but they will come back as they are now."

"So what should he and his wife do now?" asked the radio host.

"It's time to get back in. As I said, the market is coming back. Always remember that over the past forty years, the stock market has gone up 9 percent per year, on average."

"You believe now is the time to get back in?" asked the host.

"That's right," said the financial expert. "Get back in before you miss the next rally."

"Good advice," said the host to the seventy-eight-year-old man. "Thanks for the call. Next caller, please."

The taxi was now approaching the airport and my blood was boiling. "How can they keep handing out that same old advice . . . and get paid for it? How do they sleep at night?" I muttered to myself as I headed for the gate. As I waited in line to board the plane, I read a headline on a discarded newspaper that screamed, "Investors Pouring Money into Real Estate." Quietly, I shook my head and said to myself, "From one boom and bust to the next boom and bust."

The Same Old Advice

As the plane pulled away from the terminal, I began to recall when I was a first-time investor that knew very little about investing. My mind drifted back to 1965, when at the age of eighteen, I purchased my first shares of mutual funds. I purchased the shares even though I did not really know what a mutual fund was. All I knew was that mutual funds were connected to Wall Street and investing in Wall Street seemed like a cool idea at the time.

I was at school in New York, attending the U.S. Merchant Marine Academy, a federal school that trains students to be ship's officers on freighters, tankers, passenger liners, and other ships of commerce. Being a military academy, we were required to wear military uniforms, polish our shoes, and march to class. And being from Hawaii, where all I wore were shorts and T-shirts, I was finding the adjustment to this new life very difficult. It was fall, leaves were turning beautiful colors and falling, and I was getting ready to experience my first winter.

One afternoon, I received a note that a Mr. Carling wanted to see me. I did not know a Mr. Carling, but when you're a plebe, a freshman, you learn to do what you are told and do it promptly, without questioning what you are being asked to do.

"Start investing while you're young," said Mr. Carling's smiling face sitting across the table from me. "And *always* remember the secret of great investors. The secret is to buy and hold, and invest for the long term. Let your money grow. And *always* remember to be smart and diversify."

To this advice, I just nodded and said, "Yes, sir." I really did not know what he was talking about, but after four months at the academy, I was well trained in sitting or standing tall and straight and saying "Yes, sir."

Mr. Carling was an alumnus of the academy who had stopped sailing ships and had gone into the field of financial planning. He knew what hell we as plebes were going through. He had gone through it himself. Instead of simply saying "Yes, sir" I really should have been questioning how he got on campus, since he was no longer a student or in the merchant marine, and how he got my name. All I knew was that he had contacted me and had set up an appointment to talk to me during study hall and I was saying "Yes, sir" to another authority figure even though he was in a suit and tie, not a military uniform.

"How much do I have to invest?" I asked.

"Just $15 a month," the smiling face said.

"Fifteen dollars," I said. "Where will I get that kind of money? I'm in school full-time, you know." Remember, this was 1965 and $15 was a lot of money to a college student.

"Be tough," said the smiling Mr. Carling. "The academy will teach you discipline. With that discipline of putting a little bit of money away each month, you'll soon have a sizable nest egg. Remember, *always* invest for the long term." Even though I agreed with everything he said, I still noted how much he was emphasizing the word *always*. For some reason, the word and how he said it made me feel just a little uneasy.

Time was precious. I needed to get back to my studies, so I simply agreed to everything he said. After selecting the mutual fund company he recommended I invest in, I signed an agreement to send a check in once a month to purchase more shares. Once the paperwork was completed, I hurried back to my studies and pretty much forgot about the investment plan. Once a month, starting in November of that year, I began to send in my check.

Christmas Vacation

The first six months at the academy were difficult. They were some of the toughest days of my life. I was adjusting to being away from home for the first time, and in New York for the first time . . . my head was shaved and the course load was heavy. On top of that, as plebes we were not allowed off the academy grounds, except for Thanksgiving and now Christmas. As the cold winds of winter whipped across Long Island Sound, I counted the days remaining to Christmas break. I had just enough money left in my savings account to afford the price of a military personnel discount ticket home.

Finally I was back in the warm weather of Hawaii. The first thing I did was join my former high school classmates and go surfing from early in the morning to late into the night. Although my friends were laughing at me for my lack of hair, it was still nice to have this break and to be a kid again. Although I was badly sunburned, my tan was coming back.

A few days into my vacation, I stopped by my rich dad's office with his son, Mike. Mike and I had been surfing and he said his dad wanted to see me. After the usual pleasantries and catching up, I happened to mention to my rich dad that I had made my first investment . . . an investment in a mutual fund. I only mentioned the investment in passing. For me, discussing my mutual fund investment was just idle conversation. But for my rich dad, what I had done required far more than just idle conversation.

"You did what?" he asked.

"I invested in a mutual fund," I replied.

"Why?" he asked. He did not ask me which fund I had invested in. He only wanted to know why.

Rather than answer, I just stumbled and fumbled with words and thoughts, searching for a logical-sounding answer.

"And who did you purchase the shares from?" asked rich dad before I could reply. "Do you know him?"

"Well, yes," I responded assertively and a little defensively. "He is a graduate of the academy. He is an alumnus, class of '58, who has permission to come on campus and sell investments to the midshipmen."

Rich dad smirked and asked, "And how did he get *your* name?"

"I don't know. I guess the academy gave it to him."

Again rich dad smirked. Rather than saying anything, he pushed back into his chair, extended his legs, placed his hands in a praying position under his chin, and just sat there searching for the words he wanted to say.

Finally, I broke the silence, asking, "Did I do something wrong?"

Again there was just silence for a long ten seconds. "No," rich dad said finally. "First of all I commend you for taking the initiative to invest. Many people wait till it is too late, or never invest for their future. Many people spend everything they make and then expect the company they work for or the government to take care of them when their working days are over. At least you did something—you invested some of your own money."

"But did I do something wrong?"

"No—what you did is not really wrong."

"So why the concern?" I asked. "Are there better investments?"

"Yes and no. There are always better investments and there are even more bad investments," rich dad said, sitting up straight again. "It's not what you invested in that I am concerned about. Right now I am concerned about you."

"Me?" I asked. "What about me?"

"I am concerned about what kind of *investor* you are becoming more than what *investment* you have invested in."

Sales Pitch Rather Than Investment Education

"I'm not a good investor?"

"No, it's not that," said rich dad. "He advised you to 'invest for the long term, buy, hold, and diversify.' Is that correct?"

"Yes," I said softly.

"The problem with that advice is that it is a sales pitch," said rich dad. "It's not a sound way to invest much less learn to invest. It's not a good way for you to gain the education you need to become a smart investor."

"Why is it a sales pitch?" I asked.

"Well, think about it," replied rich dad. "How much do you learn about investing by simply sending a check in every month?"

Thinking about the question for a moment, I finally replied, saying, "Not much. But why is it a sales pitch?"

"You keep thinking about it," smiled rich dad. "You keep thinking about the advice of 'Invest for the long term, buy, hold, and diversify.'"

"You're not going to tell me?" I asked.

"No. Not now anyway. You're only eighteen years old. You have a lot to learn about the real world. Right now you have the opportunity to learn one of life's most important lessons. So think about it. When you think you have figured out why 'Invest for the long term, buy, hold, and diversify' is a sales pitch rather than sound investment education, you let me know. Most people never learn the difference between a sales pitch and investment education. That is why so few people ever become rich and why so many people lose money as investors. They lose because they think a sales pitch *is* investment education. And because they think that 'Invest for the long term, buy, hold, and diversify' is investment education, they actually believe it is the smart thing to do. There is a big difference between a sales pitch and true education."

As rich dad was talking, I was beginning to understand why the salesperson put such an emphasis on the word "always."

Millions Lose Trillions

As mentioned earlier, between March of 2000 and March of 2003, it is estimated that millions of people lost $7 to $9 trillion in the market crash. Those losses do not include the loss of jobs and the emotional pain that such losses bring with them. Why did so many people lose so much money? While the reasons are many—reasons such as a weakened economy, terrorists, corruption, bad analysis reports, fraud, market trends, and other oversights— one little-known underlying reason is because millions of people mistook a common industry sales pitch for sound financial education. Many *always* sent their check in, or did not sell . . . investing and holding on for the long term, even as the biggest stock market crash in history was crashing all around them.

The Money Was Not Lost

Michael Lewis is a respected financial writer best known for his best-sellers *Liar's Poker, The New New Thing,* and *Moneyball.* He has been the American editor of the British weekly *The Spectator* and senior editor at *The New Republic.* He has also been a visiting fellow at the University of California, Berkeley.

In an article written for the October 27, 2002 *New York Times Magazine,* Lewis states, "Stock market losses are not losses to society. They are transfers from one person to another."

He further describes his own experience in the market. "I should have sensed that the moment I finally decided Internet stocks were a buy is precisely when they became a sell. Instead, I jumped into Exodus Communications at $160 a share and watched it run up a few points—and then collapse. What happened to my money? It didn't simply vanish. It was pocketed by the person who sold me the shares. The suspects, in order of likelihood: a) some Exodus employee; b) a well-connected mutual fund that got in early at the I.P.O. price; or c) a day trader who bought it at $150."

In other words, between 2000 and 2003, $7 to $9 trillion was not lost . . . $7 to $9 trillion was transferred from one investor to another. Between 2000 and 20003, some investors got richer and other investors got poorer . . . which is why rich dad was more concerned about me, the *investor*, than what I was *investing* in.

When Do I Sell?

In 1965, after realizing that rich dad was not happy with my first investment, I asked, "Should I sell those mutual fund shares?"

Grinning, he said, "No. I would not sell them just yet. You may have made a *mistake* but you have not yet learned your *lesson.* Hang on for a while longer. Keep making those monthly payments until you learn what you need to learn. If you will do that, this lesson will be priceless. If you learn from this event, you will gain something more important than money. You will be on your way to becoming a better investor. One of the first things you need to learn, if you want to be a better investor, is the difference between a sales pitch and sound investment advice."

Investing for the Long Term

Once Christmas vacation 1965 was over, I returned to school in New York. It was tough leaving the warm beaches of Hawaii and stepping back into the coldest part of winter in New York. Instead of surfing I was now shivering.

Following rich dad's advice, I continued to send in my check to the mutual fund company once a month. Being in school, the extra money was hard to come by, especially since I had very little financial support from home. I still had expenses and an occasional social life to support. To make up for the shortfall there were many Saturdays I went out into the neighborhood to do odd jobs for $2 an hour. If I worked one or two Saturdays a month, I could afford to send the check in to the mutual fund company as well as pay for the necessities of life, such as fun.

Occasionally, I would open the newspaper to the investment section to find out how my fund was performing. The fund did not do much. It sort of sat at one price and stayed there, just like a sleepy old dog. Once a quarter, I received an envelope from the company with a statement verifying my contributions. After a while I began to dread opening the envelope because I was usually less than impressed with the fund's performance. The number of shares I owned was increasing but the price per share remained about the same. Truthfully I felt kind of stupid for buying such an under-performing investment.

Six months later, I was back in Hawaii, this time for summer vacation 1966. When I stopped by rich dad's office to say hello he invited me out to an early lunch. "How is your mutual fund doing?" he asked once we were seated at the restaurant.

"Well, I put in nearly $100 in six months, but the fund is not doing anything. The shares were about $12 when I first started investing in them and they're still at $12 today."

Rich dad chuckled. "Getting impatient?"

"Well, I would like to see a little more action," I replied.

"It's not good to be impatient," smiled rich dad. "Patience is important in investing."

"But the fund is not doing anything," I responded.

Rich dad laughed out loud after my last comment. He obviously found it funny. "I'm not talking about the fund," he said. "I'm talking about you. You need to learn patience if you want to be an investor."

"But I have been patient. My money has been in there for nearly ten months. The price per share remains the same."

"As I said, that is what happens when you are an impatient investor," rich dad said sternly. "Impatient investors often invest hastily—hence their impatience causes them to invest in under-performing investments."

"Under-performing investments . . . just because I invested with impatience?"

Rich dad nodded, "How long did you talk to your mutual fund salesperson before you made the decision to invest?"

"We talked for about an hour. He asked me about my goals in life. He showed me a few charts showing me how the Dow Jones Industrial Average was going up and up. He explained the value of investing a little bit of money over a long period of time."

"And you made up your mind and bought the shares," rich dad said with a smile.

"Yes," I replied.

"I'd call that impatience." Rich dad chuckled. "You invested impatiently and now you wait impatiently while your investment does nothing. How can you expect to find a great investment if you first of all don't know what a great investment looks like and you're not willing to invest the time to look for the investment? You got what you paid for. Your impatience caused you to find an investment that makes you even more impatient. And always remember this: The worst investments go to impatient investors. Got this lesson?"

"Yes, I have," I replied impatiently. "So am I wasting my money?" I asked.

"No," said rich dad strongly. "Right now, don't worry about the money you're making or not making. Right now, you're learning a priceless lesson. Most investors never learn this lesson on impatience. Don't be so impatient. Take time to learn the lesson."

"Okay," I said. "I'll take time to learn this lesson. The next time I make an investment decision, I'll be more patient."

"Good," said rich dad. "Most investors blame the investment rather than themselves. In reality, the real problem is the *investor* not the *investment.* And right now you're learning about the price of your impatience. That is a pretty good lesson to start off with—if you learn the lesson."

"But I'm a full-time student. I had to concentrate on my studies," I argued. "I didn't have time to learn more and do more research."

"And soon when you graduate and leave school, you will be working full-time. Maybe you'll get married, buy a home, and start raising a family. If that happens, expenses will go up as well as the demands on your time. If you think you're busy as a student, just wait till you're working and married with kids. If you do not make the time to learn to be a better investor now, you will be saying the same things tomorrow as you are today. You'll still be saying 'I didn't have time to learn more and do more research.' Because of your impatience, your laziness, and your lame excuses about not having enough time, you will do the same thing you just did, which is to hand your money over to total strangers and have no idea what they are doing with your money."

Sitting silently, I let rich dad's words sink in. I did not like what he was saying to me. I was getting angry. If only he knew how hard it was to attend a military academy, to carry a full academic load, play sports, and try to have a social life.

"Just admit you're impatient," said rich dad. "Just admit that you are not willing and too busy to invest the time to learn to be an investor. That would be more honest than to just say you're too busy. Then admit that you're not patient enough to find a great investment."

"And if I admit that, then I won't complain about my investment not performing well," I added.

"Or complain when your investment loses money," said rich dad with that smirk of his.

"You mean I can lose money in mutual funds?" I asked.

"You can lose money in anything," rich dad replied. "But you know what is worse than losing money?"

"No," I replied, shaking my head. "I don't know. What is worse?"

"The worst thing about not learning to be an investor is that you never see great investments," rich dad said matter-of-factly. "If you never invest the time to learn to be an investor you will live in fear of investing, constantly saying 'investing is risky.' By believing that investing is risky, you avoid investing, or you turn your money over to people you hope are investing wisely. But the worst thing is that when you avoid investing, you miss out on the hottest deals in the world. You live in fear rather than live with the excitement of searching for and finding great deals. When you play it safe, living in fear of *losing*, you miss out on the excitement of *winning*. You miss out on the excitement of getting richer. That's the worst thing about being impatient and not investing the time to become a real investor."

Thinking for a moment, again letting rich dad's words sink in, I began to recall the sales pitch of the financial advisor who sold me the mutual fund investment plan.

As if reading my mind, rich dad asked me, "Did your salesman friend tell you that the stock market goes up on average 10 percent per year? That's the standard canned sales pitch most salespeople in his business use. Did he tell you something like that?"

"Yes, he did say something like that," I replied.

Rich dad roared laughing. "He probably thinks that's a great return. A 10 percent return is peanuts! On top of that, ask him if he will guarantee that tiny return. Of course he won't. He'll just send you a birthday card once a year to say thanks for the business. He wins, you lose. But the biggest loss to you is that you will never see the great investments because you will never become a great investor if you follow his advice of 'Invest for the long term, buy, hold, and diversify.' And on top of all that, while the best investments go to the most educated, the worse and riskiest of all investments go to the least financially educated investors."

"You're saying that mutual funds are the riskiest of all investments?" I asked.

"No . . . that is not what I am saying," replied rich dad, now in a frustrated tone. Taking a deep breath and gathering his thoughts, he said, "Listen to me. I'll say it again. I am not talking about the *investment*. I am talking about the *investor*. If the investor is uneducated, anything he or she invests in will be risky. They may get lucky now and then, but generally in the long run, any money they make they end up giving most of back to the market. I've seen an uneducated investor take a great real estate investment and turn it into a run-down foreclosure. I've seen an uneducated investor buy a profitable well-run business and soon bankrupt it. I've seen an unsophisticated investor buy shares of stock in a great company, watch that stock climb in value, and fail to sell at the top. After the stock crashes, they hang on to the dead stock. So it's *not* the investment that is risky . . . it's the investor."

I was beginning to understand what rich dad was saying. He was doing his best to get me to see a world very few people see . . . the world of a real investor.

Catching his breath, rich dad continued, "I've also seen a professional investor take over an investment that a bad investor has ruined and make it a good investment again. So the bad investor loses money and the smart investor makes money."

"Are you saying the smart investor never loses money?" I asked.

"Of course not," replied rich dad. "We all lose now and then. The point I am making is that a smart investor focuses on becoming a smarter investor. The average investor focuses only on making money. I'm not here to tell you how to run your life. Right now, I want you to stop, take a moment, and think about what you are now learning . . . *not* how much money you are making or not making. Don't focus on the money. Focus on learning to be a better investor."

"So I don't learn much about investing if all I do is write a check, stick it in an envelope, lick a stamp, and drop it in the mail . . . investing for the long term?"

"That is exactly what I am saying. You're not learning to be an investor. You're learning to be a saver and stamp-licker."

Rich dad stood and stretched. I could tell he was tiring of drumming this simple but important lesson into my head. Glancing back at me, he asked, "So what have you learned from your mutual fund investments and about yourself?"

"I've learned I'm impatient. I've learned that I make excuses for not taking the time to learn to invest."

"Which causes what?" asked rich dad.

"Which means that I do not always get the best investments. It means I miss out on an exciting world, a world that very few people see. It also means that if I do not make some changes, I am a gambler more than investor."

"Good insight," smiled rich dad. "And what else?"

Thinking for a while, I could not come up with any more answers. "I don't know what else."

"What about turning your money over to a total stranger?" rich dad replied. "And what about not knowing who this stranger turns your money over to and what these even-more-faceless strangers do with your money? Do you know how much money in fees is being taken out of your money? Do you know how much of your money is actually invested and how much of your money is going into the pockets of the people who manage your money? Is any money coming back into your pockets? What happens if they lose your money? Do you have any recourse? Do you know the answer to any of these questions?"

Shaking my head, I replied with a faint, "No."

"Did you ever ask the guy who sold you these mutual funds if he could live off of his own investments or was he living off the commissions from the money you invested with him?"

"No," I replied softly. "I never asked."

Conflict of Interest

When I realized that I may have made a mistake, I wanted to blame Mr. Carling, but I knew better. *I was the investor.* I made the choice to invest in mutual funds without doing enough due diligence about the investment.

Financial planners make their commissions through selling investments and other financial products (like insurance) to the average investor. We need to learn how to ask the right questions. Like, What are the fees related to this mutual fund? What is your commission from this sale? Rich dad was trying to impress on me that I needed to be in control of my own financial decisions and not give that power over to someone else.

A *Slap* on the *Wrist*

In 2002, some of the biggest companies on Wall Street were fined $1.4 billion by New York State Attorney General Eliot Spitzer for fraud and conflicts of interest. In a news conference, Spitzer said, "Every investor knows that the market involves risk. . . . But what every investor expects and deserves is honest investment advice—advice and analysis that is untainted by conflicts of interest." A $1.4 billion fine after $7 to $9 trillion was lost to investors is equivalent to paying a $1.40 fine for causing $7,000 to $9,000 in damages, a mere slap on the wrist—and less than the commissions these big companies earned from the investors who lost the $7 to $9 trillion.

As part of the settlement by which the $1.4 billion fines were levied, reforms were agreed to that establish a set of rules aimed at eliminating conflicts of interest between Wall Street research groups and stock-offering groups. The firms' stock analysts will be barred from being paid for stock research by the firms' investment banking arms.

A *Bonus for a Job Well Done*

Soon after the slap on the wrist and fine for fraud, *The Wall Street Journal* ran an article entitled:

"Merrill Lynch Awarded Officers Big '02 Bonuses"

To paraphrase the article: Merrill Lynch & Co. rewarded both its chairman and its chief executive with $7 million in bonuses last year despite the continued stock market rout that has eaten into many of the firm's key businesses.

The article continued: During 2002, Merrill reduced its ranks by 6,500 employees, bringing its total job cuts to 21,700 since its employment peaked in 2000.

As I put the newspaper down, I could not help but wonder how a company could award millions of dollars in bonuses to company executives when this very same company had assisted investors in losing trillions of dollars, been charged with fraud, and rather than growing the business, the company's executives had fired nearly 22,000 employees.

To be fair and not seem to pick on Merrill Lynch alone, *The Wall Street Journal* article also posted the annual paychecks of other CEOs from other financial institutions:

Morgan Stanley CEO	$11.0 million
Goldman Sachs CEO	$12.1 million
Lehman Brothers CEO	$12.5 million
Bear Stearns CEO	$19.6 million

Some of these companies were also in the group that was fined by the state of New York for fraud.

More Lawsuits Follow

In June and July of 2003, many smaller investors banded together to file lawsuits against Merrill Lynch. The little investors lost even though there was substantial evidence that misrepresentations were made. Although I do not like to see the little investors lose, I tended to agree with the judge's decision that all investors need to be aware when entering the world of investing. In other words, the judge said, "Tough luck."

Mutual Fund Fraud

The New York attorney general turned his attention to the mutual fund industry in early 2003. He stated, "There are undisclosed financial motivations in damn near every transaction involving mutual funds." He is looking into unseen fees charges by the funds and conflicts of interest in the way funds are sold. He is investigating two practices called "late trading" and "market timing." *Late trading* involves purchasing mutual fund shares at the 4:00 P.M. price after the market closes, allowing the favored investor to take advantage of after-market events not yet reflected in the closing price of the fund. *Market timing* involves short-term trading of mutual funds, which has a detrimental effect on the long-term shareholders of the mutual fund. While more is being revealed every day during this investigation, the inherent conflicts of interest and insider trading have shaken the average investor's confidence.

Become an Educated Investor

As stated earlier, in the world of investing, money is not lost. It just changes hands. That is why I am hesitant to tell someone what to invest their $10,000 in. If a person does not know what to do with their money, they should first invest some *time* in their investment education before investing their *money*. In my opinion, one of the primary reasons why millions of people lost trillions of dollars is because they invested their *money* but were not willing to invest their *time*.

So my answer to the question of "I have $10,000. What should I invest it in?" is invest the time learning to be a better investor before investing your money in what you hope and pray is a good investment. Always remember what my rich dad told me years ago. He said, "People without much financial education most often fall for a sales pitch . . . mistaking the sales pitch for advice." Hence, this book is about what my rich dad thought was important for me to invest my time in—seeking real investment education—before I invested my money. Rich dad also said, "The better your investment education the better [the] investment advice you will receive."

=========== **Sharon's Notes** ===========

Recognizing a sales pitch from good investment advice is the subject of the first chapter of this book because it is a huge distinction that successful investors must learn. Is the advice you are paying for the best advice for you and your investments, or is the advice the best advice to generate more fees for your advisors? The salesman's goal is to make money *from* you, while the advisor's goal is to make money *for* you.

Park It or Accelerate It?

Most of the average investor's financial education today comes from financial institutions like banks and salespeople. They are telling the investor to invest, or "park," their money for the long term and to expect the market to increase each year. This advice of "saving for a rainy day" is the right advice for many people.

When you look at the table "Why the Rich Get Richer" in the introduction, the left side is where most people live—with the salesmen. They follow the advice of the financial institutions and salespeople and make the decision to save, or park, their money in the following ways and hope that the market will go up and that these investments will be there for them when they are ready to retire:

- Savings
- Personal residence
- Mutual funds
- Equities
- 401(k)s, IRAs, and SEPs

In addition, the most common answer to the question *Who Took My Money?* is *the government,* since most people are employees and see their largest expense—taxes—disappear from their paychecks (through withholding) *before* they get paid.

Rich dad teaches an alternative to the traditional savings and employee mentality. He teaches building or buying assets *today* that generate cash flow for you *today*—the method of professional investors. Do you feel trapped working hard for a paycheck? Is it hard to imagine having your money working hard for you? *Who Took My Money?* will help you make the transition from saver to investor.

Professional investors want to know how fast they can move their money from one asset to acquire the next asset. They choose to invest in all three asset classes and utilize as many of the related accelerators as possible. Their goal is to constantly keep their money moving and increase their returns on investment.

Business	OPM (other people's money)
	Entity selection
	OPT (other people's time)
	Tax laws
	Charity

Real Estate	OPM (other people's money)
	Entity Selection
	Tax laws
	• Depreciation
	• Passive loss
Paper	Tax-exempt
	Hedge Funds
	Options
	PPMs (private placements memorandums)
	IPOs (initial public offerings)

These methods and vehicles used by professional investors are available to everyone. With the right financial education, the right advisors, and the willingness to take action, you can start making your money work for you.

Chapter 2

Ask a Cattle Rancher and Then Ask a Dairy Farmer

"My favorite time frame for holding a stock is forever."

—WARREN BUFFETT

After correcting me on my hasty leap into mutual fund investing, rich dad reminded me of an earlier discussion (which he had to do often) about his method of investing. He recalled a financial lesson on the difference between a cattle rancher and a dairy farmer.

The Beautiful Big Island

On the Big Island of Hawaii, where I grew up, lies the Parker Ranch. While I was in high school, Parker Ranch was the *largest* privately owned ranch in America. When I was sixteen years old, rich dad took his son and me to visit the ranch. The ranch was, and is today, a beautiful place to visit. Far from the madding crowds of Waikiki Beach, the ranch encompasses tall mountains, rolling green hills, and large expanses of land that reach out to the spectacular blue waters of the Pacific Ocean, where some of the biggest marlin in the world live. Today, the little town of Kamuela, at the heart of the ranch, is a place I often dream of living, once my life slows down.

On this visit to the ranch we happened to see the cowboys herding the cattle from the feed yard to the slaughterhouse. Although rich dad took us away before we could see any cattle being slaughtered, we knew what was going to happen and so did the cattle. It was an experience I never forgot.

A few months later, rich dad took us to a dairy farm. Early in the morning, we saw the farmer herding his cows into the barn for milking. These cattle behaved very differently.

The financial lesson rich dad wanted us to learn was that while both the cattle rancher and the dairy farmer count their cattle as assets, they treat their assets differently and they operate via different business models.

The visits to the ranch and the farm were to emphasize the very important difference between:

Capital Gains

versus

Cash Flow

Simply put, a cattle rancher can be compared to a person who invests for capital gains. A dairy farmer is more like an investor who invests for cash flow.

One of the reasons so many people lose so much money investing or think that investing is risky is because they invest like ranchers. They invest to slaughter rather than to milk.

Conversations with a Capital Gains Investor

You can tell a person who invests for capital gains by what they say and the words they use. Some examples are:

1. "My net worth has gone up."
2. "My home has appreciated in value."
3. "I paid $10 a share, the price went to $15 and I sold."
4. "I bought a house, fixed it up, sold it, and made $23,000."
5. "The company's earnings are up so I expect the share price to follow."

Conversations with a Cash Flow Investor

You can also tell a person who invests for cash flow by their words. Some examples are:

1. "What is my cash-on-cash return from the property?"
2. "The stock is paying a 56 cent-per-share dividend."
3. "Did you factor in your income from depreciation?"
4. "It is a tax-free municipal bond paying 7 percent interest."
5. "I receive 16 percent interest from my tax lien certificate."

Conversations with a Financial Advisor

When you talk to most financial advisors they say, "When you are young, I recommend an aggressive growth fund. After you retire, I recommend you switch to an income fund."

Translation: "When you are young, invest for capital gains. When you are old, invest for cash flow."

The Greatest of Fools

One of the primary reasons, other than greed and corruption, so many people lost so much money in the late 1990s is because they were investing for capital gains. During the latest tech bubble it became so bad that investors were investing in companies without earnings or profits, much less dividends. They were investing in the *greater fool* method of investing, which means they were hoping for a fool greater than they. At the peak of the bubble the fast money moved out and the greatest of fools emerged. Is this still going on today? The answer is, "Absolutely."

National Television

In September of 2003, while in New York, I went on the set of a nationally televised financial show for an interview. The well-known financial commentator came at me immediately, calling into question my investment strategy. With a smirk he said, "The Dow is up nearly 50 percent. What do you have to say about that?"

Reeling from his rather aggressive posturing, I replied, "So what?"

Obviously, he was a capital gains investor and I am a cash flow investor. He invests like a rancher and I invest like a dairy farmer. Obviously, the rest of the interview did not go well.

Warren Buffett says, "The dumbest reason in the world to buy a stock is because it's going up."

A Very Important Distinction

Whenever I hear someone say, "Invest for the long term," I often ask, "What are you investing for? Are you investing for capital gains or cash flow? If I am investing for cash flow, I really do not care about price. I'll pay the price if I get my cash flow . . . my return of my money . . . now . . . not tomorrow . . . not in the long term. In other words, "Show me the money—now."

A Ridiculous Example

The question is, if you gave me $10 today, and I gave you back $1 a month for years, would you think that was a good investment? I hope you do. In other words you would have your $10 back in ten months. From then on, it's free money.

One of the reasons so many investors lose so much money is because they pay $10 a month into a fund for forty years and do not know if it will be there forty years from now. That is what I call "reparking you money." Obviously, in most cases there will be something there . . . but how much? Will it be enough?

Now I can hear some of you saying, "That example of investing $10 and getting back $1 a month is a ridiculous example." Let me assure you, the example is not ridiculous. Since most people have been trained to invest for capital gains, they often fail to see the power of investing for cash flow.

Made a Killing in the Market

One of the reasons rich dad was upset with me when I invested in the mutual fund was because I was being lured in to invest for capital gains. The reason he took his son and me to both a ranch and a dairy farm was because he wanted to teach us the difference between slaughtering and milking. He often said, "When someone says they made a killing in the market, they really did. Some poor investor got killed. The slow investor lost and the fast money got out. It happens all the time, in all markets . . . not only the stock market."

Made a Milking in the Market

As you read on in this book, you will find how the example of investing $10 now and receiving $1 a month for years is very possible . . . but you have to think like a dairy farmer not a rancher.

As you go through this book, you may begin to understand why Warren Buffett said, "My favorite time frame for holding a stock is forever."

Warren Buffett thinks and invests like a dairy farmer. I know my rich dad did. It does not matter what asset class you invest in. Many people invest in a business only to fatten it up and slaughter it, selling it to the next guy. The same thing happens in real estate and paper assets. To best understand the message from this book, the slaughterhouse mentality needs to be replaced with the milking barn mentality.

The Slaughter Goes On

One of the reasons I do not particularly care for most mutual funds is because they remind me of feed yards, the place where cattle are held to be fattened just before slaughter. The difference is the mutual fund feed yards are filled with little investors . . . getting plump as the value of their diversified portfolio increases . . . and then the cowboys ride in and take their money.

To Be Fair and Balanced

Many people think I am anti–mutual funds and the stock market. That is not true. I am against ignorance, excessive greed, and stupidity. This fattening up of the little investor goes on in any and all markets. I see it every day in the real estate market. Today in Phoenix, Arizona, the fastest-growing major market in America, foreclosures are up. Many people are losing their homes. Investors are bailing out of properties that they paid too much for. In Australia, interest rates are on the rise again, which will mean the greater fools of the property market will be led to slaughter.

The reason I said "So what?" to the famous TV host on prime-time national television is because I do not want to be led to slaughter. I do not want to be sucked into a market just because share prices are rising . . . or real estate prices are rising . . . or interest rates are falling.

The News

For the last few months of 2003, I have heard stock market reports that go like this:

> One day: "The stock market is up today. It looks like a very big rally."
> Next day: "The stock market is down today. It seems that investors are taking profits from yesterday's rally."
> Next day: "The stock market is up today. I think this is the rally we've been waiting for."
> Next day: "The stock market is down today on reports that insiders are selling."
> Next day: "The market is up on news of high earnings."
> Next day: "The market is down on a rumor that the Fed will raise interest rates."

The Reality

What the news is really saying is that the slow investors continue putting (or "parking") their money into the market, hoping the prices go higher. Each time the prices go higher, the fast money takes their money out of the market.

Investing for Capital Gains Is Gambling

Anytime you invest with the hope that something in the future will happen, you are gambling—and that is what investing for capital gains is. Not that it is wrong. The important thing is to recognize what your investment goals are and not delude yourself.

Betting on the Super Bowl

Investing for capital gains is like betting at the start of the football season on which team will win the Super Bowl. In fact, it would be less risky to bet on which team will win the Super Bowl before the season starts than to invest for capital gains. Why? Because there are only a few teams in the National Football League and there are thousands of stocks or mutual funds to pick from.

A *Matter of Priorities*

All this being said, I do invest for capital gains. I do have some money in managed funds. Occasionally, I do gamble and, occasionally, I do invest on a hot tip. The difference is priorities. In this book you will find that rich dad's method of investing followed this order of priorities:

1. Cash flow
2. Leverage
3. Tax advantages
4. Capital gains

Most investors invest only for capital gains. In most retirement accounts, you will find the average investor with cash flowing away from them, they have little to no leverage, few tax advantages, and their money sits in the feed lot, getting fat. Once the market sentiment changes, the cowboys arrive, the fast money gets out, and it is those with retirement accounts who take the biggest losses.

Even the Prince of Wales Got Out Early

The Tuesday, May 27, 2003, edition of the *Sydney Morning Herald* ran a headline stating:

> "Prince Makes Quiet Killing in Prudent Move to Property"

Again, you may notice the word *killing* and also the word *quiet*, which indicates that he did not tell anyone until after the move was done. The article goes on to say:

> London: The Prince of Wales will unveil record profits for his 700-year-old estate next month after making a timely switch out of shares and into the property market.
>
> The Prince's new status as "property king" will become apparent when he announces that the Duchy of Cornwall, the estate which gives the heir to the throne his income, has been recording profits of almost $25 million for the latest financial year.
>
> The figure is an increase of about 25 per cent on the previous year and comes when many businesses have recorded annual falls in profit because of the economic downturn.

This article illustrates one more reason why the rich get richer. While the rich are quietly moving their money, the little guy is in the feedlot waiting to be slaughtered.

There is nothing wrong with being in the feedlot getting fat. But you have to remember to get out before the cowboys arrive.

This Book Is About the Power of Cash Flow

Rather than teach me to slaughter my assets, rich dad taught me to grow my assets by using the cash flow to increase the size of my herd. Rather than take the cows to market, each year the cows have more calves and the cash flow increases.

In book number 2, *Rich Dad's CASHFLOW Quadrant*, I wrote about building a pipeline, rather than hauling buckets forever. In this metaphor, building a pipeline is investing for cash flow and hauling buckets is investing for capital gains.

Often I meet a person who says, "I found a great house, bought it, fixed it up, and sold it. I made $25,000." While I know this person is proud of what they have done, to me it sounds like hard work. To me, that is hauling buckets rather than building a pipeline. How do I know? I know because I have done the same thing. Now if this person was following the principle of investing for capital gains with the intent to build up equity for investing in cash flow, it would be more consistent with rich dad's teachings. (In fact, that principle is built into our board game CASHFLOW.)

This Book Is About Building Pipelines

This book is about building pipelines so the cash can flow and you can find freedom. This book is also about expanding the diameter of your pipeline. When I begin a business, often the only cash flow is the flow from my wallet. Later on, the flow becomes a drip coming out of a pipe the size of a garden hose. As time goes on, my job as a businessperson is to expand the diameter of the pipe . . . not kill the business, the property, or paper asset and then look for a new business, property, or paper asset . . . which, to me, is an example of hauling buckets of water rather than building a pipeline.

As the cash begins to flow, it flows into the next asset class, and then to the third asset class. Rather than buying and selling, trying to outguess or crystal-ball the market, my job is simply to build the pipelines and continually expand the diameter of the pipe.

The Best-Known Example

One of the reasons I spotlight McDonald's in *Rich Dad Poor Dad* is because McDonald's is one of best-known examples of this three-asset-class formula with interconnecting pipelines. Not too long ago, Ray Kroc started with a business plan where the hamburger business bought some of the best real estate in the world. After the company was up and running, and purchasing some of the best real estate in the world—street corners at busy intersections—the company went public on the stock market. Every time you look at a McDonald's sitting at a busy intersection, remind yourself of the business of hamburgers, buying real estate, the street corner, and selling millions of shares, paper assets, worldwide. That is the real way the rich invest.

In 2003, Ray Kroc's wife, Joan, passed away. The business they built has spread across the world, provided millions of jobs, and has made many people rich. More than rich, Joan Kroc was known for her generosity. It is estimated that she donated billions of dollars to worthy causes and charities. When I hear people say the rich are evil or greedy, I often ask them to read the story about McDonald's.

It's Not the Easy Road

Is it the easiest way to invest? The answer is no. Is it the most profitable way to invest? In my opinion, the answer is yes. Personally I started on this journey, in earnest, at the age of twenty-five. As some of you know, I was a miserable failure till I was thirty-five. But from thirty-five on, the task of building pipelines between assets got easier and even more fun. Today, as I enter the fourth quarter of my money game, the pipelines are strong, getting bigger, and more cash is flowing. To me, this is investing for the long term. As rich dad said, "There are two kinds of money problems. One problem is not enough money and the other is too much money." Which problem do you want?

Warren Buffett says, "People would rather be promised a winning lottery ticket next week than an opportunity to get rich slowly."

Why Don't More People Invest for Cash Flow?

In my seminars, I am often asked, "Why don't more people invest for cash flow?" While I am certain there are many answers, I believe there is one primary reason . . . and that reason is, good cash flow at a good price is hard to find.

If you ask most investment advisors, whether they sell businesses, real estate, or paper assets, they will say it can't be done. The reason so many say it cannot be done is because they probably cannot do it. If they could, they would do it. Their job is not to invest. Their job is to sell so they can put food on *their* table. When their compensation is based on the "buying and selling" of assets, they are in the business of assets that generate capital gains, not assets that generate cash flow. (In fact, they get their sales commission even when the investor has a capital *loss* from the sale of the underlying asset.)

One of my friends was recently talking to me about the mutual fund scandals and he said, "The mutual fund industry has been skimming funds forever that the average investor didn't realize. I am glad it is finally coming to light." While the word "skimming" sounds a little severe, these fees are charged to the fund whether it is going up or down in value in the market. While the Securities and Exchange Commission requires all mutual funds to disclose their fee structures in a standardized fee table at the front of the fund prospectus, how many fund prospectuses have you studied? If you invest through a broker, ask how they will get paid. They may be compensated by the funds through front-end sales charges or back-end loads, which are triggered if you sell during an initial period, during which the fund may also compensate the broker by charging you higher expenses. Or the broker may get a management fee for managing your money, typically 1 percent to 1.5 percent of your account value annually for mutual funds. In addition, you may be paying advisory fees to a financial intermediary, such as a brokerage firm for maintaining an account, or to an investment advisor. These fees may be in addition to the fees disclosed in the mutual fund tables.

Mutual Fund Fees

Shareholder Fees—charged directly to an investor for transactions:

- Maximum Sales Charge (Load)—Charged for purchases.
- Maximum Deferred Sales Charge (Load)—Charged for shares sold or redeemed.
- Maximum Sales Charge (Load) on Reinvested Dividends—Charged when dividends are reinvested in the purchase of additional shares.
- Redemption Fees—Charged when investor redeems shares.
- Exchange Fee—Charged when investor transfers money from one fund to another in same fund family.

Annual Fund Operating Expenses—deducted from fund assets *before* earnings are distributed to investors:

- Management Fee—Charged by fund's investment advisor for managing the fund.
- Distribution Fee—Pays marketing, advertising, and sales professionals. By law cannot exceed 1 percent of the fund's average net assets per year. May include a service fee of up to .25 percent of average net assets per year payable to sales professionals for servicing investor accounts.
- Other Expenses—For example, transfer agent fees, toll-free phone service, Web site info, recordkeeping, printing, mailing.
- Total Annual Fund Operating Expenses (Expense Ratio)—Sum of all the fund's actual operating costs, as a percentage of average net assets.

Why Are Capital Gains So Easy to Sell?

The next question I am often asked is, "Why are capital gains so easy to sell, if investing for capital gains is risky?" My answer is that it is easy to sell a *dream*.

Rich dad often said, "The problem with dreams is reality."

Warren Buffett says, "The propensity to gamble is always increased by a large prize versus a small entry fee, no matter how poor the true odds may be. That's why Las Vegas casinos advertise big jackpots and state lotteries headline big prizes."

Why This Book Is Different

If you have read our other books, especially *Rich Dad's Guide to Investing: What the Rich Invest in That the Poor and Middle Class Do Not!* and played our board games, you will see this theme of three asset classes throughout our material. You may have also read about the pipelines versus buckets before. If you have not read the previous books or played the CASHFLOW games, you may want to, if you want to better understand how you can acquire or create assets of your own in all three asset classes.

Why this book is different is because it focuses not only on the synergy of the three asset classes, *it primarily focuses on the speed of cash flowing.* One of the most important lessons I learned from rich dad was to not let my money sit in a bank or in a cattle feedlot for years. The job of my money was to work hard for me, acquiring more assets.

In order to accelerate the speed of money through the different asset classes, a person needs to understand and use the power of:

1. OPM (other people's money)
2. Entity selection
3. Tax laws

These subjects will be covered more fully as the book goes on. It is these powers that give your money speed as well as protection.

Why Speed Is Important

One of the reasons the velocity of my money is important is because if it does not move quickly, it is often attacked by predatory taxes, has less chance of being leveraged with other people's money, and becomes a target for thieves. People who have their money sitting in a retirement account for years have very little velocity and therefore pay excessive taxes—and have their money susceptible to thieves, faster investors, and market forces. So why is this book different? This book is different because it is about the speed of your money, more than the asset you invest in.

To Better Understand the Message in This Book

To understand the rest of this book you need to understand that investing for cash flow is different from investing for capital gains.

The mentality of a capital gains investor is very different from that of a cash flow investor. As stated at the start of this chapter, the rancher and a dairy farmer both count their cattle as assets. The difference is, they treat them differently.

Most People Invest for Capital Gains

Another reason I have dedicated so much time to the difference between capital gains investors and cash flow investors is because most people invest for capital gains. That is what the investment advisory industry has trained the masses to do and is why most investors think investing is risky.

Skill Versus Luck

While there are many capital gains investors who have tremendous skills, most capital gains investors count on luck, not skill. To be a person who invests for cash flow does, however, require tremendous skill and knowledge. The moment a person begins to invest for cash flow, they will soon find out that most investments do not cash-flow—at least for the right price. The moment a person begins to search for cash flow, they begin to find that most investments are bad investments.

It is really easy to walk into a financial planner's office and purchase a diversified portfolio that costs you money. It is really easy to buy a piece of real estate and lose money. You do not have to be a rocket scientist to start a business and have it go bust. The real skill of real investors is to acquire assets that cash-flow—putting money into their pockets rather than taking money out.

Acquiring an asset that cash-flows takes skill and a little bit of luck. Although I like being lucky, I would rather count on my financial skills to secure my financial future, rather than my luck.

Improving Your Luck

Most people believe they are lucky . . . that is until they are unlucky. Most people tend to believe, "That will happen to someone else . . . it won't happen to me."

While I also feel lucky to have this gift called life, I do not count on luck when it comes to my financial security and my financial freedom. In the following chapters of Part I, you will find out not only how to increase and protect your cash flow, but how to improve your luck by being smart rather than by being lucky. You begin to be smart when you seek the right advice from the right advisors.

The Right Advice from the Right Advisors

I was watching a TV show where a woman was onstage, baring her soul, saying, "I seem to attract the wrong type of men." The female host smirked and said, "Attracting men is good. Your problem is, you give the wrong type of men your phone number."

Rich dad said, "Just because a person has a business card with a major financial corporation and a great title, such as VP, does not mean they know anything about investing. Too many people call the wrong people and leave their number with them."

The purpose of this book is not to blame anyone for losing people's money. Rather than blame a person or a group for personal losses, in my opinion, it is better to take personal responsibility for what happens to us, learn from our mistakes, and seek the right advice from the right advisors. That is what rich dad did after I invested in my mutual fund. He took me to the right advisors. But he also taught me that each advisor has his or her own point of view. I needed to learn to identify which advice was right for me.

A Word of Encouragement

Most people would rather work hard and then turn their money over to a money manager and hope and pray the money manager is a smart investor. While I recognize that this may be the right thing to do for most investors who are not willing to educate themselves financially, to me that is not only risky, it is not much fun and not very profitable.

Before going on, I would like to offer a few words of encouragement. When it began to dawn on me that I was probably not going to get rich quickly and I had to start building or buying assets, I became very discouraged. So I understand how some of you may be feeling at this moment thinking about building two or three asset classes, especially when you may not have even one today.

My words of encouragement are these: Think of building or acquiring assets in two or three asset classes as taking the time to learn two to three different games. For example, saying to yourself, "I will invest ten years learning how to play tennis, racquetball, and golf." Even if you are not good at any of those sports today, in ten years you could be pretty good at all three. You would be far better than your friends, especially if they never practiced any of the games for the same ten years.

And that is what happens with money and investing. For years, I struggled. After ten years, I was pretty good at the game, even if my scores were not that good. After twenty years, I am better at my games and my scores prove it. In other words, today I make much more money than some of my friends who made more money when we were younger.

For those of you who do not feel you are that smart, neither am I. Yet I studied hard but slowly, and I surrounded myself with people who were smart. For those of you who are afraid to start, so was I. So again, I found friends who helped me start. If you read my book *Retire Young Retire Rich,* it begins with my best friend Larry Clark, Kim, and me sitting in a log cabin covered in snow, and making plans for the next ten years of our lives. Ten years later, we were all financially free.

As rich dad said, "Anything is possible if you give yourself enough time."

What Makes Sense to You

Many people have said, "What you recommend is risky."

My response is, "I don't recommend. I simply explain how the rich get richer."

They then say, "Well, for most people, what you write about is impossible."

To which I respond, "It's not impossible, it's improbable. People have done what I write about. I have done it and so have many other very rich people. I believe it's up to the individual to decide if it's impossible. I know

I thought it was impossible when I started out and for years I struggled. But today, I have made more money in a day than many people make in a lifetime. It is a matter of personal choice. We do live in a free country."

What makes sense to you? I realize that what I do and what I write about is not the easy road. I chose the *hard road* because the *easy road* made no sense to me. To me, it made no sense:

1. To have a job and be an employee, working hard for something I would never own and could never sell. And if I stopped working, the cash flow would stop.

2. To start putting my money into a pension plan at twenty-five, parking it, and not to see it again till I was sixty-five. I want my money back in less than five years and I want to keep the asset. I did not want to slaughter the asset to get my money back.

3. To leave my money in the feedlot for forty years, exposed to the ravages of cowboys, crooks, and convulsions of the market. Never mind the crooks and market convulsions, most managed funds take an average management fee of 1.5 percent per year, even if they say they don't. Over forty years compounded, that adds up to a lot of money, regardless if you make any money in the fund or not.

Whatever makes sense to you often determines your choices in life. What made sense to me was to seek the right advice from the right advisors, rather than just salespeople, to start building my own assets and my own pipelines between the assets, to expand the volume of cash flow, and to increase the velocity of my money. The rest of the book is about what finally made sense to me when I was twenty-five years old. I wrote this book in hopes that some of what I write about makes sense to you and your future as well.

Sharon's Notes

Cash flow is to our financial lives what air is to our bodies. Cash flow is the basis of rich dad's teachings and the underlying foundation of our books and financial products. Teaching people to look for and create positive cash flow is what sets rich dad and Robert Kiyosaki apart from many other financial experts and educators.

Cash flow	vs.	Capital gains
Dairy farmer	vs.	Cattle rancher
Cash in my pocket every month	vs	Cash in my pocket when I sell
System	vs.	Single transaction
Pipeline	vs.	Buckets

The concept is simple, so why doesn't everyone invest for cash flow? Are we trapped in a world of "buy low, sell high"? Is your only source, or major source, of monthly cash flow your paycheck? What would happen to your cash flow if you became ill or unable to work?

We have been programmed as a society to "save" as opposed to "invest." The concepts we introduce in *Who Took My Money?* about the three asset classes and accelerators may seem overwhelming and complex, but take them one at a time.

A business asset could be a single vending machine, a Laundromat, an Internet company, a network marketing business, or a business franchise. Real estate could be a single-family rental home or condominium. We recommend you start small and learn from your mistakes.

In *Rich Dad Poor Dad*, our first book, there is a chapter called "Mind Your Own Business." It says that what you do FOR your paycheck is your job or profession, what you do WITH your paycheck is your business. The cash flow from your job or profession can help you buy or build assets that can generate additional cash flow for you.

In addition, analyze how you spend your time. Are you working for money—or are you working to buy or create assets that will generate money for you? You may want to adjust the way you spend your time.

Rich Dad's objective in starting businesses and owning real estate is to generate positive monthly cash flow. The object of our board game CASH-FLOW (notice the name of the game is also the object of the game!) is to accumulate assets that build your passive income (income generated by your assets, not by you) to the point where it exceeds your monthly living expenses. It is at that point you are "Out of the Rat Race."

Chapter 3

Ask Your Banker

"Most people only use their banker to get poorer. You need to learn
to have your banker help you get richer."

— Rich Dad

In my search to find the answer to the question "What is the difference between a sales pitch and financial education?" rich dad asked me to go with
him and interview his banker. On a weekday during one of my visits home, he
took me over to his bank and introduced me to his favorite loan officer. Sitting down in front of the loan officer's desk, I did as rich dad had instructed
me. I asked the banker if he would lend me money to invest in mutual funds
for my retirement.

The banker smiled when he heard the question. "You're trying to teach
this young man a lesson, aren't you?" he asked, glancing over at rich dad.

Rich dad nodded, saying, "Yes. I thought it best this young man got the
answers straight from the source."

Jim, the banker, smiled, turned to me, and asked, "And what are you going to do with these mutual funds?"

On cue, doing as rich dad had instructed me to, I said, "I'm going to invest for the long term—buy, hold, and diversify these funds."

The banker nodded and grinned. "I'm glad to see you're beginning your
investment career early."

"So will you lend me the money?" I asked.

"I'm afraid not," Jim said gently. "As a matter of policy we rarely lend money for mutual funds. If you had a job and excellent credit, we might lend you some money as a personal line of credit, and then you could invest in mutual funds, or anything you wanted to spend your money on."

"If I came to you to invest in real estate, would you at least look at the investment before saying no?" I asked.

"Yes, I would definitely be more inclined to consider the investment. But I would still want to look at your personal finances and credit history. We always want to know who we are lending our money to, regardless of what the money is used for."

"So why real estate over mutual funds?"

"There are many reasons," said Jim the banker.

"Is it because mutual funds are riskier than real estate?" I asked.

"That is definitely one of the reasons," Jim said quietly. "But as I said, there are other factors to consider."

"If your bank won't lend me money for mutual funds, then why do so many people invest in mutual funds?" I asked.

"Good question," smiled Jim. "I should ask myself that. I invest in mutual funds."

"Do you invest in real estate?" I asked.

"No, I own my house . . . well the bank owns my house, but no, I do not invest in investment property."

"But why don't you?" I asked, now very puzzled. "If your bank will lend you money to invest in property but not mutual funds, why not use your bank's money to invest?"

Jim was now getting flustered. I could tell he was more used to asking the questions than being the person being asked. "Look," he said courteously, "I have other customers waiting." Pointing at rich dad, he said, "Your friend here owns a lot of investment property. Maybe you should ask him those questions."

"I will," I said, nodding. "I will."

Rich dad and I walked silently out the door and headed for the car. I could tell that my lessons on becoming a better investor were well under way. "He's not really an investor, is he?" I said to rich dad as I closed the car door.

"No, he's a professional banker. He'll probably be a banker for the rest of his life. But even if he isn't an active investor, as a banker he holds a vital and important key to your investor education," rich dad said as he turned the ignition and began backing out of the bank's parking lot. "If you're going to become a rich and successful investor, your education begins by understanding the world of investing from a banker's point of view. Bankers are careful who they lend their money to. Did you notice that he wanted to know who you were before he would loan you the money? They don't lend money to strangers and neither should you."

No Free Lunch

We drove in silence to a small coffee shop. Since it was too early for lunch, the place was empty. After ordering our sandwiches at the counter, rich dad and I sat down at a small table and my education continued. Breaking out his yellow legal pad and pen, rich dad began by asking me, "As I have told you many times, there are three types of education that are important for your success in the real world. What are those three types of education?"

As I spoke, rich dad wrote. "The three types are academic, professional, and financial education."

"Very good," said rich dad as he listed them on his legal pad.

1. Academic
2. Professional
3. Financial

"Presently, what kind of education are you pursuing?"

"Professional education," I replied immediately. "When I finish the four-year program at the academy, I'll have my bachelor of science degree and a third mate's license to sail commercial ships throughout the world."

"Do they teach you much about finances or investing?" asked rich dad.

"Not yet," I replied.

"What do they tell you about retirement planning?"

"So far the general attitude is that when we graduate we will work for a large shipping company, companies such as State Lines, U.S. Lines, or Matson Navigation, and the company will provide the funds for our retirement."

"Old corporate entitlement thinking," rich dad said softly with his usual smirk.

"What did you say?" I asked, since I did not hear clearly what he had just said.

"Never mind," smiled rich dad. "You'll understand someday. It's just my attitude against the "take care of me" mentality so many people have today. Too many people expect the company or the government to take care of them once their working days are over. It's really kind of a welfare state of mind. These people often say, "If I work for you, then you have to look after my long-term welfare." But instead of calling it *welfare* they call it *entitlements* or *benefits.* I predict that when you're my age, the problem of too many people expecting to be taken care of will financially cripple many companies and many governments. Too many companies and governments are making promises they may not be able to keep in the future."

"How did this problem begin?" I asked.

"When I was a young man in the mid-1930s," said rich dad, "a federal program we now know as Social Security was implemented. Even though we were in the Great Depression at the time, there were many people who thought the idea of a guaranteed government pension was a good idea and many others who thought it was a bad idea. Unfortunately, as you know, Social Security is one of the most popular government programs today . . . even though it will someday greatly damage our economy. So the few individuals that thought Social Security was a bad idea put up a strong fight, but were outvoted. Today Social Security and this new program Medicare are turning into monsters of government *welfare* . . . better known as *entitlements* or *benefits.*"

AUTHOR'S NOTE

President Franklin D. Roosevelt signed the Social Security Act into law on August 13, 1935. In addition to several provisions for general welfare, the new act created the social insurance program designed to pay retired workers age sixty-five or older a continuing income after retirement commonly referred to as "Social Security." Medicare was signed into law by President Lyndon B. Johnson as part of the Social Security Amendments of 1965.

"Why do you stress the importance of the difference in names? What is the big difference between welfare, entitlements, and benefits?"

"Because when the programs were presented as *welfare*, most self-respecting individuals rejected the program. To most people, *welfare* is something only for poor people or helpless people. But when the same programs were renamed and presented to the public as *entitlements* or *benefits,* the public was more willing to accept the programs. That is the power of words. It's still a form of social *welfare,* just under a different name."

"So welfare is for poor people but *benefits* and *entitlements* are for working middle-class people."

Rich dad just nodded and said, "And the rich too. In fact many of the rich have another form of welfare, which is corporate welfare."

I shook my head, indicating that the conversation was way over my head. Getting back to a level I could understand I asked, "Why do you think Social Security is a bad idea?"

"Back in the 1930s, many people thought it was a bad idea. In protest, these people kept saying, "Social Security will create a nation of *spendthrifts.*"

"And has it?" I asked.

AUTHOR'S NOTE

Credit cards were not yet in use in 1966. We have progressed from a nation of spendthrifts to a nation of debtors.

"In my opinion it has," said rich dad. "For many people of my generation, when we came back from World War II, we no longer had to worry much about saving for retirement. After all, we now had a government pension, Social Security, and many of us had a company pension. So rather than learning about investing, preparing to take care of ourselves after we retired, we as a nation began spending like there was no tomorrow. In many ways it was a good idea because the economy expanded at a tremendous rate . . . but nonetheless we did become a nation of spendthrifts . . . and the spending is getting worse. But that is not the biggest problem caused from welfare, entitlements, and benefits—a nation of cultural welfare."

"What is worse than cultural welfare?" I asked.

"It has created a nation with a large group of people who expect someone else to take care of them."

"Is it a bad idea?"

"There is always good and bad to everything. There will always be those who want their free lunch and expect someone else to pay for it. Unfortunately, the numbers who expect the free lunches are increasing. Someday, as I said, probably during your lifetime, your generation will have to pick up the tab for all the free lunches that my generation is serving today. I'd sure hate to be running for president in 2012 or later."

"Why the year 2012?" I asked.

"Because that is when your generation begins to retire and will expect to collect the money you contributed into the system for years."

"What is wrong with that?" I asked.

"The money will be gone. All there will be are IOUs in the U.S. Treasury. Because we are becoming a nation of spendthrifts, we will go from the richest country in the world to the biggest debtor nation in the world. So I suspect your generation will find that all the money you have contributed will be gone. Your money has been spent. You are truly entitled to the money, but someone else has already spent it. How the government will explain the missing money to you, the first generation to fully pay into the Social Security system, will be a big problem."

"So how will that problem be solved?"

"As I said," smirked rich dad, "that's the challenge of your generation, not mine."

Our sandwiches were delivered to our table and the conversation on welfare, debt, and a growing financial problem ended.

Hitting the Wall

What Mr. Greenspan is saying is that the U.S. government is in deep trouble financially. In a few years, the U.S. economy will hit the wall if the problem of spending too much money and making too many promises is not fixed. By 2012, we will need to be changing our financial strategies dramatically. Financially, things will be very different. In a few years, there will be a battle

---

AUTHOR'S NOTE

In a *Business Week* magazine article dated February 24, 2003, Alan Greenspan, chairman of the Federal Reserve Board, states, "The march of baby-boomers into retirement will put a tremendous strain on the budget. It's a demographic time bomb that Washington can ill afford to ignore." According to White House calculations, "Social Security is in the hole to the tune of almost $5 trillion, while Medicare is in the red by more than $13 trillion." Greenspan ends by saying, "At the present time, there seems to be a large and growing constituency for holding down the deficit. But I sense less of an appetite to do what is required to achieve that outcome."

---

between those who think that other people should take care of them and those who think people should take care of themselves.

The Banker's Point of View

As we munched away on our sandwiches, rich dad began to further explain his ideas on investor education. "Let me show you some differences between how a banker thinks and your mutual fund salesperson thinks."

"Okay," I replied.

"First of all," said rich dad, "let me explain to you what is involved with financial education." Tilting the yellow legal pad closer to me, he began to write:

> 5. Exit
> 4. Protect
> 3. Leverage
> 2. Manage
> 1. Earn/Create

Looking back up at me, rich dad said, "Most people go to school to learn how to earn or create money. The problem is, that is where their education ends."

Turning the legal pad back toward him, rich dad then drew the following:

5. Exit	
4. Protect	
3. Leverage	
2. Manage	Financial education
1. Earn/Create	Professional education
	Academic education

Pointing at "Earn/Create," rich dad said, "Presently you are in school for your professional education. You're learning to be a ship's officer . . . a very high-paying profession."

Nodding, I said, "One of the highest-paying professions today. The problem is, there are fewer and fewer jobs available."

Continuing, rich dad said, "If you are going to be rich and prepared for the rough financial seas that your generation is heading for, you will need to learn the following areas of financial education." Pointing to the topic of "Manage," rich dad said, "Most people earn money from their work, but struggle financially, regardless of how much money they make, simply because they never learn to *manage* their money properly. Many people are smart when making their money but are foolish when spending it. Do you understand that?"

"Yes, I do," I replied, reaching over for rich dad's legal pad. "That is why you spent so much time teaching Mike and me how to read a financial statement and the differences between assets, liabilities, income, and expenses." As I spoke I drew the diagram on page 51.

"I remember in high school you saying to me, 'My banker has never asked to see my report card from school. My banker wants to see my financial statement. A banker does not care about my grade point average or what school I attended. A banker just wants to see how smart I am with my money . . . how well I manage my money.'"

The Power of Leverage

"Very good," said rich dad as he took back the legal pad. Pointing to the next topic, the word "Leverage," rich dad said, "The next step in your

Income

Expense

Asset	Liability

financial education, after *managing your money,* is learning how to *leverage your money.*"

"You mean I need to learn how to make money with my money . . . to have my money work harder than me."

"Not only your money, you want your banker's money working hard for you also."

"I want to invest with my banker's money?"

Nodding, rich dad said, "There are many people who manage their money well, but they fail to become very rich simply because they never learn to harness the power of financial leverage. Most people attempt to leverage their money by *saving* money or trying to become *debt-free.* While these are simple forms of leverage, they are not really forms of *power leverage.*"

"Is the reason you took me to meet your banker because a banker is a source of power leverage?"

Nodding again, rich dad continued on, saying, "When you invested in your mutual funds, whose money did you use?"

"I invested my own money."

"If you truly want to understand investing with leverage, you need to learn how to invest with someone else's money—someone like your banker."

"But your banker said he would not lend me money to invest in mutual funds."

"That is why I wanted you to talk to him. If you want to become a great investor you need to see the world through a banker's eyes. Did you ever ask your mutual fund salesman if he would lend you his money to invest in the mutual funds he was selling you?"

"No, I didn't ask."

"Professional investors are always searching for some form of leverage. One form of leverage is using OPM, or other people's money. That is why I want you to learn to see the world of money through a banker's eyes. A banker can be a wealth of information on how they evaluate risk and returns on investment. Most people just go to the bank to save money or borrow a few dollars for their home loan or consumer loans. Very few people ask a banker about how to use the bank's money as leverage, as leverage to become rich."

"That is why you say I need to know the difference between *good* debt and *bad* debt. Most people only see the banker for bad debt, debt that makes you poorer."

"Getting this lesson?" asked rich dad. "The lesson on the importance of leverage and investing?"

I nodded, took a deep breath, and looked back at the list on his legal pad. Over the years, I had heard much of this and I had observed him dealing with his bankers, often borrowing large sums of money. Now that I was older, the lessons had more impact . . . new meaning to me. "So the first reason people struggle financially is because they mismanage their money. The second reason is that they fail to leverage their money."

Nodding, rich dad said, "And in just those two steps the rich begin getting really rich while everyone else works hard and struggles financially. That is why I want you to continue to learn more about managing your money and how to leverage your money. Each step is a course of study in itself."

"How do I continue to learn more about those two steps?" I asked.

"From your banker . . . one who wants to help you," smiled rich dad. "Where do you think I learned it from? As you get older, make it a practice to talk to your banker. Take him or her to lunch. Pick their brains. Find out how they think, what they think is important, why they say yes to certain people and why they say no to others. All it will cost you is a lunch now and then. A lunch now and then is a lot cheaper than a college education."

Protection

Nodding was all I could do for the moment. For years I had watched rich dad invite his banker and other advisors to lunch. I remember him asking them questions and noticing how willing his advisors were to share their wisdom with him over lunch. Although rich dad did not have a formal education, he never stopped getting educated. Rich dad always surrounded himself with smart people from different professions and *listened* more than *talked.* He often shared his financial problems or challenges openly with them and asked their opinions on how to solve the problem or challenge. That is how he learned, how he gained his knowledge, and how he got ahead financially. He got smart and got rich over lunch. I got the lesson one more time. "And what about protection?" I asked, pointing to the word "Protect" on the legal tablet.

"That is a very big subject," replied rich dad. "But let me do my best to make it simple. Would you drive a car without insurance?"

Shaking my head, I said, "No."

"Can you own a home without insurance?"

Again I shook my head and said, "No. Besides, even if you could, that would be foolish."

"So why do so many people invest without insurance?" asked rich dad.

"I don't know," I replied. "I didn't think you could buy insurance for investments."

"Yes you can," said rich dad. "Professional investors invest with insurance but amateur investors do not. That is why amateur investors say investing is risky. Did your mutual fund salesperson offer you insurance for your mutual funds?"

"No he didn't," I replied.

"Besides telling you to 'buy, hold, and diversify,' did he tell you that the stock market goes down as well as goes up?"

"No. He just said that the stock market goes up by 9 percent per year, on average."

"Was he willing to guarantee that?"

"I don't know. I didn't ask. Would he have guaranteed me a 9 percent return?"

Rich dad just shook his head with a disgusted look on his face. "Now do you understand why I said that you made your investing decision based upon a sales pitch rather than sound investor education?"

"I'm beginning to," I said feebly. Thinking for a moment, I hesitantly asked, "Do you mean to say that professional investors invest with insurance?"

"That would be a great question to ask Jim, the banker," said rich dad. "Ask him if he would lend you the money without insurance . . . insurance such as mortgage insurance, title insurance, fire insurance, and so on.

"That is why you want to see the world of investing through a banker's eyes. Bankers often tend to be too cautious, but that is their job. After all, it's their job to protect the bank's money. That is why they ask for financial statements, credit reports, employment records, pay stubs. They don't turn their money over to strangers, like you did. They want to know who you are and how smart you are financially. They don't care about your grades or what school you went to. They want to see your financial statement, your financial report card. They want to know if you are financially savvy and so should you. That is why you need to start keeping accurate and neat financial records. Most people do not and that is another reason most people struggle financially. And no matter how confident they are in you, they still require insurance, or protections against risk. You should do the same things—if you are to become a professional investor. That is why I took you to the banker first. Your banker is one of your best teachers on how the game of money and investing is really played. Not that financial advisor who only sells you mutual funds, mutual funds that your banker won't lend you money on."

Rich dad had made his point. He now just sat and grinned at me in silence.

"Okay," I finally said. "I'm getting the message."

Rich dad kept grinning and finally said, "One of the reasons so many people think that investing is risky is because they know little to nothing about asset protection. Professional investors need to learn how to protect their investments from predatory taxes, predatory lawsuits, market ups and downs, disasters, and economic cycles."

"You mean you don't just buy, hold, and pray," I added sarcastically.

"No," smiled rich dad. "To a professional investor, insurance and protection are very important subjects. If you cannot protect the asset, you really should not buy it. As I said, you do not drive a car without insurance or buy a house without insurance. You should never invest without insurance."

Frustrated at how much more there was to learn about each subject, I said, "Let's move on to the subject of the exit."

Exit

"Besides buying, holding, and praying, what was your exit strategy?" asked rich dad. "Why did you ultimately buy that mutual fund? Did you have an exit strategy in mind?"

"No, not really," I answered sheepishly. "I just wanted to sign the papers and get back to my studies."

"I understand," said rich dad. "For professional investors, the *exit* is a very important area of study. Most amateur investors buy but fail to think about the exit. And because they do not know much about exits, the words 'invest for the long term' are comforting. It delays thinking or looking into the future, which is hard work for most people. Most people live only for the moment, thinking about today and not tomorrow. Suddenly they wake up, they are over fifty years old, and it begins to dawn on them that their days are numbered. That is when you hear them saying, 'If only I had done this earlier.'"

Realizing that time was getting short and lunch was over, I needed to ask for a quick lesson. "Give me an example of exit," I asked.

"Sure," said rich dad. "If I sell an investment and exit in one way, I pay taxes. If I sell it another way, I pay nothing in taxes. That is one of many examples of an *exit*. Did your mutual fund sales person discuss your different exit strategies before selling you the fund?"

"No. He just said to keep putting money into the account and watch the account grow in value."

"So he took your check and never discussed exit, protection, leverage, or management."

"If he did, I don't remember."

The Difference

With that, rich dad reached for his wallet and paid the waitress when she presented the bill. Before standing, he took hold of his legal pad and wrote the following words:

	exit
	protect
	leverage
	manage
Earn money	Earn money
Salesperson	Banker/Investor

"When you go to a salesperson for investment advice, most only want to know how much you can afford. That is true regardless if it is mutual funds, real estate, or a new car. That is why I drew nothing above the topic of earning money in that column. But a professional investor and someone like a banker needs to know more. That is why I wrote the words "manage, leverage, protect," and "exit," above "earn money" in the banker/investor column. A professional investor and a banker will be concerned with your knowledge of money management, how much leverage you are using, your protection strategy, and your exit. All your salesperson friend told you to do is "buy, hold, and diversify." In the long run, even if you buy, hold, and diversify for years, how much do you learn by doing that?

"What kind of investor do you become in the process if all you do is turn your money over to strangers and then do as they tell you to, which is to buy, hold, pray, and lick stamps . . . for years?"

I did not need to say anything. I just sat quietly, thinking.

Two Professions

Rich dad stood and headed for the parking lot. Turning to me he said, "If you are going to be successful in the real world, you and your generation will need more than just *academic* and *professional* education. Your generation has some very rough financial times ahead . . . maybe even rougher than the depression my generation went through. You will find out that the prestigious military academy you are attending will teach nothing about financial education. That education you have to get on your own. That education begins by seeing the world of money through a professional banker's eyes. Bankers are not necessarily great investors, as you found out, but they sure do know how to tell a good money manager from a bad one and they always require assurances and insurance. You should too."

"So I need to know a little about a lot of different professions," I said, tagging along behind rich dad.

"You don't have to learn those professions," said rich dad. "But you have to have friends who are professionals in the required professions. That is why who your friends and who you go to lunch with is so important. Most people only spend time with people who are in the same profession . . . birds of a feather flocking together. You may recall I often had lunch with my banker, accountant, attorney, financial planner, insurance broker, real estate broker, and stockbroker. All I did was pay for lunch and I got the best financial education in the world. And it was education for the real financial world, not the academic financial world."

Rich dad had reached his car. Getting behind the steering wheel, he said, "Your generation and generations beyond will have to have at least two professions . . . one for you and one for your money. As you get older, you will want your money to work harder than you. My profession is business owner. My money's profession is real estate. That is where I keep my money and leverage my money—safely. My money and my banker's money is very safe because I watch over it—not some stranger."

"Two professions?" I said with a puzzled tone to my voice. Silently I was saying, "I'm having trouble getting this first profession."

Nodding as he started the car, rich dad said, "My generation has passed on the idea of welfare . . . today called *benefits* and *entitlements*. Many people actually think there is a free lunch and that someone else is responsible for their welfare once their working days are over. The problem is, there are millions of people who think that way in this country and the numbers are growing. Your generation is the generation that is already picking up the tab for this free lunch that is not really free. That is why I suggest you *not* follow in the footsteps of my generation. Don't expect someone to take care of you with a secure job, a pension, medical benefits, Social Security, and Medicare. Those entitlements and benefits are too expensive. Soon companies and governments will not be able to afford them. So learn to take care of your-self. I predict the U.S. economy will hit the wall just about the time your gen-eration begins to retire. If and when that happens, your generation will ask, 'Who took my money?' That is why you need two professions—one for you and one for your money."

Becoming a Better Investor

Rich dad shook my hand and began to drive off. I waved goodbye and headed for my car. The idea of taking care of myself rather than depending upon a company or the government was easy to accept. I did not want to be dependent upon anyone or any organization in any way. What was sinking in was that *investing* had little to do with the *investment*. Rich dad was not pro or against any asset class . . . assets such as mutual funds, stocks, businesses, bonds, or real estate. What he was adamant about was having me learn to be a better investor. To him, being a better investor was far more important than what asset class I was investing in. I was beginning to realize that the best in-vestment of all was to learn to become a better investor and that education began with my banker. Why my banker? Because if I was to use my banker's money to invest, I needed to be a student of money management, leverage, protection, and exits . . . *the fundamentals of a sound financial education.*

═══════ Sharon's Notes ═══════

The world of banking has changed dramatically in the last few years, but its primary business is still lending money and providing financial services. Robert's poor dad put his money in the bank or his retirement account, which is what many people do today. His rich dad, on the other hand, kept his money moving. He wanted his money buying investments, giving him a return where he would get his money back quickly so he could move it into even more assets. He did not like the idea of "parking" his money in a bank.

When you put your money in a bank, the law allows the banking system to lend out that money many times (it's called leverage of your deposit; the bank is required to keep reserves that are only a fraction of their total de-posits). As an example, you put $100,000 in the bank and receive 1 percent interest on your deposit, which would be $1,000. The banking system turns around and turns your $100,000 into loans totaling, for example, $1 million. If they charge interest at a rate of 10 percent on those loans they will earn $100,000 on your original $100,000, and pay you $1,000 for the use of your money. The bankers net $99,000 income from leveraging your deposit. This is a very oversimplified example of the complex banking and monetary system and is shown to illustrate the difference between saving your money in a bank and the leverage that the banks receive from using your money. However, the bank will also loan you the money to allow you to use this concept of leverage to your advantage.

Rich dad used the bank to leverage his money and to keep it moving. In effect, he wanted to become the bank. In a later chapter you will see how you can use $100,000 of your money to purchase a property for $1 million using the bank's money. You have the choice of saving your money or keeping it moving through the power of leverage.

As we said, the banks are in the business of lending money. Get to know your banker, have him or her as part of your advisory team and keep in regular contact.

We send updated financials to our banker regularly. By having an established relationship and keeping him updated on our financial condition, it allows us to move quickly when investment opportunities arise. In addition, he will let us know of investment opportunities that become available through the bank.

Your banker, or mortgage lender, can provide this tremendous source of leverage for you in your investments in several ways. Three examples are:

1. *Securing the investment:* You can secure a loan for a business or piece of real estate that allows you to leverage the cash you have on hand. We share an example in the book's introduction where we purchase a $1 million property with only a $100,000 down payment. The $900,000 bank loan provided us with a 9:1 leverage. The underlying tenant or business should provide not only sufficient cash flow to pay the debt service to the bank but also generate positive cash flow for you.

2. *Depreciation of the entire asset:* The tax law allows you to depreciate the value of the real or personal property involved in the real estate or business investment. So even though you only put 10 percent cash down, you will get the benefit of the depreciation of the entire investment. The

tax law allows you to offset your income by depreciation so you pay less tax. This will be explained further in Chapter 5.

3. *Ownership of the appreciation:* By leveraging through debt with your bank or lender, you still maintain 100 percent ownership of the underlying asset. As long as you pay the debt service to the bank as required, you will enjoy 100 percent of the appreciation of the asset (even the appreciation for the 90 percent purchased through the debt!).

All three of these leverages accelerate your return on investment dollars. It does pay to get to know your banker.

Chapter 4

Ask Your Insurance Agent

"Most people think investing is risky simply because they invest
without insurance. It's not investing that is risky. It's the investor
without insurance that is risky."

— RICH DAD

Summer vacation 1966 was quickly coming to an end. I had not seen rich dad in about two weeks and I wanted to continue with my financial education, so I gave him a call.

"Okay," he said, "meet me on Bishop Street. I'll take you to lunch with my insurance agent. I have a meeting with him anyway, so you might as well come along."

This time the meeting was at an elegant downtown Honolulu restaurant, the kind of restaurant that businesspeople frequent . . . the kind of restaurant where deals are made or lost. Rich dad was already there. He had arrived earlier to conduct his business with his insurance agent and was now ready to have lunch. Rich dad stood, shook my hand, and said, "I want you to meet Dan. Dan handles all the insurance for my properties."

Dan was tall, well-dressed, distinguished-looking, and a little older than rich dad. "Glad to meet you," he said as he stood and shook my hand.

"Robert is home on vacation from his school in New York. I'm helping him with his financial education," said rich dad.

"That's good," said Dan. "The earlier you learn about money the better. What are you teaching him?"

"Well, today, it's not what I'm teaching him. It's what you're going to teach him," said rich dad, smiling. "That's why I wanted to have lunch with the two of you."

"What do you want me to teach him?" asked Dan.

"Well, for starters, what is the first rule of the insurance profession?"

Dan chuckled and smiled. "Okay, let's begin there." He then paused to collect his thoughts and said, "The first rule of insurance is: 'You can't buy insurance when you need it.'"

"So when do you buy insurance?" I asked naively.

"Before you need it," said both rich dad and Dan, laughing out loud.

Dan took over from that point and said, "I really shouldn't be laughing because it is really tragic. Do you know how many people come to see me *after* they need me? For example, it's tough to buy auto insurance the day after you crash your car. It's tough to buy property insurance after the building has burned down. The sad thing is that if a person really does need insurance, in most cases I can't help them."

"So you buy insurance before you need it?"

"Yes," said Dan. "Before you need it."

Rich dad then spoke up, saying, "If you are to be a good investor, regardless of what you invest in, you need to understand insurance . . . or protection from losses. Investing is far less risky when you have insurance."

"So the people who say investing is risky often do not have insurance?" I asked.

"Yes," rich dad continued, "As we have been discussing, many people turn their money over to total strangers, believing as you did in the sale pitch of 'Invest for the long term, buy, hold, pray, and diversify.' When a catastrophe occurs—and there are always catastrophes—they lose their money, then they come looking for insurance. That's not only risky, that is ridiculous."

Dan just sat there nodding. This time he was not smiling. He was actually pretty somber.

"Do you insure mutual funds?" I asked.

"No," said Dan.

"Do you insure stocks and bonds?"

Again, Dan said, "No."

"What do you insure?"

"In the world of business and investing, I insure people. Key people such as your rich dad."

"What is a key person?" I asked.

"Someone who is vitally important to the management team of the business. In case something happens to him, his businesses will have the funds to hire someone to replace him. But there are many other types of personnel insurance other than what is known as *key man* insurance. Basically there are types of life or disability insurance. People insurance."

"What else do you insure?"

"We insure real estate and other forms of property such as cars, boats, planes, and equipment."

"But you don't insure mutual funds or stocks?"

"No," said Dan. "Someone might, but I do not know of anyone who does. People have asked, but we tell them the same thing I am telling you."

"Why don't you insure mutual funds?" I asked.

"Because they're too risky," said Dan. "But as I said, someone might insure your stocks, bonds, and mutual funds against market losses. I just don't know who they are. There is insurance for anything—if you are willing to pay the price."

"So you don't insure pensions?"

"No. But I'll look into it for you if you want. Maybe there is a company that does. I suspect it might be pretty expensive insurance."

Turning to rich dad, I said, "So your business and real estate investments have insurance against catastrophic losses?"

"Yes," said rich dad.

"But my mutual funds do not."

Both Dan and rich dad nodded.

"So a smart investor needs to think of insurance or protection against losses *before* the loss happens. That's the lesson?" I asked.

Again both Dan and rich dad nodded.

Naked Investors

As stated earlier, between March 2000 and March 2003, millions of people lost trillions of dollars . . . and that does not include the losses of jobs, other forms of income, and emotional trauma. Why did millions of investors lose trillions of dollars? Simply put, most investors did not have any insurance against catastrophic losses and the price was measured in trillions of dollars. That is the price of taking advice from investment salespeople rather than real investors.

Did some investors have insurance? Absolutely. In the world of professional investors, they use such words as "covered." When an investor says his position is *covered* or *hedged,* he or she means they are protected from a change in market conditions. If they say they are "naked," they mean they are *not covered,* not insured. A professional investor is very aware when they are naked. Just as a banker will require you to have multiple types of insurance when they lend you money to invest in real estate, a professional investor in the stock market will insist on insurance, although different types of insurance from real estate. The lesson is, professional investors are *covered* and amateur investors are *naked.*

The Witch Hunt Begins

As Dan, rich dad's insurance broker, had said, "You can't buy insurance when you need it. "After the crash, when many investors realized they had no insurance against a market crash, rather than say, "I should have had insurance," they went looking for someone to blame and burn.

Historically, after any market crash, some of the more obvious crooks float to the surface and angry investors go on witch hunts, looking for someone to blame. Back in the late 1980s, investors went after Ivan Boesky and Michael Milken, the Drexel Burnham Lambert junk bond king. They also went after real estate developers such as Charles Keating, when the savings and loans began to crash.

Ten years later, instead of hunting for witches who dealt in bonds and real estate, people are hunting witches who dealt in stocks and mutual funds and CEOs such as the executives of Enron, WorldCom, Global Crossing, Tyco, Adelphia, and other corporations who are accused of cooking their books with the help of accounting firms such as Arthur Andersen. The biggest investment houses in the world, firms such as Merrill Lynch, Solomon Smith Barney of Citigroup, Goldman Sachs, Credit Suisse First Boston, Deutsche Bank, Morgan Stanley, JP Morgan Chase, Lehman Brothers, UBS Warburg, and Bear Stearns agreed to individual settlements with securities regulators in an aggregate of $1.4 billion, $900 million in fines, $450 million to pay for independent research and $85 million for what regulators called "investor education." Individuals were sent to jail, such as Sam Waksal, CEO of ImClone Systems. Others lost their professional positions, such as Kenneth Lay, Bernie Ebbers, and Dennis Kozlowski. Mutual funds continue to be under intense investigation for fraud. Insider trading at some of our largest corporations is being scrutinized by securities regulators. Angry investors are still looking for someone to blame.

When it comes to understanding insider trading I recommend Arthur Levitt's book *Take on the Street*. For those that do not know who Arthur Levitt is, he was the head of the Securities and Exchange Commission for eight years during President Bill Clinton's term of office. In his book, Mr. Levitt explains how Wall Street really works and why the little investor has very little chance of winning in the stock market. In his book he explains in detail:

1. How legal and illegal insider trading really works.
2. How he fought to stop insider trading—and who fought him.
3. He actually names the people who fought him, such as leading politicians, many of whom are Democrats; bankers; the heads of brokerage houses, large financial institutions, such as mutual funds and pension funds; and of course, the large accounting firms. I thought it courageous of him to actually name some of the people who are still operating behind the scenes, took a lot of money, and will never be charged for any crimes.
4. In detail, he exposes the lies that mutual fund companies tell. He calls them their *dirty little lies*.
5. He also tells you how the little investor can still beat the big investors . . . the investors that control the game from the inside.

The point is, if you are going to invest in stocks and mutual funds, and I do, Arthur Levitt's book is a must read. To naively hand your money over to those very rich strangers and not know what they are doing with *your*

money is foolish. In the movie *Wall Street*, Michael Douglas played Gordon
Gekko. In that movie, Gordon Gekko said it best. His line goes, "If you're not
on the inside, you're outside." Arthur Levitt's book gives a glimpse into the
inside . . . the dark side of the inside.

For me, the most interesting section of Levitt's book is the section
where the former chairman of the SEC describes his battle to get Regulation Fair Disclosure into law. Basically, Reg FD, as it is called, is about stop-
ping the trading of inside information with the rich and powerful. I found
it interesting how many already rich, successful, and influential people do
not want the public to know how the inside of the stock market really
works. Simply put, many of the rich and famous in America and the world
had insider information long before the little investor did. In other words,
there was no *fair disclosure* . . . which meant insider trading was legal for
the rich and powerful. The little investor never really did have a fair chance
of making money. If they did make money, it was only after the rich and
powerful did.

When the market started to crash, the big investors were getting out
while at the same time telling the little investors, through their network of financial advisors and journalists, to stay in the market, invest for the long
term, and buy more. In other words, the little investors were instructed to
buy the shares the rich and powerful were selling. Although this is not necessarily illegal, to me it is deceptive, unethical, and immoral.

After much of a fight, Regulation Fair Disclosure was finally passed into
law on October 23, 2000. You may notice how this date also coincides with
the beginning of the market crash, March of 2000. The bubble burst for many
reasons. One of the little-known reasons the market crashed so hard is because the insiders could no longer obtain and withhold information from
the little investor. Hence, the big investors sold in mass at the same time the
little investor was still being told to buy, hold, and diversify.

Who Are the Real Insiders?

In early 2003, I was invited to listen to former SEC chairman Levitt speak at
the Phoenix Country Club, in Phoenix, Arizona. There were about two hundred people invited and each was presented with an autographed copy of
his book. Maybe it was because I had already read his book or because I was

listening to him in person that his message had a stronger impact on me. As he spoke, it began to dawn on me that many of the insiders who stack the deck in favor of the rich are not the flamboyant characters like Gordon Gekko in the movie *Wall Street.* Many of the insiders are obscure people from professions we tend to trust, never guessing they are working primarily for and fulfilling the wishes of the rich and powerful.

During his talk, Mr. Levitt said, "It is the big accounting firms that are continuing to fight the rule changes that would make the market more fair for the little investor." In other words, the big accounting firms are working for the big corporations, not the little investor. Many people think of lawyers as being unfair, not accountants.

As I've said, I found Mr. Levitt very courageous in actually naming names in his book, a lot of names, including Democrats, Republicans, as well as former friends and business partners. He clearly states who he believed was on the side of the rich and who was on the side of the little guy.

In sum, sometimes in the real world of investing, you might need insurance protection from the people you think are on your side.

More Than One Kind of Insurance

As you may be beginning to understand, there is more than one kind of insurance when it comes to investing. There is insurance for people and property. There is also insurance against market cycles. And there is also insurance against mistakes, omissions, and lawsuits. The lesson that rich dad wanted me to get was that professional investors are always concerned about protection. When you turn your money over to a financial expert, one very important question is, "How safe is my money?" Professional investors do not simply "Invest for the long term, buy, hold, diversify, and pray."

The rich also use legal entities as forms of insurance. My poor dad was very proud that his house, his car, and his other belongings were in his personal name. In contrast, my rich dad held most of his valuable assets in the name of legal entities such as corporations, trusts, and limited partnerships. Because we live in a litigious society, he wanted to personally own as little as possible. To my rich dad, a legal entity was a form of insurance. Today there are even more types of entities available and different entities are appropriate for different types of assets. You may want to refer to our Rich Dad's Advisors book by Garrett Sutton, called *Own Your Own Corporation*, for more information.

Two Kinds of Insurance

In the second half of this book, I will go into the different types of insurances an investor should consider. But for now, I will just state that insurance can be broken into two distinct categories. They are:

1. INSURANCE YOU CAN PURCHASE
When I purchase a piece of commercial real estate, acquiring insurance is easy. I simply pay for it. It is the same for insurance on my car or on my life. I don't have to do anything much more than find a good agent and purchase the appropriate type of insurance.

2. INSURANCE YOU HAVE TO LEARN IN ORDER TO ACQUIRE
Choosing the right legal entity is very important to a professional investor. They seek advice from experts like their attorneys and tax advisors to make sure they are achieving the maximum protection for their investments.

I also use intellectual property as another form of insurance. It protects what I write and develop by not allowing others to use it without my permission. We have many copyrights, trademarks, and patents that protect our intellectual assets. You can learn more about this form of protection through the Rich Dad's Advisors book by Michael Lechter, *Protecting Your #1 Asset*.

When investing in the stock market, I have to also learn to use insurance. For example, in the stock market, I need to learn how to use put options or call options. Options are not only a form of insurance, they are also a form of leverage.

The problem with this second form of insurance is that you have to really invest the time to learn how to use these types of insurance or find the right members of your team with this expertise.

Most People Do Not Learn

Since most people do not want to invest the time to learn how to trade options, futures contracts, or other forms of stock market insurance, most people are safer investing in real estate . . . at least when it comes to insurance protection.

Even fewer people want to invest the time to build a B quadrant business. Yet if you do and you are successful, building and owning a B quadrant business in the right entity can give you the most leverage and protection in the world. If you are interested in starting your own B quadrant business, I suggest you keep your daytime job and start a part-time B quadrant business. If this sounds like something you would like to do, I recommend you look into a network marketing business. The reason I recommend network marketing is because some of them, not all, have excellent training programs that prepare you to be a B quadrant entrepreneur.

We also have a book entitled *The Business School for People Who Like Helping People*. This tiny book may give you some insights into some of the other benefits of building a B quadrant network marketing business.

What if I Do Not Want to Learn or Build a Business?

If you do not want to learn the insurance of hedging skills used by professional investors, such as options, or build a B quadrant business, do not worry. Just read on and you will find out what you can do and which investments are best for you. There are many ways to invest and many investments to invest in. I simply started with the highest leveraged and most protected forms of investments I know.

Investing the time to learn how to build a B quadrant business was the best investment for me. I do not recommend it for everyone, yet owning your own business could be the best investment of all, if you are inclined to build one.

Good News

Whatever you decide, the lesson of this chapter is that professional investors are proactive when it comes to asset protection. Always remember, the first rule of insurance is "You can't buy insurance when you need it." The millions of investors who lost trillions of dollars between 2000 and 2003 needed insurance . . . but had none.

Sharon's Notes

The definition of the word "insure" is "to guarantee against loss or harm." It would seem to be understood that as you create or build assets you would want to protect them through insurance.

I was discussing this book the other day with a friend who owns an insurance company and he panicked that we would be accusing the insurance companies in *Who Took My Money?* As we discussed it further, he had a great comment worth sharing. "In my twenty-plus-year professional life, I have never had a claim recipient complain that they had spent too much in insurance premiums."

Own Nothing but Control Everything

The term *insurance* includes far more than the typical insurance instruments that you can buy that come to mind. One of the most important types of insurance you can have is how you hold title to your investment assets. Some of the choices include:

- C corporation
- S corporation
- Limited liability company (LLC)
- Limited partnership (LP)
- General partnership
- Sole proprietorship

Sole proprietorships and general partnerships can be recipes for disaster. Our Rich Dad's Advisors book *Own Your Own Corporation* by Garrett Sutton reveals the legal secrets, strategies, and structures that the rich have used for generations to run their businesses and hold and protect their assets. By planning properly and utilizing the appropriate entities you can save thousands of dollars in taxes and protect your family assets from the potential attack of creditors.

In addition, once you start building a business or creating assets, you may want to review other ways to protect them, such as through copyrights, trademarks, or patents. Find a good intellectual property attorney and review your business and your ideas for ways to protect them and ways to insure others can't use them without your permission. Robert mentions the Rich Dad's Advisors book *Protecting Your #1 Asset,* which is a great place to start. It will help you know the right questions to ask your own intellectual property attorney.

Chapter 5

Ask the Tax Man

"The tax laws were written for business owners and investors."

— Rich Dad

After you earn or create income, one of the most important elements of managing, leveraging, and protecting your money is understanding the tax laws and taking full advantage of the tax deductions and tax deferrals available to you. These tax advantages serve as accelerators to your income and help you keep your cash flow moving and increasing.

We were not created equal under the tax law. Taxes are our largest single expense . . . and employees have the least number of legal tax deductions. Maybe you've heard talk about Taxpayer Freedom Day, which is in mid-May each year. It means that all the money earned from January 1 through mid-May goes to pay your income taxes for the year—*before* you get to start earning income for yourself. Because owners of businesses create jobs, the government offers many tax incentives to business owners, but not to employees. When you analyze the CASHFLOW Quadrant, the truth of the difference in the tax laws becomes even more clear.

If you are not familiar with rich dad's CASHFLOW Quadrant, it is introduced in book number 2 in the Rich Dad series of books. *Rich Dad's CASHFLOW Quadrant* is an important book for anyone seeking to make financial changes in their lives. The E stands for employee. S stands for self-employed, small business owner, or specialist. B stands for business owner, and I stands for investor. The book points out the mental, emo-

tional, and technical differences between the individuals found in each of the quadrants.

As a quick review of the difference between the left side and the right side of the CASHFLOW Quadrant: The left side E and S represent individuals working hard for money, while on the right side, the B represents teamwork and the I is where your money works for you. The goal is to have as much of your income coming from the right side of the quadrant, where your money works for you. Here are some more of the differences between the left side and right side of the Quadrant:

E-S	*B-I*
Individual	Team
You working	Other people's time and money
You working	Systems working for you
School prepares you	Experience teaches you
Benefits are important	Return on investment is important

Security is important	Freedom is important
Success makes you busier	Success gives you more time
Income is limited	Income is infinite
Few tax advantages	Many tax advantages

One frequently asked question is what the difference is between a businessperson in the S quadrant versus the B quadrant. The differences are significant and many. For one thing, if an S quadrant business owner stops working, their income often stops. For example, if a plumber stops working, their income stops coming in. A B quadrant business would be the type of business defined by *Forbes* magazine as a business with over five hundred employees working in support of the business. Another difference is that a B quadrant business can operate in multiple locations at the same time. An example is McDonald's versus a mom-and-pop hamburger stand that Mom and Pop have to be there to operate full-time.

We recommend that employees start a part-time business to take advantage of the tax deductions offered to business owners. Starting an S quadrant business is often the first step to creating a B quadrant business.

Different Tax Laws for Different Quadrants

The tax laws are significantly different for each quadrant. Different tax laws have been enacted that have significantly impacted the left side of the quadrant. Even highly paid employees and self-employed individuals are penalized based on the source of their income.

In 1943, the U.S. government passed the Current Tax Payment Act, which introduced income tax withholding for employees. The result is that the employee's income taxes are withheld by the employer and remitted directly to the government. It is often a shock to a new employee when he or she compares his or her gross pay to the actual amount of his or her paycheck. The employee only receives his or her net pay, the amount left after all the taxes have been withheld. Who Took My Money? The government makes sure it takes its share first from employees.

The employee can only invest or spend what is left after taxes, which greatly limits his or her options. Today there are only a very few tax-planning options available to employees. Other than certain itemized deductions, including an interest deduction on your personal residence and deductions for contributions to retirement accounts such as 401(k)s, IRAs, and SEPs, the employee has few tax deductions available.

Then in 1986, the government passed the Tax Reform Act of 1986, which took away tax shelters and deductions, which had previously been allowed. The limitation on the deduction of passive investment losses severely impacted highly paid individuals and professionals such as doctors, lawyers, accountants, architects, and other licensed individuals in the S quadrant. In addition, highly paid individuals now frequently lose even the normal itemized deductions due to a little-known phase-out of deductions. As your income increases, you start losing a percentage of your itemized deductions.

As a result, today there are few tax-planning opportunities available to the E and S quadrants. However, the tax code provides many advantages to individuals who operate out of the B and I quadrants. This is why I recommend people keep their E or S daytime jobs but start a part-time business on the side so you can begin building a business asset and take advantage of the tax laws created to support the business owner and investor.

During 2003, a major tax revision called the Jobs and Growth Tax Relief Reconciliation Act of 2003 was enacted that impacts all four quadrants by reducing income tax rates. However, many people claim the lion's share of the breaks went to the B and I quadrants—the quadrants of the very rich. This may be true, as the B and I quadrants are where new jobs and growth are generated.

While all taxpayers received reductions in tax rates and other benefits, my concern is that without proper education tax savings will be spent on consumption rather than on buying or building assets.

Whom the Tax Break Was For

The tax cut was advertised as a major break for investors, because in addition to reductions in the income tax rates, it also reduced the tax rate for both capital gains and dividends, income generated from the I quadrant. Investors had their capital gains taxes reduced from 20 percent to 15 percent for long-term capital gains. A 5 percent tax cut is a significant percentage tax cut.

In addition, the tax rate on dividend income paid was reduced to a top rate of 15 percent (5 percent for individuals in the 10 percent and 15 percent federal income tax brackets). Previously, dividend income was taxed as ordinary income, with rates running as high as 38.6 percent. That is a 23.68 percent reduction in income tax on dividends for people in the highest tax bracket. Now that is what I call a major tax break.

The reduction in dividend tax rates was intended to address the problem of double taxation on corporate earnings and shareholder dividends. Double taxation results from the income being taxed first at the corporate level and then again at the shareholder level when dividends were paid. Many B quadrant businesses structured as C corporations have had to carefully monitor and plan for their yearly earnings to reduce or eliminate this double taxation.

For those who have read my other books, you may remember that I tend to use C corporations when doing business. Many accountants criticized me for this, stating that utilizing a C corporation was double taxation . . . which it wasn't if you knew what you were doing and did your proper tax planning a year in advance. These same accountants were still recommending their clients use sole proprietorships and general partnerships for their businesses and real estate.

If you do not know much about the use of corporate entities, you may want to read Garrett Sutton's book, *Own Your Own Corporation*, a Rich Dad's Advisors book. This book explains the difference between C corporations and limited liability companies (LLCs) and S corporations and when each may be appropriate. It may save you a lot of time, a lot of money, and help you ask your accountants and attorneys the right questions.

Selecting the proper entity for your business or real estate is essential in protecting your investment. Garrett's book also explains why sole proprietorships and general partnerships are very risky ways to hold your investments, providing the least protection to you.

Different Tax Laws for Different Assets

You can further distinguish tax law advantages by reviewing each of the three asset classes: business, real estate, and paper:

Asset	Advantage
Business	Deduction of business expenses
	Deduction of business losses
Real Estate	Depreciation
	Passive losses
	Tax-free exchange
Paper	Tax-exempt securities
	Capital gains tax rates
	Dividend Tax Rates

Consider a Part-Time Business That Gives You Business Training

One of the reasons I recommend starting a network marketing business, even though I am not in network marketing, is simply because a network marketing business gives the little guy a chance to build a B quadrant business. Many network marketing businesses offer the little guy the opportunity to use a system that has the potential of unlimited expansion. You may start as an S quadrant business, but with their systems and guidance you can build it into a B quadrant business. As stated earlier, a B quadrant business is a business of over 500 people. If the network marketing company is good, the individual not only receives moral support, he or she receives business skills training not taught in schools, but which are necessary for success in the real world. That is why I often recommend network marketing for people who are serious about their financial success and independence. Now the government has given the industry an even bigger tax break.

That is why I often say that the best investment you can make is an investment into your own B quadrant business. It offers you the most protection in this uncertain world. Is starting a B quadrant risky? The answer is yes. But when you look at what is certain, what is certain is that the people in the E and S quadrants have very little protection. Their losses aren't uncertain—their losses are guaranteed.

Good Losses and Bad Losses

One of the reasons so many people are afraid of investing is because they are afraid of losing money. Yet not all investment losses are equal. Just as there is good debt and bad debt, good income and bad income, there are also good losses and bad losses.

I have a friend who's a medical doctor who lost over $1 million in the stock market in 2001. Although he felt terrible about losing the money, he thought he could find some way to offset those losses in tax write-offs. In other words, he thought he could turn those losses into some kind of advantage.

Returning from his tax accountant, he called me, saying, "Did you know the most I can write off each year is $3,000 in losses? At that rate, it will take me 300 years to write off the million-dollar loss." For my friend, his losses in the stock market were bad losses. He lost money and the tax man did not allow him much of a tax break for those losses.

The Biggest Loss of All

Among the saddest losses of all are losses to the average investor with a retirement plan such as a 401(k). People who lost money inside a 401(k) have no tax advantage from the loss. At least the doctor who lost $1 million was able to take a $3,000 write-off. People who lost money inside their retirement plans got no break at all from the tax man.

Accountants have argued with me that there is no tax advantage from the loss because the moneys put into the retirement plan such as a 401(k) were not originally subject to tax. This is because the contributions would have been deductions to the individual's taxable income in the year contributed. However, if you ask individuals who today see their retirements cut in half by the losses in the market, you would know that the losses were real.

Losses in Real Estate and Business Are Good Losses

Interestingly, a person who invests in building a business or in real estate can take advantage of certain losses. For example, let's say a business owner loses several million dollars in his business; this business owner may be able to deduct these losses against other income. If the losses are in a C corporation, the business owner may be able to sell the company with the net operating loss, NOL, to another business that is profitable and can utilize the loss. Of course, there are strict rules that need to be followed.

I often hear people say that building a business is risky. Yet if you look at the asset from the point of view of the tax man, investing in stocks and mutual funds is far more risky. If I lose a lot of money building a business, I can deduct or otherwise benefit from the losses. If I lose a lot of money in paper assets, in most cases those losses are real losses for which there is little tax benefit.

For real estate investors, the tax man offers a tax incentive known as *depreciation* to investors. Depreciation looks like a loss on many investors' financial statements but it really is not a loss, it creates a phantom deduction . . . which may result in a paper loss. A good real estate investment will be generating positive cash flow for you, but you may be able to shelter your rental income with the depreciation deduction, thus paying no income taxes on the rental income. In addition, you might be able to offset other income with the passive loss from your real estate up to $25,000, or even more, if you or your spouse qualifies as a real estate professional. (An added advantage is that the property may actually be appreciating in value, even though the tax man allows the investor to claim that the property is going down in value through the depreciation deduction.)

When I was first starting out as an investor, this bonus from the tax man made very little sense to me. Even today, I find myself twisting my brain around the concept in an attempt to understand it. One of the reasons I can attain a higher return on my investment dollars is because the tax man gives me a bonus deduction known as depreciation.

Tax Strategy for Paper Assets

The tax law treats long-term investments in most paper assets favorably through reduced tax rates for long-term capital gains and dividend income. One of the very few tax deductions available to employees relates to contributions to retirement plans. Again, rich dad referred to this as saving, not investing, or parking money versus accelerating money.

In addition to the reduced tax rates for capital gains and dividends, there are other strategies related to paper assets. My rich dad's plan was to build businesses, invest in real estate, and then invest in paper assets. The overall strategy included considerations of cash flow and taxes, as well as protection. In general I prefer tax-exempt securities, hedge funds, and options to equity investments.

A person who invests in equities, stocks, often talks about EBITDA (pronounced ee-bit-dah), which stands for earnings before interest, taxes, depreciation, and amortization, or the P/E ratio, which is the price to earnings ratio. Even though these have become popular terms, do they really tell you what you need to know to make an informed investment decision?

Sharon's Notes

The subject of taxes can be complicated and confusing. A situation may be treated differently depending on many different factors, including your personal tax situation, the entity being taxed, and the timing of the taxable event, just to name a few of the variables. It is vitally important to find competent tax advisors.

As a recap of the importance of understanding the tax law:

- You can maximize the protection of your assets and minimize your taxes by selecting the appropriate entity in which to hold your assets.
- You can reduce your taxes by proper tax planning on a regular basis with your tax advisor.
- Anytime there is a change in the tax law you should meet with your advisor to analyze its impact on you and your investments.
- Consider starting a part-time business if you do not already have one. (It should have a legitimate business purpose other than saving taxes.)
- Review your personal expenses to see if any qualify as legitimate business expenses.
- Learn the vocabulary of investing so you can better know what questions to ask your advisors.
- By properly planning your investment strategy and minimizing your taxes, you can maximize your cash flow.
- Reinvest your tax savings into buying or creating more assets.

Chapter 6

Ask a Journalist

"There is a fine line between lying and *not* telling the truth," said rich dad.

"What is the difference?" I asked.

"The fine line," rich dad replied. "When you find the fine line,
you will find the truth."

The Freedom to Lie

During my four years at the academy, the required course of study included Admiralty Law, which is law of the seas, Business Law, and International Law. While we were not training to be lawyers, as officers of ships transporting cargo to different ports throughout the world, the awareness of the different types of laws was essential to our professional training.

My International Law instructor was a U.S. Constitution fanatic. Every chance he got he wove in something about the Constitution, especially when he compared our laws with the laws of other countries. He was particularly enthusiastic about the First Amendment, which protects the freedom of speech and the freedom of the press. To him, it was this guaranteed right that made America great. He would often say, "In other countries of the world, the press is not free . . . speech is not free. In America, your right to say what you want is guaranteed. That is what is great about America."

Being young, naive, and idealistic, I was filled with admiration as this instructor spoke of the brilliance our forefathers had when they drafted the Constitution, the law of the land. The instructor did his best to have his class realize how revolutionary the ideals granted by the Constitution, to all people, were. Only after leaving school and entering the real world did I realize that the *ideals* the Constitution assures on paper are often less than *ideal* in the real world. Being young and naive, I actually assumed that freedom of speech meant we *had* to tell the truth. It took me a few years to finally realize that the freedom of speech protected the right to lie as well as other less than desirable types of communication.

Do Politicians Lie?

In recent history and in my lifetime, there have been at least three presidents of the United States who will be remembered for single statements:

1. "I am not a crook." (President Richard Nixon)
2. "Read my lips. No new taxes." (President George H. W. Bush)
3. "I did not have sex with that woman." (President Bill Clinton)

A Research Project on Lying

A political scientist at Britain's University of Strathclyde conducted an intensive research project and concluded that politicians lie. Glen Newey, the political scientist, whose findings were published by the government-funded Economic and Social Research Council, states, "Politicians need to be more honest about lying."

As an American taxpayer, it is heartening to know that the English government also spends their taxpayers' money promoting such valuable and informative research projects. It's good to finally have the truth on politicians. I always wondered if politicians were lying or telling the truth. Now I know.

The Freedom to Lie, Deceive, Damage

Now that I am older and a little bit wiser, I begin to realize how big and massive the ideals of freedom of speech and freedom of the press are. In my calm moments, I often sit quietly, doing my best to expand my awareness in an attempt to include the boldness and the brilliance the forefathers had to allow such an ideal to be granted to all people of a nation. I am also more aware of the good and the bad such freedoms allow and why we each need to be ever more vigilant as to what we read, see, or hear.

Today, with the advent of the World Wide Web, we as a people and a global community have even more challenges with a borderless world without rules, or rules without enforcement. The World Wide Web has taken the freedom of speech and the freedom of the press to whole new dimensions. If there was ever a time for greater personal responsibility, respect of the different laws, ethics, morality, and kindness, it is now. While there will always be those who choose to lie, deceive, and damage, regardless if it is in person or electronically, it is even more important today to remember to *not* be like such people, even though we may want to be.

Management of Information

In the model for building wealth, the word *manage* is number two on the list:

    5. Exit
    4. Protect
    3. Leverage
    2. Manage
    1. Earn/Create

When I do my classes, many people think that I am referring only to the management of money when I refer to management. In reality, "management" is a very big word, encompassing management of money, time, people, resources, and especially management of information. In my opinion, one of the most important assets an investor needs to *manage* is their flow of information—especially their financial information. One of the reasons so many millions of investors lost trillions of dollars is because they received financial information that was of poor quality, late, often biased, and sometimes dishonest. An example is the investment advice of "Invest for the long term, buy, hold, and diversify." It is financial advice about on par with the advice of "Eat at Joe's." While eating at Joe's may be good for Joe, it may not be good for you. Poor-quality food affects one's health and poor-quality information affects one's wealth.

Truth and Money

When it comes to money, the freedom of speech allows any of us to say just about anything we want to say, even if it is not true. Some of the other things our freedom of speech allows:

1. We can make promises we do not have to keep.
2. We can spread rumors and ruin someone's reputation.
3. We can pretend to be an expert speaking about things we know nothing about.
4. We can criticize.
5. We can deceive.
6. We can hurt.
7. We can have a hidden agenda and not disclose it.
8. We can exaggerate.
9. We can say "I love you" or "I'm sorry" yet feel no love or sorrow at all.
10. We can be factual and still lie.

Not only are individuals granted this freedom. So is the press.

You Don't Have to Say "I'm Sorry"

Between 2000 and 2003 there were many financial journalists, journalists for newspapers, magazines, the Web, radio, and television, who handed out very bad financial advice . . . advice that caused millions of people to lose trillions of dollars. Most of those professional journalists continue to dish out financial advice today. Never once have I heard any of those journalists say "I'm sorry. I was wrong." Not having to say "I'm sorry," or having to admit they had no idea what they were talking about, is another right granted by freedom of speech.

An article by Michael Lewis called "In Defense of the Boom" in the October 27, 2002, *New York Times Magazine* referred to the journalists as well. "Like every other newspaper, *The Wall Street Journal* was once interested mainly in fantastic success and added its share of fuel to the Internet boom. Now, like every other newspaper, *The Journal* is interested mainly in failure. Failure, even in Silicon Valley, is suddenly a form of corruption. And that's a pity. Because the other, earlier attitude produced some real, measurable returns."

The power of the press is not to be understated. That is why one needs to be careful about the management of financial information one accepts as from a competent source.

Wine Experts in One Hour

Speaking of competent sources, a friend of mine owns a vineyard in the Napa Valley. It has been in his family for three generations. He has told me many funny stories of tourists walking into his wine-tasting room and pretending to be wine experts, attempting to impress him and his workers with their knowledge of wine. He said, "Many people today think it important that they also be a wine expert." He said, "The good thing is that the more importance a person places on the need to be a wine expert, the easier it is to sell them the more expensive wine, even though there is not much difference between the expensive wine and our lower-priced wines."

Asking him if there is much difference from one wine to another, his reply was, "Yes, there is, but most people cannot really tell the difference. When it comes to wine, many people are faking it . . . pretending they know something . . . pretending to be experts. The vineyards make a lot of money catering to that pretense, playing along with the pseudo-sophisticated charade. If we make them feel they are intelligent and sophisticated, they tend to buy more of the expensive wine, even if there is not really much difference from one vintage to the next. The more we cater to their egos, the more wine at higher prices we sell. We know the primary motivation of most amateur wine connoisseurs is not really to become wine experts but more to impress their friends at their next dinner party."

"So how do you know a good wine from a bad wine?" I asked.

"The best way to buy a wine is, if it tastes good to you and you like the price, buy it," he replied. "I do not pretend to be a wine expert although I have been in the wine business all my life. When it comes to wines, there are really very few great experts . . . but there *are* a lot of people pretending to be experts selling to people who are also pretending to be experts."

"Sounds like the world of investing," I replied.

Poor People Teaching You to Be Rich

Rich dad often said, "When it comes to money, there are many poor people telling you how to get rich."

In 2003, while on a trip to Australia, I was interviewed by a writer who writes a financial column for a local newspaper. "Obviously, getting out of debt is your best investment," he said.

Withdrawing a little, I politely said, "Well, sometimes getting out of debt makes sense, and other times debt can be good, even beneficial."

"You're crazy," he stormed. "You don't know what you're talking about. All debt is bad. That is why I tell all my readers to get out of debt. Then after paying off their debt, they should invest in a diverse portfolio of managed funds."

"Okay," I said. "You write what you think is right."

"I do," he said.

"But don't you think your readers might like to know about the difference between good debt and bad debt?" I asked.

"There is no such thing. What you are saying is a load of rubbish. If you want to get rich, the first thing you have to do is pay off your bills, get out of debt, and start saving money."

I then asked the journalist, "Do you make your money as a journalist or as an investor?"

"That is none of your business," said the journalist. The interview was over and my point of view on using debt to get rich was never published.

The Definition of Intelligence

Rich dad often said, "The definition of intelligence is, if you agree with me, you're intelligent. If you don't agree with me, you're obviously an idiot."

Ask Your Financial Advisor

One way to manage your source of financial information is to ask your financial advisor a question similar to the question I asked the journalist in Australia. A question you can ask each financial advisor is "Do you earn most of your money as a financial advisor or as an investor?" You would be surprised how many financial advisors will respond exactly as the journalist did.

The problem with financial journalists is that you as a reader cannot ask them that question. And if you did, would they publish their answer truthfully?

How Long Does It Take to Become a Licensed Advisor?

One of the reasons there is so much bad financial information is simply because it does not take much education or training to become a licensed financial authority. In fact, in many places, it takes longer to become a licensed massage therapist than it does to become a licensed financial advisor.

Will You Guarantee It?

In late 2002, while on tour publicizing *Rich Dad's Prophecy,* I ran into a heated debate with a financial advisor who had his own radio program. For those of you who understand marketing and lead generation, having your own radio program is a great way to find new clients. The financial planner said, "Your book is wrong. The stock market isn't going to crash."

"How can you say that?" I asked.

"Well the reason the baby boomers will not pull their money out of the stock market when they retire, like you say they will, is because the baby boomers will soon be inheriting millions of dollars from their parents. Also, the Chinese will begin investing in the U.S. stock market and that will cause the market to boom, not crash as you think it will."

"Sounds good. That definitely might happen," I said. "Will you guarantee it?"

"Guarantee it?" The financial advisor scoffed and sputtered . . . not sounding too intelligent to many of his listeners. "Well, of course not. How can someone guarantee something like that? No, I won't guarantee it."

Will I Guarantee It?

The financial advisor finally recovered his composure. My words "Will you guarantee it?" had taken him by surprise and caught him in his deception. He then turned to me and asked, "Will you guarantee what you say? Will you guarantee a stock market crash?"

"Absolutely," I replied.

"You will?" he asked feebly.

"Sure," I said.

"How can you do that?"

"Easy," I said. "Any investor knows that markets go up and markets go down. Guaranteeing a market crash is the same as guaranteeing that it will snow in Alaska next winter. A professional investor knows there are always changes in the market cycle just as there are changes in the weather. It is foolish to believe that Chinese investors or baby boomers' parents have the power to prevent a market crash . . . a market cycle. There are certain things that always happen in the world of investing . . . and market crashes are one of them. That I will guarantee. That is why I know the premise of my book is accurate. The exact date of the crash may be inaccurate, but trust me, there is another crash coming. Market crashes have always followed market booms. No market can go up forever. That is an idea that flies against the laws of nature. As an investor, I would rather bet on the laws of nature than Chinese investors or baby boomers putting their inheritance into the stock market."

"So you recommend real estate instead?" asked the financial advisor, attempting to draw me off the subject.

"No," I replied. "Real estate also has cycles. I am recommending your listeners increase their financial intelligence and astute investors know that there will always be market cycles. That is why I will bet on the market cycles, not Chinese investors or baby boomers inheriting money and saving the stock market from crashing."

"We're out of time. Thank you for your comments," said the financial advisor politely.

One of the things I like about live radio or TV interviews is that it is difficult to change what I say. The audience hears exactly what I am saying and they are able to judge for themselves if they like what I say or do not like what I say. However, print journalists—people who write for newspapers, magazines, or the Internet—have the power to take what I say and change it, distort it, and yes, even lie. While the press I have received has been 95 percent favorable, there is always that 5 percent that is unfavorable. While I am a big boy and understand that one takes the bad with the good, I am always more fearful of journalists who are writers. Of the 5 percent of the press that has been unfavorable, most of that press has come from journalists who are writers . . . writers who have the power say you said something . . . even if you did not say it.

The Four Magic Words

One of the things rich dad taught me was to use the four magic words "Will you guarantee it?" anytime I heard someone speaking as an absolute authority. You would be surprised how many times I have used those magic words and caught an expert in their exaggerations and sometimes their lies.

Rich dad said, "The fine line between lying and not telling the truth is personal responsibility." When you ask someone to guarantee their statements, you begin to discover which side of the line they are on—yours or theirs.

This Sounds Contradictory

Earlier, I stated that you should be aware of someone who sounds too certain . . . someone who sounds like they know all the answers. I am aware that when I guaranteed a market crash I was sounding like a person who is also too certain and someone you should be cautious of—which you should. Yet, there is a lesson to be learned from this obvious contradiction. The lesson is that an investor must know when a person is being *certain* about:

1. Facts
2. Opinions
3. Principles

When the financial planner who had his own radio program assured his listeners that the market would not crash because the Chinese and baby boomers would save it, he was being certain about an *opinion.*

When I said, "The market will crash," I was being certain about a *principle*.

Rich dad said, "In your management of information, you need to know the difference between facts, opinions, and principles." When you inspect the reasons why millions of investors lost trillions of dollars, one of the reasons is because many investors based their investment decision upon opinions—not facts and principles.

Ask yourself this. Is the investment sales pitch of "Invest for the long term, buy, hold, and diversify" a fact, opinion, or principle? My answer is that it is an *opinion*, void of facts, and definitely not a principle. Any investor who invests only upon an opinion, confusing it with a fact or a principle, is delusional and often loses their money.

Increasing Your Financial Success

In previous books I emphasized the statement from the Old Testament "And the word became flesh." In other words, "You are your words." After my investment in mutual funds, rich dad was adamant that I know the difference between opinions, facts, and principles. My definitions for these words are:

1. Fact—something that can be proven to exist via some sort of evidence.

2. Opinion—something that may or may not be based on fact. The key words are *may or may not*. That means something may be a fact, but until I verify it, it remains an opinion. For example, if someone says "I have ten puppies," that statement remains to me an opinion until I can verify it. You may notice that bankers follow this gem of wisdom. If you list on your credit application $25,000 in savings, the banker will verify it even if they think you're an honest person.

3. Principle—something that is true in *all* cases—no exceptions. An example of a principle is the principle of *precession*. An example of precession is that when I throw a stone in the water, there will always be ripples or waves. The reason I can predict a crash with certainty is due to my certainty on the principle of precession.

The point is, when someone is certain of an opinion, be very careful of that person. Always remember that millions of people lost trillions of dollars because they listened to opinions they thought were facts or principles. Always remember rich dad's four magic words. If you suspect something is an opinion rather than a fact or principle, simply ask, "Will you guarantee it?"

The other day, I was looking at a very expensive apartment in Hawaii. When I said, "The price of this unit seems high," the salesperson said, "Yes, but when they add on the new golf course, the price of this unit will double."

All I said to that was, "Will you guarantee that in writing?"

"Of course not," said the salesperson. "I can't do that."

As obvious and as innocent as this little conversation sounds, it happens millions of times a day. Every day, millions of people buy upon opinions, rather than facts and principles. Just using those four simple magic words will help you find out what and whom you are dealing with.

Ask a Journalist

The reason this chapter is entitled "Ask a Journalist" is because if you decide to become a professional investor, you will need to be careful what publications you read and choose carefully what publications you get your information from.

I was having lunch with my mortgage banker, Scott, who happens to be one of the biggest mortgage bankers in America, lending several billion dollars a year. Out of the blue, Scott asked, "Why do these fancy money magazines not write about real estate investing? Most of those glossy money magazines only talk about stocks, bonds, and mutual funds. The only kind of real estate they talk about is fixing up your home, or buying a vacation home, or investing in REITs, real estate investment trusts. That's not real estate investing."

Agreeing, I said, "Because they need to keep their advertisers happy."

Whom Does the Journalist Write For?

One of the best ways to check the validity of your investment information is to first check who the advertisers are in the publication you read. Many publications that support the idea of investing for the long term in mutual funds have mutual fund companies as their primary source of advertising revenue. That is why before the crash, during the crash, and after the crash, these publications continued to write about the advantages of mutual funds.

While the magazines will state that their editorial departments are separate and distinct from their advertising departments to keep integrity in their reporting, it would have been financial suicide for those financial publications to boldly state on their front covers, "Mutual Funds Are Terrible Investments" or "Get Out of Mutual Funds Now." Instead, these publications continue to run year after year, issue after issue, the same tried-and-true cover headlines as "Which Mutual Funds Are Best?" or "The Top Performing Funds for 2002" or "Is It Time for Bond Funds?" or "Which Sector Funds Will Make More Money?" The question is, can such publications be fair and unbiased? Can they provide you with sophisticated financial information? Are they writing for you or for their advertisers? What is

the financial sophistication of their readers? I'll let you find your own answers to those questions.

In his book *The Future of Money*, Bernard Lietaer discussed the decline in
Americans' belief in the credibility of the media. He refers to Noam Chomsky's
claim that "the purpose of mainstream media . . . is not so much to inform or
report on what happens, but rather to shape public opinion in accordance with
the agendas of the prevailing corporate power." Lietaer goes on to say, "It has
become a practice for many magazines to submit articles for prior review by
the advertisers. The *Los Angeles Times* has even reorganized its management
structure in order to maximize advertiser-editor cooperation."

Managing Your Financial Information

The reason I wrote this chapter is because the quality of financial information you receive is vitally important, especially when it comes to your money.

One assignment I give people is to call a journalist, especially a print journalist, and ask him or her two questions. Question number one is: "Is everything in the media truthful, factual, unbiased, objective, and free of commercial
considerations?"

People who have taken me up on this assignment report back that almost all journalists scoff at the idea that the media is honest. Most journalists will admit that much of the media is not really about the truth. Much of
what is in the media is about entertainment and selling advertising.

The second question is: "Are *you* truthful, factual, unbiased, objective,
and free of commercial considerations?"

In most cases, the answer to this question is very different. Most journalists believe that they are truthful, factual, unbiased, objective, and free of commercial considerations . . . even though they believe many of their fellow
journalists are not.

My friend who is a therapist calls this "selective delusion." He also calls it
"professional discourtesy." He explains: "All professionals tend to think that
others in their own profession are quacks but they themselves are not. Most
professionals sincerely think they hold the flag of truth and honor for their
profession—even though many of their peers think they are holding a flag
with a duck on it. That is an example of *selective delusion*. All professionals
are guilty of it."

A Market Filled with Ducks

One day while in China, I saw a duck farmer herding his flock of several hundred ducks to market. As I sat in the car, waiting for the farmer and his ducks to cross the road, I thought of the therapist and his ideas on selective delusion. Turning to my friend in the car I said, "It looks like a convention of financial experts crossing the road."

My friend laughed and then he said, "Notice that the ducks are just quacking away, following the other ducks. Rather than quacking at each other, maybe they should be quacking at the farmer, asking him where he is leading them."

Delusional Duck

In the world of financial advisors, I too am guilty of selective delusion. I too am a duck. To be honest, in my mind, I sincerely believe that I do hold the financial flag of truth and honor. I am also aware that many of my peers think that my flag has a duck on it. When it comes to my financial advice, I am very aware that I too am a delusional duck.

Regardless of what I quack about or my fellow ducks quack about, the person I am most concerned about is the farmer, that silent figure that seems to be leading much of the world to market. Also, my concern is that many financial ducks are really working for the farmer, not their fellow ducks. Many ducks working for the farmer are disguised, as are journalists, investment advisors, bankers, insurance agents, and government officials. If one of the independent ducks suddenly stops quacking at other ducks and says, "Hey, where is the farmer leading us?," the ducks that are working for the farmer start quacking louder, calling the independent duck a "quack" . . . which many ducks are . . . including many of the ducks that work for the farmer. Nonetheless, once the ducks start quacking at one another, everyone stops asking questions about the farmer.

Whom Is the Duck Working For?

To attempt to stamp out the ducks that work for the farmer is not realistic and not practical. There are simply too many of them and many of the farmers' ducks do serve a useful purpose. Yet, it is not too unrealistic to ask yourself, each time you meet a financial duck, "Who is this duck working for—me or the farmer?" Is this duck trying to lead me to financial freedom or to slaughter?

Higher-Quality Information

After my 1965 experience with the mutual fund salesperson, rich dad said to me, "Better investors seek better information." He also said, "Better financial information is not readily available. You must go in search of it."

Today, I am constantly aware of the quality of the financial publications I read. I do glance at the headlines of popular money magazines conveniently placed near supermarket checkout stands. While waiting in the checkout line, I may pick up the magazine and glance through it. Occasionally, I buy one and read a particular article that catches my attention. Even though the article may be interesting, I am always cognizant of the advertisers, the fact that most of the writers may be well educated but not necessarily financially successful. I also question whom the target market and demographics of the publication are aimed at and if the publication is funded by the farmer. Many popular financial publications are targeting the well-educated, high-income professional with very little formal financial education who has little time to invest, and so they invest in mutual funds. For many of the readers of such publications, this level financial publication is as high as they go. Farmers love this type of investor and that is why they often have their own publications. Many money magazines are the farmers' tools for locating fresh ducks.

The point is, if you want to become more financially successful, you will have to go in search of your financial information . . . because many of the best financial publications are not sold in supermarkets or even in bookstores.

Be Careful Who You Invite into Your Head

The lesson I learned in 1965 was that I had to be very careful about who I invited into my head. Rich dad said, "We have locks on our doors for a reason. You should have a lock on your brain for the same reason."

Today, while I do read newspapers, business magazines, and watch the financial news channels on television, the information I choose to let into the deepest part of my brain comes from successful and rich investors rather than journalists who are employees who earn most of their income from a paycheck. Even though I tend to invest heavily in real estate and business I enjoy reading and learning from investors who do not invest in real estate. The people I do invite into my head are people like Warren Buffett, Federal Reserve chairman Alan Greenspan, Jim Rogers, George Soros, Lord Rees-Mogg, and others. On television, I have tremendous respect for Mark Haines and Ron Insana of CNBC. They seem to have a depth of knowledge and experience that many new TV financial journalists do not have. I enjoy *Kudlow & Cramer*. They are entertaining, honestly opinionated, and very bullish on the stock market. They are the beacons of hope for the millions who are hoping. The print journalist I enjoy reading is Thomas Friedman, the author of *The Lexus and the Olive Tree*. While there are many other fine journalists, whenever I see or hear something from these individuals I just listed, I usually take the time to let them into my head . . . always, however, remaining vigilant to their bias.

As far as newspapers go, I read *The Wall Street Journal* because it is more often bullish and I read *Barron's* because it is more often bearish. Today, I love reading *The Economist*. For a number of years, I would try and read it but had to put it down because it was too far over my head. As I grew older and a little bit more knowledgeable, I could read a few more articles in *The Economist*. Now I can understand about 65 percent of what I read in *The Economist*.

As far as business news goes, I find *Business Week*, *Fortune*, and *Forbes* are good for keeping up-to-date with the trends of big business. I find *Fortune Small Business* and *Fast Company* excellent for trends in small business.

For real estate news, I find my information in the market reports put out by many commercial real estate firms. Many of these reports are free and are a wealth of information about trends and challenges facing the professional real estate investor.

For more radical and specific information, I subscribe to several investment newsletters. If you do not currently subscribe to newsletters, all you have to do is subscribe to just one. Since many of them sell their list of subscribers, you will soon be inundated with solicitations from some very radical newsletters. Although some of them are written by quacks, I still learn something from their unorthodox points of view and their obscure bits of information.

By no means do I recommend you read what I read. The point of all this is to encourage you to actively seek a higher-quality financial information. Your greatest asset is your brain and you need to keep a door with a lock on it.

Summary of Financial Information

When scrutinizing what type of financial information you accept into your head, just remember the CASHFLOW Quadrant:

1. There are publications and programs written by E and S people for other E and S people. Most popular money magazines fall into this category as well as the many popular money experts who have their own radio program or TV show. Most general newspaper articles on money and investing fall into this category. Sometimes, a general newspaper may bleed over into the next category.

2. There are publications and programs written by E and S people about B and I people. Publications and media outlets such as *The Wall Street Journal*, *Forbes*, *Barron's*, CNBC, and Bloomberg TV fall into this category.

3. There are publications written by B and I quadrant people for B and I people, or people who are striving to be B and I people. Warren Buffett has an annual report that is read by many people. You can find excellent real estate information from commercial real estate brokerage firms—information that

most residential real estate agents do not have. There are also many specialty, often highly technical newsletters that are written by real B and I people.

I would say that the Rich Dad series of books, Rich Dad's Advisors books, and other Rich Dad products fall into this category of information.

I do not know of many TV or radio programs that are created by B and I people for B and I people . . . but there needs to be.

Seek Good Advice

One of my answers to someone who wants to know where to invest $10,000 is to invest some of your money in higher-quality financial publications and read them regularly. If you do not want to improve and upgrade your financial information, then definitely keep your money in a bank.

Advice from Losers

One of the worst sources of financial information comes from losers and you can find losers everywhere. For example, once while I was teaching a simple course on investing, a person raised their hand wanting to be recognized. The person stood and said, "Real estate is a bad investment."

"Why do you say that?" I asked.

"A friend of mine at work invested in a condominium and he has only lost money. He has not made any money."

"How is he losing money?" I asked.

"Well, first of all, he paid too much for the condominium. Then he did not have enough money to invest, so he did not put enough money into the down payment. Because his mortgage payments are so high, he does not collect enough rent to cover his mortgage and other expenses."

"Well, that's not good," I said.

"It gets worse," said the speaker. "He raised the rent and his tenant moved out. A new tenant moved in, damaged the unit, did not pay rent, so he had to evict the tenant. My friend is now trying to sell the unit but no one will give him the price he is asking unless he repairs the damage. He doesn't want to spend any more money on fixing the unit up and he does not want to lower the price. Because he has no tenant paying rent, he is losing even more money. He told me he would never invest in real estate again. That is why I say real estate is a bad investment."

More Powerful than the Power of the Press

This is an example of taking investment advice from a loser. It does not make a difference what the investment is, be it stocks, real estate, mutual funds, or businesses . . . each one of these investments has losers ready to hand out investment advice. A primary reason so many people are not successful as investors is because they take advice from these losers.

Keep a Door to Your Mind

At the start of this chapter, I mentioned the importance of freedom of speech and freedom of the press. These freedoms are also extended to losers and people who are afraid of losing . . . hence those afraid of losing are often the ones that spread the news about the losses of losers.

Before going further, let me make clear that I am not against losers. I have lost many times in my life. In fact, I often encourage people to lose more so they can learn more. After all, we are designed to learn from our mistakes. What I am against are losers who blame other people or events for their losses rather than learning from them. On top of that, these losers often infect others with their lack of success.

One important reason to guard the door to your mind is because these losers are everywhere. When I see someone who is struggling financially, I often ask him or her who they are close to and what their attitudes toward money, investing, and success are. Very often, the person who is struggling is taking advice from someone who has lost or is terrified of losing financially. Rather than being honest and admitting they are afraid and responsible for their own losses, these people are often cynical, critical, unhappy, or spreaders of bad news to anyone who will listen. This right to spread bad news or lie about true feelings or blame others for their lack of success or criticize those that are successful is a right protected under the First Amendment.

A Family Affair

Families are a major source of financial misinformation, deceptions, power struggles, and lies. Some of the more common negative statements I have heard regarding families are:

1. "I want to start investing but my (husband/wife) doesn't want to. (He/she) says it's too risky."
2. "I want to quit my job and start my own business but my father insists I keep my job. He says a small paycheck is better than no paycheck."
3. "My family thinks I'm crazy. In order to keep the peace I'm just going to do nothing."

The Biggest Liar of All

One of the most important lessons of life I learned in Vietnam. I have written about this event before, yet it is worth repeating, since the lesson is applicable in many areas of all our lives.

Early one morning, my crew and I were flying into hostile enemy territory. We were a gunship helicopter that escorted troop-carrying helicopters into combat zones. Suddenly we could see tracers from enemy machine-gun fire rising up toward us. Being a pilot new to combat, I began to panic. My flying became less positive and I began to worry more about dying than flying. Sensing I was losing the battle in my mind, my crew chief tapped me on the helmet, then pulled at it so we were looking at each other eye-to-eye, and said, "Lieutenant, do you know what the problem with this job is?"

"No," I said, shaking my head from side to side.

"The problem with this job is there is no second-best. Either we are going to win or that machine gunner on the ground is going to win. Only one of us is going home today."

In the heat of battle and sheer terror, I could hear my crew chief clearly. He had been here before with green pilots like me. I knew I was terrified. He knew I was terrified. My mind was racing with thoughts of doubt, fear, and insecurity. I was thinking of myself and not the four other young men on the aircraft with me. "What should I do?" I asked.

"As I said," the crew chief stated clearly, "the problem with this job is there is no second place. It's kill or be killed. If you are afraid of dying we are all going to die. Focus on what your job is—not what you are afraid of. Listen to the winner in you—not the loser. It's okay to be afraid but you cannot let the loser in you win. Focus on winning, Lieutenant. Do your job. Get us home."

Nodding, I turned back to face the bullets coming up at us, focused on winning, and did my job.

Don't Let the Loser Win

The lesson I learned that day is that inside each and every one of us is a *winner* and a *loser*. One of the main reasons many people do not attain their financial potential is because when it comes to money, most people allow the loser to win.

Even today, after years of ups and downs, of financial failure and finally financial success, I still have to contend with the winner and the loser inside me. The other day, I was looking at a beachfront piece of land and I could hear the loser begin talking. He said, "You don't really want this. It's expensive. Besides, what if the economy changes. What if interest rates go up? If interest rates go up, then prices on real estate will come down. And if real estate goes bad, then all your other investments and business will go bad."

Now, there is nothing wrong with the loser in you. The loser in you plays a very important role. The problem for many people is that the loser is the only voice in a person's head. There is no free speech. There is no First Amendment. When it comes to money, in many people the loser has already won. The loser began to lose the moment he began to listen to someone say, "Play it safe. Get a safe secure job and don't take risks. Save money. Get out of debt. That's the smart thing to do." In my opinion, that is the voice of the loser. I know that voice well because I hear that voice every day.

The lesson I learned in Vietnam is what I was fighting for. I was fighting for freedom and one of the most important freedoms is the freedom of speech. That day in Vietnam, I granted that freedom of speech to the winner in me.

Letting Both Winner and Loser Speak

So why is the freedom of speech is so important? The reason it is important is because very often the biggest lies are the lies we tell ourselves. Lies such as . . .

1. I can't afford it.
2. I can't do that.
3. I'll never be rich.
4. I'm not smart enough.

5. It's too hard.
6. I'll invest when I have the money.
7. I'll invest when I have more time.

A favorite lie of dieters is, "I'll start my diet tomorrow."

In upholding the ideals of the First Amendment, we need to grant the winner inside all of us the freedom to also speak. Both winner and loser are important. Both have the right and the need to be heard. That is what the freedom of speech is all about.

An Exercise

In my investment workshops, I often address the issue of the winner and loser inside of us. In fact, in some of the more intense workshops, a tremendous amount of time is spent on this issue, since in many ways the battle between the winner and loser is often the primary cause of success and failure in a person's life.

On a lighter note, I often ask people to write about an incident when the loser in them beat the winner. Many of the stories told are hysterical. I believe that all of us have stories when we passed up a great deal or great opportunity because the loser did the talking.

An exercise you may want to try is to write a detailed description of a time when you talked yourself out of winning. Then invest some time analyzing the thoughts and fears that caused you to talk yourself out of winning.

One of My Stories

I have many stories of when the loser in me won. One I often share with people is the time I purchased a condominium on the cheap side of a great building in 1973. Instead of purchasing a property for $48,000 on the ocean side of the building, I purchased the exact same unit on the mountain side for $34,000. Three years later, the property market boomed, as I expected it would. While both units went up in value, the oceanside units were selling for approximately $150,000 and the mountainside units were selling for about $70,000. If you do the math, you will find that the mountainside units were far more expensive in the long run. On top of that, the $14,000 difference in purchase price would only have cost me an extra $1,400 as a down payment to buy the oceanside unit, since banks were requiring a 10 percent down payment. For an extra $1,400, I could have made $100,000. Instead I saved $14,000 and lost $65,000, only making $35,000.

My lesson from this experience is to first look at *value* rather than *price*. Today when making financial decisions, I always remember that deal. I always remind myself that the loser won because the cheap person in me did the talking.

The other valuable lesson I learned is that the loser in me speaks louder when I am afraid or doubting myself. Today, whenever the loser starts talking, I need to remind myself to start seeking the advice of the winner in me also. Although I did not make as much money as I could have on that investment, the lessons have been priceless.

This is one of many of my own personal experiences when the loser beat the winner in me. The important thing is to learn from our lessons. When we learn from the loser, rather than blame someone else for our losses, we become more responsible for the *management of information* into our brains. If you can do that, the winner ultimately wins.

Sharon's Notes

Rich dad said, "Be careful whom you invite into your head."

Understanding the differences between facts, opinions, and principles is extremely important when analyzing the information that we are bombarded with each and every day. The better you understand the source of the information, the quicker you can determine if it is applicable to you and your personal situation.

Rich dad said, "Financial intelligence is having control over your cash flow." As we compare investing for cash flow with investing for capital gains we must recognize the information we are using in making those decisions.

In analyzing an investment for cash flow, you look at the current information and decide based on the current net cash flow. *FACT*

In analyzing an investment for capital gains, you typically invest in some-

thing that you believe, or have been told, will increase in value over time.
OPINION

Investing for both cash flow and capital gains is important, investing for cash flow affects your financial situation today, while investing for capital gains is hoping it will impact your financial situation positively tomorrow.

Chapter 7

Ask a Gambler

"Don't count your money while you're sitting at the table."

— A PROFESSIONAL GAMBLER

The Worst Investment Advice of All

Millions of people lost trillions of dollars because they invested for the long term. Investing for the long term could be the worst investment advice of all.

When Is Your Money Yours?

Rich dad said, "A professional investor needs to know three things. They are, *when to enter* a market, *when to exit* the market, and *how to get their money off the table.* As an investor, you need to be looking for a market signal to enter, a plan to exit, and when to get out. An amateur investor leaves their money sitting on the table and eventually loses it all."

"Why do they lose it all?" I asked.

"Because eventually the market wins. The market gives and the market takes it all back if you just leave your money sitting there."

Breaking the Rules

Years ago, when I was in my twenties, I went to Las Vegas to have some fun. Not having much money, I started out with a small bet at the craps table.

Rolling the dice, with only $1 at risk, I won a few times and lost a few times. Suddenly I hit the hottest winning streak of my gambling life and had soon won over $300. People all around me began to yell and scream, cheering me on, because they were winning also. As my hot streak continued, I began to notice people next to me were betting hundreds of dollars and I was following the rules and playing it safe. It dawned on me that they were getting richer faster than I was . . . and it was *my* hot streak.

Greed Set In

Greed set in. I began placing bigger bets, knowing that I was breaking every law rich dad had taught me but I was hot and the crowd was on my side. By breaking the rules, I was suddenly up $1,500, so I broke the rules again and bet the $1,500, winning again. Even though my common sense was screaming at me saying, "Take some money off the table. Go back to only betting $100," I didn't listen. I continued to break the rules. Rather than following the rules and putting $2,900 in my pocket, I bet the entire $3,000. I said to myself, "When you have $6,000 in your pocket, then you can play it safe." That thought reassured me, so I rolled the dice with $3,000 on the table, and lost it all.

Losing $3,000 was painful, yet it was a valuable lesson in investing. Even though rich dad had often said, "Be disciplined and follow the rules," it took breaking the rules to learn the lesson.

Bigger Losses

Between 2000 and 2003, many people broke rules by leaving their money in their retirement plans on the table. Millions of people bet their entire financial future on the roll of the dice. Even after losing, many of those same millions of people still have their money on the table, hoping the market will come back and they can make up their losses. They continue to set themselves up to repeat the same mistakes in the future.

Chasing Losers

Every professional gambler knows that when you are betting money to make up for your losses, it is time to stop. It is time to get away from the table, take a break, and look for new options. Unfortunately, due to current rules of many retirement plans, millions of people cannot step away from the table. Many investors are in retirement plans that penalize them if they step away from the table and put their money in different investments.

Words of Wisdom from a Gambler

"Don't count your money while you're sitting at the table." Those are priceless words of wisdom followed by professional gamblers. Along those lines, having your money sitting in a standard retirement plan violates three very important rules that professional gamblers and investors follow. They are:

1. As long as your money is on the table it is *not* your money. As long as your money is in the game, the money belongs to the game, not to you.

2. The game is more important than counting money. While gambling in Las Vegas, I was winning the game of craps as long as I was focusing on the game. The moment I began to win, I took my mind off the game and began counting my money. When I was up $3,000, money became more important than the game. That is one of the reasons I lost. Counting money became more important than the game.

Between 1995 and 2000, while the stock market was going up and retirement plans were increasing in value, many amateur investors thought they were rich, and they too began focusing on the money rather than the game. Many opened the envelopes containing their retirement statements, saw their net worth going up, and thought they were rich. Many amateur investors began buying bigger houses or cars, or took money out of their savings accounts and blindly threw more money into the market. As their net worth went up, many people took on a false sense of wealth and focused on money rather than the game.

A False Sense of Weath in Real Estate

A similar false sense of wealth happens when a person's home goes up in value. Often I hear people say, "My house has gone up $40,000 in value." At this point many people feel more secure and confident, and then many lose their drive and take their mind off the game. They count their net worth and think they've won the game. It is at this point that many people begin to fall behind financially.

The Real Object of the Game

3. The object of the game is to get your money off the table and still remain in the game. A professional gambler or professional investor ultimately wants to play the game with OPM, other people's money. That is the object of the game. The moment I left all my money on the table, I lost sight of the object of the game.

Four Kinds of Money

As some of you already know, there are three types of income defined by the tax service, which are *earned* income, *portfolio* income, and *passive* income. A professional investor needs to know about the three kinds of income and the four kinds of money. The four kinds of money are:

1. Your money
2. The bank's money
3. The tax man's money
4. The house's money

The Velocity of Money

A professional gambler wants to be playing the game with *house* money as soon as possible. While in Las Vegas, if I had put my money back in my pocket and only played with my winnings that would have been an example of playing with *house* money. The moment I began betting everything, I lost the game because I lost sight of my goal, which is to stay in the game but to play with other people's money . . . *not* my own money.

As a professional investor, I want to:

1. Invest my money into an asset.
2. Get my money back.
3. Keep control of the asset.
4. Move my money into a new asset.

5. Get my money back.
6. Repeat the process.

This process is called the *velocity of money*. It is one reason why the rich get richer and the average investor risks losing it all.

Let me offer this example to better clarify this process. Let's say I purchase a rental property—a two-bedroom, two-bath condo for $100,000. I put $20,000 of my money into the asset and $80,000 of my banker's money. In this example, let's say I receive a 10 percent cash-on-cash return of $2,000 in net passive income per year. Along with the $2,000 in income, I will receive tax money in the form of depreciation and other expenses, which is additional phantom income. In this example, ten years later, I have received all of my own down payment back, from just the rents, $2,000 × 10 years = $20,000 . . . and I still have the asset, which means I am still at the table.

But my money is off the table. I am still in the game playing with my banker's money, the tax man's money, and the house's money. With my money, the initial $20,000, returned to me, I would have pooled it and then reinvested it into another property, business, or paper asset and the process would have continued.

In many ways, I have completed the object of that game, but due to appreciation of the underlying asset, the game continues. The best part is I will continue to receive the $2,000 rental income per year from the asset even though my money is off the table (all my initial investment of $20,000 has been returned to me). By financial definition, my ROI—return on investment—is infinite.

Even Higher Returns

For the sake of this example, let's say the property appreciates to $180,000. In order to follow the tax rules, I could borrow a portion of the $80,000 of appreciation in the form of an equity refinance. Refinancing this $180,000 property, I could receive an extra $70,000 in cash tax-free (since it is equity in the property, not income), while I continue to own and control the asset. So in ten years, I would get all of my $20,000 initial investment money back from passive income, which is tax-free money due to phantom depreciation deductions, possibly an extra $70,000 from the appreciation in the equity, continue controlling the asset (which keeps sending me passive income), all while I move my money into another asset.

Let's say I take my $20,000 and my $70,000, which means my money is now off the table related to the first asset, and I now use this $90,000 to purchase a $450,000 asset.

In summary, ten years later, I control the original $100,000 asset, now worth $180,000. I continue to receive at least $2,000-a-year income from that property. I have now moved $90,000 into a $450,000 asset and could be receiving approximately $10,000 a year income from the second property. My next objective is to repeat the process with both of these assets—pull additional equity from both assets through refinancing and reinvest it into the purchase of an even bigger third asset. In this example, I used an 80 percent leverage from the bank. If you were more aggressive, you could even use a 90 percent leverage and increase the velocity of your money.

This is an oversimplified example of an investor's objective to keep their money moving, aka the *velocity of money.* Obviously, these numbers all assume an up-trending real estate market. If the market is flat or going down, these numbers will not work.

Setting the Parking Brake

Whenever I hear someone say, "I have no debt," or, "I just leave my money in an account and invest for the long term," or, "I want to own my investments free and clear," to me this means this investor has moved their money into an asset or their retirement plan, set the parking brake, and begun to count their money. Many people are happy to have no debt in their investments or be happy with an increasing net worth. While for these investors this may seem a safe way to invest, for a professional investor this is a very risky, slow way to invest, and with much lower returns.

How to Get Higher Returns with Greater Safety

When someone has no debt or high equity in an investment, I often ask them to compute their return on equity. In most cases, their returns are very low. With no debt and high equity in an investment they are not using the leverage available through using their banker's or other people's money. In other words, *the more of your money that is in the investment, the lower the*

return on the investment. The less of your money you have in an invest-
ment and the more you use other people's money, the higher your returns.

I am not saying that one way is better than another. The higher leverage
allows you to speed up your return on investment and accelerate the growth
of your money. However, with higher leverage, the investor needs a higher
level of financial literacy.

Getting Rich Quicker

By understanding the object of a professional investor, which is to get their
money off the table as quickly as possible to invest in another asset, a professional investor can get ahead faster by using the velocity of money. One of
the reasons the rich are getting richer is because their money is moving and
most other people have their money parked in their homes and in their retirement accounts, investing for the long term.

Why Is It Safer?

Why is investing for the long term by leaving your money on the table so
risky? The answer is found in Newton's Laws. One of Newton's Laws states,
"For every action, there is an equal and opposite reaction." Leaving your
money on the table exposes your money to the changing forces of nature.
When I was betting on my winning streak and got up to $3,000, I forgot
about the laws of nature and that every winning streak comes to an end.
Since I do not know when my winning streak will end, the earlier I get my
own personal money off the table, the safer I become.

Occasionally, I will take friends and show them some of the buildings
Kim and I control through our legal entities. While my friends look at the
physical structure, my mind is running the financial structure of the property. I generally wear a big smile if we control the property and receive income from it, but have none of our own money remaining in that property.
To us, that is the best kind of property. In our minds, the income coming in
is basically free money, our risks are very, very low, since we have little to
lose, and our money is working somewhere else.

This idea of the velocity of money can be applied to all asset classes.
Sharon, Kim, and I initially put up $1,000 to start the Rich Dad company and
in just a few years it has generated over millions of dollars in product sales

worldwide. Our growth has been fueled through using other people's money. We have several strategic partners who fund the manufacturing and distribution of our products and all we do is collect the royalties. Our publishing partners include Time Warner Books for the English version of our books and close to forty international publishers that translate and distribute the Rich Dad books and games into their markets. By using their contacts and distribution systems we have been much more successful in spreading the Rich Dad message than if we had continued trying to do it on our own.

In stock market investments, as soon as our stock or hedge fund gets ahead in the game, we begin to take our money off the table, letting the game go on with the house's or market's money. Professional investors may be in the game long-term, but their money is short-term.

How Long Is Long-Term?

Whenever I hear someone advise, "Invest for the long term," I often ask, "How long is long-term?" In commodity futures trading, long-term could mean thirty seconds. When investing in some real estate properties and businesses, long-term could mean centuries.

Why is knowing the term of the investment important? The reason is because all markets move according to the laws of nature, which means they move up and down. Simply buying an investment without paying attention to the ups and downs of the market is not a wise investment strategy.

In the second half of this book, I will be going into greater detail on the 20-10-5 cycle of investing. For now, I will briefly explain the 20-10-5 cycle and how it affects the game. While many investors do not believe the 20-10-5 trend exists, there are other investors who do pay attention to it. Simply put, this theory states that the stock market is in favor for 20 years. When the 20 years are over, the market crashes and for the next 10 years, commodities such as oil, gold, silver, real estate, gas, soybeans, pork, rise in value. The 5 of the 20-10-5 cycle means that every 5 years some tragedy happens, such as the 1987 stock market crash or the September 11, 2001, massacre.

A Reminder That Things Change

Although I would not set my clock by this cycle, awareness of the cycle serves a useful purpose . . . and that is to constantly remind me that markets change. It also reminds me to look for investment opportunities in different markets, rather than keep going back to a well that is dry.

Between 2000 and 2003, millions of investors lost money in the stock market because the 20-year cycle of stocks came to an end. Rather than follow the 20-10-5 cycle, many investors continue to sit around waiting in the stock market, rather than moving on to the commodities market, which as I write is going strong. It is reported that in 1996 Warren Buffett stopped actively investing in the stock market and quietly moved into the commodities market, investing in hard assets such as silver. In 1996, I too moved out of the stock market and moved into the oil and gold markets. Why? . . . because market cycles were changing. Just as the moon changes phases, so does any market.

Waiting for the Long Term

Today as I write, millions of investors, even while losing a lot of money in the stock market, are still sitting around waiting for the market and the price of their shares to come back up. That is a waste of time. Although the market will someday be back, the market they lost their money in is gone. If a person lost their retirement money in the fourth quarter of their life, and they wait ten years for the next bull market, they are wasting more than money. Instead of investing for the long term, they are actually waiting for the long term.

In the second half of this book, I will also go into a little more detail on how I use this 20-10-5 cycle to help me make money rather than get caught out of phase and in the wrong market, with my money still on the table.

Guarantee of Losing

It makes no sense to me to invest for the long term knowing that one day Mother Nature can pull the rug out from under you. If you look at an individual's game of money, let's say they begin investing at age twenty-five and expect to get out of the game at sixty-five—forty years later. That means many people will have their money sitting on the table for forty years. If the 20-10-5 cycle is somewhat accurate, this plan for investing for the long term is therefore a guarantee of losing. If the stock market goes up and down in twenty years, blindly investing for the longterm for forty years is a suicide mission. You are almost guaranteed of being a loser once, maybe twice, or even more during those forty years.

Why Do Pilots Wear Parachutes?

As a student pilot in Naval Flight School at Pensacola, Florida, one of the first classes we had to attend was not about flying but parachuting. We had to learn how to jump out of a plane and land in either water or on land. Why are pilots taught to parachute before learning to fly? The answer is obvious.

Most retirement plans state that if you withdraw your money early from the plan, you will be punished financially. Rather than give you a parachute, they are handcuffing you to the plane. During the crash between 2000 and 2003, many small investors did not know that their pilots, the heads of their mutual funds, CEOs of companies, and other privileged insiders, were parachuting to safety, while the little investors were handcuffed to their seats. One of the reasons I do not have a 401(k) is because I was a pilot. I would rather wear a parachute than a pair of handcuffs.

A Common Mistake

Rather than keep their money moving, most people *park* their money. They park their money in a bank, a retirement plan, or at their broker's office. Rich dad taught his son and me to keep our money moving. If we were not investing in our business, we were taught to invest in real estate. If the real estate market was not favorable, we were taught to move it into a hedge fund or fast-moving stock for short-term gains and liquidity. Rich dad did not like his money sitting idle. He wanted his money working hard, moving fast, and with as much safety as possible. He knew that markets moved, so he wanted to keep his money moving. That is why he spent so much time looking for new investments to move his money into . . . and eventually out of.

When I hear people say "My net worth has gone up" or "My house has appreciated in value," these are people who are often counting money sitting on the table. Their money is still in the game. Rich dad said, "Your money should be working, not sitting. If your money is sitting, you are not receiving a return on your equity."

Today, Kim and I do not know what our net worth is. When reporters ask us, "What is your net worth?" We tell them we do not know. We do say, "We

may not know our net worth but we know how fast our cash is flowing."
When reporters ask "Why are you not concerned about net worth?" I reply
with two answers. Answer number one: "It is easy to lie to you and to myself
about my net worth." Answer number two: "I am not concerned with how
much money I have sitting around . . . I am concerned about how hard my
money is working, how fast it is moving, and where I will move it next. That
is why I want to know as much as I can about all three asset classes rather
than only one asset class. For example, if real estate is too expensive at the
moment, or I cannot find a great deal, I will move my money into my hedge
fund, receiving an additional 25 percent return until I see the real estate market change or a business opportunity appears. In my world, the velocity and
safety of my money is far more important than the amount of my money."

The final lesson for this chapter is: Never forget that the object of the game
is to get your money off the table *and* stay in the game. That is what every gambler knows and what every professional investor strives for. Only amateur investors put their money in their retirement plan and set the parking brake.

An Example of Increasing the Velocity of Your Money

Suppose you have $20,000 to invest. The following are three choices that
you have.

Choice 1: Invest $20,000 in a mutual fund that earns 5 percent a year.

After seven years: your $20,000 should have grown to $28,142 assuming no
market fluctuations.

Choice 2: Invest $20,000 and borrow $180,000 from the bank for a
$200,000 rental property and let your equity compound. As-
sume rental income only breaks even with expenses and the
property appreciates at a rate of 5 percent a year.

After seven years: the property will be worth $281,000 and your equity is
now $101,420, assuming no market fluctuations.

Choice 3: Invest $20,000 and borrow $180,000 from the bank for a
$200,000 rental property. Rather than letting the equity com-
pound, you borrow out the appreciation every two years and
invest it in a new property at 10 percent down.

After seven years: the total value of your properties will be worth $2,022,218 and your net equity is $273,198, assuming no market fluctuations.

SUMMARY OF A $20,000 INVESTMENT

Net Equity	Average Annual Return on a $20,000 Investment
Choice 1: $28,142	5.8%
Choice 2: $101,420	58.2%
Choice 3: $273,198	180.9%

Choices 1 and 2 are examples of people who park their money and choice 3 is an example of people that increase the velocity of their money.

(A special thank-you to Tom Wheelwright, CPA, the source of this example, for his technical contribution to this chapter and this book.)

═══ Sharon's Notes ═══

After examining the three choices of how to invest $20,000, it is obvious that increasing the velocity of your money is a better choice. Of course the investor needs to first invest in their financial education before expecting such accelerated returns.

A professional gambler is like a professional investor because they both want to use Other People's Money. The gambler wants to use the house's money while the investor wants to use the banks' or other investors' money and both want to accelerate the velocity of their money. They do not leave the money parked on the table.

The professional investor follows the following formula:

1. Invest money into an asset
2. Get the original investment money back
3. But keep control of the original asset
4. Move the money into a new asset
5. Get the investment money back
6. Repeat the process

YOU CAN DO THIS TOO!

The following paragraph is the core message of this book.

This process is called *the velocity of money*. Financial institutions understand how important it is to expand their money supply in order to increase their earning power. Most investors do not realize they too can expand their own money supply and thereby expand their earning power. Financial institutions do this by making their money move. The more times a dollar moves, the greater the money supply and the greater their earning power of that dollar.

Simply stated, the movement of money increases your money supply! The Federal Reserve understands this very well as it is the key to how they control the supply and cost of money. The Constitution allows the government to coin money, but it would be impractical to control the money supply simply by speeding up or slowing down the printing presses. If abundance were printed, it soon would be worthless.

The Federal Reserve System manages the money supply in three ways:

- Maintaining a certain portion (typically 10 percent) of all deposits as a reserve held by banks. This helps control the quantity of money in circulation.
- Adjusting the discount rate charged to banks when they have to borrow from the Federal Reserve. This can impact the borrowing ability of the banks.
- Utilizing the open market operations to buy and sell government securities. When buying securities, the Fed essentially creates new money by creating reserves to pay for more securities. This increases the money supply in the economy. The Federal Open Market Committee (FOMC) also sets a target for the federal funds rate, which is the rate the banks pay when they borrow from one another for overnight loans to cover their reserve requirements.

So how does this movement of money increase the money supply? Let's say a bank's reserves are increased by $100 million; it may loan up to $90 million of that to businesses and individuals, who in turn deposit these loans in that bank or other banks, who will then be able to loan the funds again. As a business or individual, you receive minimal interest returns of about 1 percent on your "parked" deposits while the banks enjoy the greater return on the ability to continue to loan (move) the funds to others.

Our tax advisor, Tom, has provided the previous example of comparison investments to demonstrate how you can apply these same principles to your money and expand your money supply. The example demonstrates the differences of how your money increases when invested in a mutual fund, a rental property, and a rental property where you borrow the appreciation every two years.

In lieu of parking your money and saving, you become your own banker with the ability to increase the velocity of your money. This allows you to benefit from the same system that the government benefits from, and enables you to take control of your financial situation. Consider *control* and how it differs among the different types of asset classes.

Owning your own business	You are in control.
Owning real estate	You are in control.
401(k)s	Who is in control?
Mutual funds	Who is in control?
Equities (stocks)	Who is in control?

Other than being able to change investment allocations or buying and selling, you have little to no control over investments in 401(k)s, mutual funds, and stocks. The individual companies have presidents and boards of directors who have control over the operation of the underlying business.

Professional investors want CONTROL over their assets and their cash flow.

AUTHOR'S NOTE

About Ongoing Education

Learning how to find the right investment and knowing my exit strategy has been a lifelong study. I have made a lot of mistakes, yet those mistakes can be priceless if I learn from them. If you are interested in undertaking a long-term study on how to be a better investor, learning more about entry and exits, then you may want to consider our free Web site or our subscription-based Web site. For more information, just go to richdad.com and find out how you can learn, meet people like you from all over the world, and find out about investments from all over the world. You may be interested in *Rich Dad's Insiders*, a subscription-based Web site where you can play the electronic version of CASHFLOW 101 with people around the world, as well as have private discussion forums and educational programs only available through *Rich Dad's TV*.

Chapter 8

Ask Newton

"For every action, there is an equal and opposite reaction."

— Sir Issac Newton

"When you drop a stone in the water, a wave is generated at
90 degrees to the line of the stone dropping."

— Dr. Buckminster Fuller

"It's not nice to fool Mother Nature."

— Mother Nature

Apples Always Fall from Trees

When I was in school, my teacher said, "Sir Isaac Newton discovered the law of gravity by sitting under an apple tree. When the apple hit him on the head, he realized apples always fall toward the earth. Apples never fly to the sky."

In 1996, as the stock market soared skyward, many people actually seemed to believe that Mother Nature had repealed the laws of gravity. Whenever I heard someone say "This is the new economy," they may as well have been saying "Apples don't fall from trees anymore."

Rich dad often said, "I do not know if history repeats itself, but I do know that generation after generation of new investors always repeat the same mistakes. Two common mistakes they always make: 1. Leave their money on the table too long. 2. When markets get hot, many get greedy and forget about the laws of nature. Both mistakes are expensive."

Who Loses Money

Between 2000 and 2003, millions of people lost trillions of dollars because they violated the laws of nature. One of the primary laws or principles they violated was Newton's Law *For every action, there is an equal and opposite reaction,* and the law of *gravity,* or in simpler terms, *what goes up eventually comes down.* Average investors, by leaving their money on the table for the long term, and investing in vehicles, such as 401(k)s, that did not allow them to exit without severe penalties, were setting themselves up to lose by violating the laws of nature.

A professional investor, on the other hand, knows to respect and use the laws of nature. When the professional investor goes against the laws of nature, which many do, nature will win. That is why a professional investor pays attention to the laws of nature rather than follows the financial advice of financial salespeople. Following the laws of nature requires a professional to pay attention to the trends.

Trends to Watch

One big reason why the velocity of my money is important is because trends are constantly changing. Rather than diversifying into one asset class such as paper assets, rich dad encouraged his son and me to learn to move our money in and out of different asset classes. If I could get a higher return in my business, my money moved in there. If real estate opportunities appeared, I would be in that market. If I had excess cash, and needed a temporary home, my money went into paper assets such as a hedge fund or a tax-free bond paying at least 7 percent. Rarely do I park my money in a bank, especially at today's interest rates. Money sitting in a bank at 1 percent interest is a guaranteed loss because its value is being robbed via taxes and inflation, and it's not working hard, which means I have to work harder.

As stated in the previous chapter, I tend to be an investor, which means I move my money in to acquire the asset, and then move my money out, while still holding on to the asset. A trader, by definition, buys and sells the asset, for money. I simply move my money, in most cases.

I know that most financial advisors say this is a risky strategy. Yet let me explain why it really is not, if you have the experience and education to invest in three different asset classes. One of the reasons investing in different asset classes is less risky than the average retirement plan is again because I get my money out as quickly as possible, rather than leaving the money on the table. That means, if the market does crash, or I do make a horrible mistake, the asset may get damaged but my cash has moved on. The object is to acquire assets and keep my money moving.

How Fast Is Your Cash Moving?

For example, in 1996, when gold was around $280 an ounce and the dollar was strong, I began trading dollars for gold coins. When gold hit $380 an ounce in 2003, I sold some of the coins, got all my cash back, and came out with a sizable number of one-ounce gold coins left over. If gold had not gone up in value, my cash would still be safe in a tangible asset, because I bought the coins when the price of gold was low and value of the dollar high. When the trend changed and the price of gold went up and the dollar went down, dollars and gold coins traded places.

If you would like to learn more about the velocity of money, simply play my CASHFLOW 101 and 202 board games, the CASHFLOW for Kids board game, or our electronic games, CASHFLOW THE E-GAME and CASHFLOW for Kids at Home (found on our Web site at www.richdad.com) on a regular basis, and soon your mind will begin to see how to speed up the velocity of your money. The CASHFLOW games are the only games that have the lessons about velocity of money designed into them. If your money has velocity, you can move your money out of harm's way and into the next market before the new market picks up speed.

Diversification Versus Trends

A few days ago, I listened to a television ad that said, "The number one strategy for investors is to diversify." That may be true for amateur investors, but not for all professional investors. To me, *diversification* is just part of the sales pitch to get the average investor to buy more shares of stocks and mutual funds. It would be the same as going to a used car dealer and asking, "What if the car I buy is a lemon?" Naturally the used car salesman would say, "I recommend you diversify. Buy six cars instead of one. That way if one car is a lemon, you can still get to work on time."

Trends Can Be Your Friend or Your Enemy

If *diversification* is not number one, then what is? The answer is *trends,* because trends are the movement of nature's laws through the market. Professional investors often say, "The trend is your friend." Rich dad said, "Trends can be your friend *or* your enemy." Between 1980 and 2000 the trend of the stock market was bullish. The trend was up. It was easy to make money. Just put your money into the market and, like magic, the value of the asset went up in value. But suddenly, in March of 2000, the trend changed directions and investors who did not change with the trend lost trillions of dollars, even if they were diversified.

Who Took Their Money?

There are many reasons why so many people lost so much money. Some of them are:

1. They did not pay attention to the trend.
2. They left their money on the table.
3. They invested in plans that handcuffed them to the table.
4. They had bad advisors who did not tell them to get out.
5. They did not know where else to go.
6. They continued to leave their money in the same asset class waiting for the trend to return.

The Trends to Watch

The reason this chapter is entitled "Ask Newton" is because all trends follow the laws of nature. Long before 9/11, rich dad trained his son and me to pay close attention to trends. He said, "Just as surely as you can see a ripple moving across a still pond, a professional investor can see a ripple in the market and take action on it. If you take action early enough, the ripple can help you. If you ignore the ripple, the ripple can hurt you."

In the world following September 11, 2001, it is more important than ever to notice trends and not violate the laws of nature. The following are some of the trends I watch today, and use to make some of my financial decisions. If you watch these trends, you will have a better chance of making money rather than losing money.

TREND TO WATCH #1: DEMOGRAPHICS

"Demography is destiny," said Auguste Comte, a nineteenth-century French philosopher. One reason I am bullish on investing in real estate in America, even though there will be booms and busts in the real estate market, is because America has a growing population. In the year 2000, the last time the census was taken, there were 281 million Americans. The forecast by demographers is that by 2025 the population could be 350 million to as high as 400 million.

To give you an idea on how fast the population of the U.S. has grown, the following numbers show the trend:

1867	37 million
1900	76 million
2000	281 million
2025	350–400 million?

If these forecasted numbers are close, by 2025, what do you think will happen to the price of real estate? If you think it is expensive today, I am betting that by 2025 the price of real estate will be higher.

Japan, on the other hand, has a declining population. According to an article titled "Japan: Population Aging and the Fiscal Challenge" in the March 2001 *Finance & Development*, a quarterly magazine of the International Monetary Fund, by 2025 there will be one elderly person for every two people of working age in Japan. The article also states:

Demographic changes will be a defining feature in Japan for the foreseeable future. A sustained decline in fertility rates underlies a rapid aging and dwindling of Japan's population that can be expected to continue well into this century. This dramatic demographic shift is likely to have profound social and economic implications, including slower growth in output for some time. High public debt and adverse population dynamics increasingly constrain the government's room for maneuver, suggesting that strong policy adjustments will eventually be required to put public finances back on a sustainable footing. Reforms currently being implemented in the pension and health systems are a step in the right direction, but further measures will be needed to avoid a large increase in payroll taxes and government transfers that would distort incentives and hamper growth.

If these predictions for both countries come true, in which country do you think real estate would be a better investment?

TREND TO WATCH #2: DEBT

One of the reasons for the explosion in government and personal debt is because today *money is not money—money is debt.* One lesser-known fact is that years ago, the U.S. dollar was real money. As a kid, I would look at my dollar bill and it would say "Silver Certificate" across the top of the bill. That meant the U.S. dollar was real money backed by silver or gold, tangible assets. On August 15, 1971, President Nixon announced that the United States would no longer redeem currency for gold. Today a U.S. dollar has the words "Federal Reserve Note" across the top. That means our dollar is no longer real money backed by assets. Today our money is *debt* . . . a liability, an IOU, a lien against the U.S. government.

One Reason Why the Rich Are Getting Richer

The action of changing the backing of the U.S. dollar from silver and gold to debt has had many results. One is that the gap between the rich and everyone else has gotten wider and deeper. Over the past thirty years, some of the changes are:

1. *The New York Times* reported that today in America, 13,000 of the richest families have almost as much income as the 20 million poorest.

2. The annual salary in America, expressed in 1998 dollars (that is, adjusted for inflation) went from . . .

Workers' Compensation

| 1970 | $32,522 |
| 1999 | $35,864 |

An increase of approximately 10 percent over thirty years. Over the same period, according to *Fortune* magazine, the average real annual compensation of the top 100 CEO's went from . . .

CEOs' Compensation

1970 $1.3 million, or 39 times the pay of the average worker
1999 $37.5 million, or more than 1,000 times the pay of the
            average worker

The reason the change in currency in 1971, from silver and gold to debt, is so important is because once the dollar became debt, government and big business had to encourage everyone to get into debt. If the little person did not get into debt, the economy would not expand. If the little person cannot take on any more debt, then the economy begins to contract. That is why this trend is so important to watch.

America in the 1950s to the 1960s was really a middle-class society. It was close to the world portrayed in the popular TV show *Leave It to Beaver.* There was a sense of fairness to the society even though highly educated professionals, middle managers, college teachers, often claimed they earned less than unionized blue-collar workers. After 1971, the middle-class world of America began to disappear. Those who could accelerate their income faster than the devaluation of the dollar did well. Those who worked for the dollar began to fall behind in earning power and used personal debt to supplement the gap.

Today, as I write, with interest rates so low, millions of people are in even greater debt. The reaction to easy and cheap credit will be a dramatic increase in bankruptcies, foreclosures on homes, and lives financially ruined because they will have substantial blemishes on their credit records. While the economy will grow, it will grow at a dreadful cost to those that continue to work hard for money and have very little financial education.

Two Careers: One for You and One for Your Money

This is one more reason why I ask the question "Isn't it about time we began teaching financial intelligence and financial responsibility in our schools?" Today, too many young people are leaving school and getting off on the wrong financial path early in life. If they knew a little bit about money, money management, taxes, credit, and investing, they might have a better chance at a better life.

Today, we all need to have two careers . . . one for us and one for our money. For example, while I make my money as an author, which is my career, my money works in real estate. If a child knew that the government taxes workers' *physical labor* harder than it taxes money's *financial labor*, many more children might be more inspired to have their money work harder for them.

In my opinion, this little-noticed change in the value of money in 1971, has caused one of the biggest financial ripple effects in the world. Once our dollar was no longer backed by real assets the gap between the rich and everyone else accelerated. This change in the value of our currency is one of the primary reasons why the rich are getting excessively rich and the poor and middle class work harder and harder for less money, fall deeper into debt, and pay higher taxes.

Printing Money Rather Than Working for Money

Backing the dollar with debt rather than a hard asset has had the same effect as you going to work every day while your neighbor sits at home and turns on his printing press, printing money rather than working for it. You work harder and harder because the money he is printing causes the money you work for to be worth less and less. While millions work harder and pay more taxes, many of those in power have the ability to play games with money, which makes things worse for those that play by the rules.

To make up for the lack of wage increases, inflation, and to keep up with the Joneses, millions of people have had to go into debt. The chart on page 131 reflects the increase in debt as a percentage of GDP (gross domestic product).

Why Debt Increases

After the U.S. stopped backing the dollar with real assets, the national debt began to grow. The reason debt will increase is because that is how the economy now grows. Since our dollar is no longer an asset but an instrument of debt, in order for the current money system to work, people and businesses have to take on more and more debt. If people and companies stop borrowing, the entire Federal Reserve System stops growing and begins to implode.

That is why, even though the chart above shows Americans being in even greater debt, lending institutions keep finding new ways to keep people borrowing. Most of us have heard the new car dealer in your home-

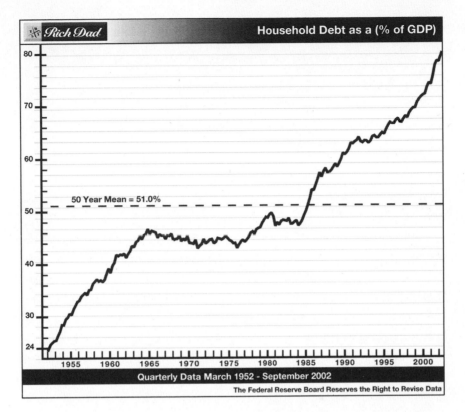

town say, "Even if you have bad debt, a bankruptcy, a foreclosure, come on in. We'll help solve your credit problems so you can drive out in a new car today."

Always remember that since money is now debt, debt must increase. The question is, if increasing debt is the action, then what is the equal and opposite reaction? Also, what happens if people stop taking on more and more debt?

How Much Is a Trillion Dollars?

One of the questions often asked is, "How are we going to pay off the national debt?" Since the average person in America is earning less than $50,000, most people have a difficult time imagining how much a trillion dollars is. The following is a comparison between a million, a billion, and a trillion dollars.

How Long Would It Take to Count?

If you began to count dollars at the rate of one a second, it would take:

12 days	$1 million
32 years	$1 billion
31,688 years	$1 trillion

As stated earlier, Alan Greenspan acknowledged that the U.S. is in debt $18 trillion to Social Security and Medicare alone. How are we going to pay for all this debt? Who is going to pay for it? What happens to America if this trend continues?

Although not a trained economist as Alan Greenspan is, my crystal ball says the answer to excessive debt is to print more money. One reason for printing more money is to pay off the government's debt with cheaper, less valuable dollars. If that happens, that means the price of your house will go higher, your savings will be worth less and less, and most people will have to work harder just to keep up with the cost of living. If prices rise because your dollar becomes worth less and less, this is called *inflation*. When there is inflation, debtors are winners and savers are losers. If there is excessive inflation, can you afford to retire? Can you afford to simply park your money for the long term and hope your mutual fund manager can outperform the market and inflation?

What if Deflation Is King?

Of course, *inflation* might not happen and things could go the other way, which would mean *deflation*. I have a friend who fled Buenos Aires in 2002 with nothing but the shirt on his back. He said, "One day I was rich and the next day I was poor. One day my house was worth $450,000 and today it might be worth $45,000, if I can find a buyer." His final words were, "What surprised me was how fast the change came. We had no warning. The change came overnight." Although the conditions in Argentina are not the same as in America, there are similarities that concern me.

Debt Is Worse Than Being Poor

In 1929, after the market crash, the government dried up the money supply. In other words, there was no money and the Great Depression was on. In my opinion, one of the reasons why the money supply dried up was because in those days money was real money. It was real money because it was backed by precious metals. As a country, we were still on the gold standard. Because it was real money, anytime there is fear or doubt or distrust, real money goes into hiding.

In 2000, when the market crashed, rather than drying up the money supply, the Federal Reserve flooded the world with money. One of the reasons we may not have the kind of great depression we had in the 1930s is because today many people have money, so they are not poor, but more importantly it is much easier to get into debt. Credit cards were not around during the Great Depression. The problem is, since there is so much fake money and debt, many people are in even worse financial shape than being poor. Today, millions of people are deeply in debt, which means we have a different kind of depression. It is the emotional depression of having a lot of material wealth but tons of debt.

As Newton's Law states, "For every action, there is an equal and opposite reaction." One of the reasons you want to be a better investor with very little of your own money on the table is because you want to be prepared for the reaction to all this debt. When that reaction comes, have your cash ready to start moving and picking up real assets, which will increase the velocity of your money, if you know what you are doing.

TREND TO WATCH #3: INTEREST RATES

When the stock market began to fall in March of 2000, the Federal Reserve lowered interest rates. One reaction to falling stock prices and interest rates was a rise in real estate prices. Not only did lower interest rates encourage people to move into real estate, lower interest rates punished savers. By lowering interest rates, the government was sending a signal to savers to get their money out of the bank and into the marketplace.

Bankers Do Not Like Savers

While most people believe that savers are smart and good, the reality is your banker does not like savers . . . your banker loves borrowers. Bankers would rather have a customer who borrows $10 million than a customer who has $10 million to deposit. Why? Because your savings are an asset to you but a liability to the bank. That means the bank makes more money by lending you money than holding your money. So the lower interest rates have encouraged more and more people to borrow rather than save. The question is, What happens when interest rates go back up . . . if they go back up?

In the late 1970s and into the 1980s, as gold, silver, and oil prices rose, interest rates went over 20 percent before coming down again. Will that happen again? Only time will tell. If after years of a low-interest-rate environment the pendulum swings the other way, and interest rates begin climbing again, stand by for massive changes in the economy.

Why do I think interest rates will climb, even though they are at record lows today? One reason is again due to Newton's Law. My crystal ball senses that the U.S. government will have to print more and more money to keep the economy afloat. If the government goes into hyper-printing of money, those that work for money will fall further behind financially. More than just losses of money from stocks, one of the greatest losses to Americans has been the loss of the value of their money. Not only was the stock market coming down between 2000 and 2003, so was the value of the U.S. dollar. Relative to value of other currencies, Americans took an additional 20 percent loss in wealth. That is why it is important to pay attention to inflation, interest rates, the price of gold, and government debt.

TREND TO WATCH #4: PRECESSION AND LAG

When a stone is dropped in the water, not only is there an equal and opposite reaction, but there is also a reaction at 90 degrees, which is the ripple we see moving across the pond. That is an example of *precession*. The delay in time from when the stone hits the water until the ripple hits the far shore is known as *lag*. Both are universal principles or laws of nature.

The reason that precession and lag are important is because too many investors watch only the stone's action and not the entire omnispherical time-delayed reaction. A crude example would be a driver of a car watching the car in front but failing to see a train coming at him from the side.

In 1990, very few investors had a direct line to the financial markets. The only people who had access to the market were banks and other large institutional traders. Today, due to the Internet, millions of investors now have real-time access to the market. If a price moves a penny, many investors are reacting in one way or the other almost instantaneously. Does this mean you have to watch the market that closely? The answer is no, not if you don't want to.

One of the reasons why the laws of precession and lag are important is because you can take a longer view of the market, rather than watch it second by second. For example, when you look at the trend in population, you can plan your real estate investments accordingly. Rather than panic when housing prices rise, you can wait patiently, knowing that over the long term, prices will come down again, before going up again. Or you can buy a piece of raw land inexpensively, and wait for the town to grow out to it. When Kim and I moved to Phoenix, Arizona, we did so because Phoenix was the fastest-growing major city in America. That was twelve years ago. Over that twelve-year period, it has not always been number one, but it has always been first or second in growth.

When it comes to my business, I use the same longer view on the trend. As the baby boomers get closer to retirement, and the reality of not having enough money set aside for retirement sets in, the demand for financial education will only increase. Rather than investing my time in an industry that is crowded and mature, such as the automobile and airline industries, I would rather invest my time building a business where demand for its product or service will only increase over the long term.

An Increase in Small Personal Businesses

With an aging population combined with massive corporate layoffs, people are beginning to realize that job security is a myth and their 401(k)s and other retirement plans may not provide long-term financial security. I believe that the trend toward small business creation will increase exponentially. Many midlevel managers are becoming self-employed consultants when their efforts to seek reemployment are unsuccessful.

This trend will be in people starting new businesses, in buying franchises, or looking at starting businesses within industries, like the network marketing industry. I often speak to network marketing businesses because they provide low-cost entry for people to start businesses while also providing them valuable training and mentoring. Building a successful business allows people to take control of their long-term financial security. Remember, though, it is always important to do your due diligence before joining any network marketing group, or buying any franchise.

TREND TO WATCH #5: FINANCIAL INTELLIGENCE

One of the more important trends I have learned to watch is the relationship between my money and my financial intelligence. When I struck it rich in my early twenties due to my business and real estate investments, I sincerely thought I was a financial genius. I actually thought that since my income was going up that my financial intelligence was also going up. Again, I was violating Newton's Law. Instead of my financial intelligence going up with my income, my financial intelligence went the other way.

Although it is a painful lesson, I have come to realize that the more financially successful I become, the more I need to keep my ego and arrogance in check. Instead of becoming more arrogant, which is not financial intelligence, I remind myself to become more grateful and humble, so I can continue to learn and earn more, rather than give it all back to the market, which I have done. I have learned the hard way that not only does my money follow Newton's laws, so does my intelligence.

A Final Word

Rich dad said, "Obey the laws of nature. Always remember that Mother Nature does not care if you are a millionaire or a poor person. If you both jump off a tall building without a parachute, the law of gravity will treat both people equally."

Sharon's Notes

Researching and analyzing trends has never been easier. With the search engines now available on the Internet, trend information is easy to find if you take the time to look for it. The problem is often having *too much* information and not knowing how to find what you are looking for. It is also important to check the timeliness of the information and to determine if the information is being provided as *information* or as a *sales tool*. Remember to analyze this trend information with experts in the fields. Your advisors will help you determine how to structure your investment strategy to take maximum advantage of the trends.

Some of the places where I find valuable information in addition to those listed by Robert in Chapter 6, "Ask a Journalist" are:

Business trends	NFIB Research Foundation
	Small Business Administration Office of Advocacy
	SCORE
	Kauffman Foundation
Real Estate Trends	reis.com
	National Real Estate Investor (www.nreionline.com)
	Local real estate newsletters
Paper Asset Trends	*Wall Street Journal*
	Bond Market Association (*www.investinginbonds.com*)

As a reminder, when working with any information determine if there is a *salesman* or *sales pitch* involved. Their information may still be valuable, but you will be better prepared to make your investment decision with full knowledge of the transaction. Robert often talks about paying your brokers well—just know what they are getting paid for and know that the remaining return on your investment is within your investment strategy.

Chapter 9

Ask Father Time

"Every investor must know when a flower is about to
bloom . . . and how long that bloom will last."

— RICH DAD

One of the unique advantages of attending the U.S. Merchant Marine
Academy in New York was sea year. Each student spent one year at sea as a
junior officer on various merchant ships carrying cargo to ports throughout the world. I spent a lot of time on freighters, tankers, and passenger
liners. I wanted to spend some time on a tugboat, but never got the assignment.

During my sea year, between the ages of nineteen and twenty, I traveled
to Japan, Hong Kong, Thailand, Vietnam, Tahiti, Samoa, and other islands of
the Pacific. Other classmates sailed to Europe, Canada, Africa, South America, and Australia. Although I wanted to sail to Europe, Africa, and South
America, my primary interest was sailing through the islands of the Pacific,
which I did and would love to do more of.

Being at sea afforded me a lot of time to read. Not only did I read my professional textbooks about ships, as a requirement for my correspondence
curriculum at sea, I also read books on money, gold, the great explorers, investing, and international trade. The problem was that I soon found myself
more interested in money, gold, investing, explorers, and international trade
than I did in ships, navigation, and cargo operations.

Classmates Were Not Interested in Investing

After my lesson on investing from rich dad and spending so much time reading about money and investing at sea, I found it increasingly more difficult to relate to my classmates. One day, during a break back at school in New York, I began telling my classmates what I was learning about the world of investing.

"Why are you wasting your time studying investing?" asked Jeff sarcastically. "Investing is risky. It's gambling."

"Investing is my future," I replied defensively. "I don't plan on working all my life."

"Well, I'm not planning on working all my life either," said Jeff. "I'm going to get a job with a big steamship company, become captain of a ship someday, and retire on the company pension. I'm not going to worry about my retirement. Somebody else will do that for me."

One or two of my classmates were interested in what I had been learning about investing, but for the most part, most were focused on their professional education rather than their financial education.

The Times They Were A-changin'

My time at the academy spanned four years, 1965 to 1969. It was common during this era for people to not be concerned about investing or their retirement. My generation was still living under the umbrella of my parents' generation, the World War II generation. My parents' generation, for the most part, did not concern themselves with retirement or investing since most expected to get a job with a big corporation or a government agency. They were also counting on Social Security and Medicare. As a generation, most did not put much importance on their financial education, investing, and their investment portfolio. The educational system we were going through at that time reflected that attitude toward retirement, which was that retirement was someone else's responsibility. Many schools today still reflect that antiquated attitude toward money.

In the 1960s and into the 1970s, the Beatles, Bob Dylan, the Vietnam War, college protests, and the resignation of President Nixon were on the minds of young people . . . not investing and retirement. Little did we know that as a generation we were heading into one of the most volatile economic times in history. In 1971 when President Nixon took the U.S. *off* the gold standard, it meant that the U.S. dollar could be printed at will. The reason the shift off the gold standard is so significant is because prior to the change, each dollar was backed by a precious metal, either gold or silver. Today, the U.S. dollar is backed by *debt* and the promise of U.S. taxpayers to pay that debt, which is substantial and growing.

The Biggest Changes of All

During the 1960s and 1970s, President Nixon worked to open the doors to China. The impact of that change in foreign policy decades ago is only beginning to be felt today. Today, while there are many good things happening due to Nixon's efforts in China, there are also millions of people who are losing their jobs to workers in China. While I do support trade with China, I am concerned about the high-paying manufacturing jobs we are losing and the people these losses of jobs affect. During the 1960s, when some of my classmates said they were not interested in investing, these financial changes had not yet happened and the impact of those changes would not be felt for years.

Then, on November 11, 2001, trade ministers from across the world officially approved China's entry into the World Trade Organization (WTO) after fifteen years of negotiations. This brought a market of 1.3 billion people into the global trading system. This one event will have a tremendous impact on our economy for years, even decades.

A Very Big Change

In 1974, when President Gerald Ford signed into law the ERISA, the Employee Retirement Income Security Act, which later led to the 401(k) and other such pension plans, the financial changes began to accelerate. The reason the 1974 ERISA and the pension reform that followed it are so symbolic is because this act put employees throughout America and the world on notice that employers were no longer going to be responsible for the employee's financial well-being once the employee's working days were over. In other words, looking at the CASHFLOW Quadrant:

The B quadrant was now saying to the E quadrant, "You employees have to become investors in the I quadrant." Like it or not, this change in pensions will have long-term effects on all of us for years to come.

The Problem Is Bigger Than I Imagined

In the fall of 2002, I released *Rich Dad's Prophecy*, a book that attracted a lot of negative press from financial journalists working for the Wall Street machine. While I did expect the criticism, it was disappointing to witness firsthand how far these journalists were willing to go to distort the truth and even lie in their efforts to discredit me and the message inside *Rich Dad's Prophecy*.

The interesting thing is, *Rich Dad's Prophecy,* written in 2000 and 2001, while accurate, was inaccurate because it understated how severe the problem really is. By 2003, as more of the truth began to leak out, I began to realize that the problem is far greater than I imagined.

Rich Dad's Prophecy is about the change from a DB, a defined benefit pension plan, to the DC, a defined contribution pension plan. For those who may not have read *Prophecy*, a DB pension plan is the pension plan of my mom and dad's generation, the World War II generation. Simply stated, a DB pension plan assured the employee a steady dollar amount in retirement income after they retired and for as long as they lived. In many ways,

Social Security and Medicare today are government DB plans. The problem is, with expenses going up and global competition increasing, DB pension plans became too expensive. Hence in 1974, the big B quadrant businesses encouraged the U.S. government to pass ERISA, which became the start of a shift away from DB plans and led to defined contribution plans, where the employee became responsible for his or her own retirement—a DC pension plan.

A DC pension plan is just that. The employee's benefits are *defined* to what the employee and the employer have *contributed.* If the employee and employer have contributed nothing, or the stock market crashes and the matched contributions have been wiped out, the employee receives what is left—if anything is left. If the employee runs out of money at age ninety-two, that is not the employer's problem as it would have been if the employee had a DB pension plan. There is one more major difference between most DB and DC pension plans. Employers offering DB pension plans from major corporations often also had medical benefit plans available for their employees for their retirement. A DC does not. If you are aware of the rising costs of health and medical care, you might begin to realize how much of a change this 1974 law triggered. So today, employees throughout the world have these new DC pension plans, which can run out of money, and the responsibility for medical and health care for these retirees has been passed on to you know who . . . you guessed it, the taxpayers.

Why the Stock Market Will Crash

Rich Dad's Prophecy was about how this 1974 change in the law will lead to the biggest stock market crash in history. The reason the stock market will crash is because all throughout the world, there are millions of people who will begin retiring about the same time. Now, you do not have to be a rocket scientist to realize that stock markets go down if people begin pulling their money out. In America alone, there are an estimated 83 million baby boomers, an age group that will begin retiring in force around 2012. Not all of the 83 million have money in the stock market, but millions do. On top of that, there is a flaw in the law that later created the 401(k). The law states that when a person with a 401(k) turns seventy and a half, they *must* begin withdrawing their money. Why? Because the tax department, the IRS, wants to be paid the taxes that have been deferred for all the years the employee was working. In the year 2016, the first baby boomer turns seventy and a half and that is the approximate time the house of cards will come tumbling down, leading to the biggest stock market crash in the history of the world. The book was not meant to be a doom-and-gloom book. It was meant to be a doom-and-boom book. The second half of the book was about alternative investments one could invest in, other than the stock market.

Now you may understand why the financial institutions had their journalists do their best to discredit me and my book.

Why It's Worse

As I said, *Prophecy* was written in 2000 and 2001. In the book, I assumed DB pension plans were safer and better for employees. By 2003, news began to leak that DB pension plans, the plans of my mom and dad, were also in bad financial shape. In *Prophecy*, I stated that employees with DB pension plans were better off than employees with DC pension plans. How wrong I was. Many DB pension plans are in terrible financial condition and employees do not know it. Why don't employees know it? Because no one has to disclose to workers the condition of the pension plan, even if the employee asks.

What's Good for General Motors

There is an old saying that goes, "What is good for General Motors is good for the country." Well, General Motors is in trouble. Why is it in trouble? The answer in one word is *pensions.*

In June 2003, the Associated Press issued a press release stating that Moody's Investor Services had lowered GM's long-term debt rating because of increasing competition and large pension benefits. Moody's downgraded GM's credit rating from A3 to Baa1. So is it true that what is good for GM is good for America? Is it time to reduce employees' pensions or is it time to keep borrowing more and more money to pay those benefits? Both GM and the U.S. government are facing this same problem simultaneously. Later in the chapter there is a list of some very large companies all facing underfunding in their pension plans.

Classmates Now Worried?

Back in the late 1960s, most of my classmates were not concerned about investing. They were not worried because most were smart and most knew they would find good high-paying jobs with big corporations. The problem is, time has moved on and the rules of employment have changed. As you may have noticed, President Ford signed ERISA into law in 1974, five years after my class graduated. Since then, the financial changes that have hit the baby-boom generation and the generations that follow have been massive. The reason this chapter is entitled "Ask Father Time" is because Father Time has moved on. I wonder how many of my classmates and my generation have moved on with the march of time? I wonder how many people are waiting for a rise in the stock market to fatten their 401(k) plans for retirement? I wonder how many are working for big corporations that have DB pension plans that are in financial trouble . . . and do not know it?

Bye-Bye, Pensions

As mentioned earlier, I had no idea how understated the problem described in *Rich Dad's Prophecy* was. Nor did I realize how much rich dad's prophecy affected all pension plans—both the DB and the DC plans.

The March 17, 2003, edition of *Fortune* magazine ran an article entitled "Bye-Bye, Pension." The subtitle read "Soon hundreds of corporations may slash pensions by half." It is an important article on the potential final demise of the DB, the defined benefit pension plan. Due to the high costs of DB pension plans, the article says, "To get out completely, a number of companies are simply going to slash benefits." The article quotes a Vermont congressman who says, "What we are seeing is a massive assault on the pensions of millions and millions of workers."

The assault is already on. The *Fortune* article offers an example of Larry Cutrone, fifty-five years of age, a former tech worker at AT&T, who recently had his pension slashed from $47,000 a year to $23,000 a year. You do not have to be a math wizard to notice that this is a 50 percent cut in benefits. So who took Larry Cutrone's money? Was it the corporation who changed the plan or was it Father Time just moving on?

Another example from the *Fortune* magazine article states: "On a cold

Philadelphia day this past February, 50-year-old Janice Winston received something that warmed her considerably: a $400,000 payment from her former employer Verizon Communications. The money represented the pension benefits Winston had earned during her twenty-nine years on the job. It is also about $215,000 more than the company had hoped to pay her."

A full seven years earlier, Winston's employer, Bell Atlantic (which later merged with GTE to form Verizon), had made an elegantly simple, barely noticeable change in its pension plan that would have slashed the anticipated retirement benefits not only for Winston but also for thousands of her fellow employees.

What Bell Atlantic (and, for that matter, what IBM and some 300 other big companies) had done was switch its dowdy defined benefit pension plan to an exciting new type of plan being touted by benefits consultants. Even its name had a dollar-happy ring to it: "cash balance."

The article goes on stating that the difference between a "cash balance" account and a defined contribution plan such as a 401(k) is that a cash balance account cannot be slammed by the stock market. The problem for the employee is how the benefit is calculated . . . and as expected, the calculation is designed to have the benefit be cost-effective for the employer and less of a windfall for the employee. In this case, Winston received a final payout of $400,000, which to some may sound like a lot of money. But the questions I have are: Can she manage it properly? Will it last her the rest of her life? And what happens if she loses all of it, as many people with lump-sum payments do?

Peter Stealing from Paul

This problem of employee pension plans is not only a U.S. issue. It is a worldwide problem. From the Web site InvestorDaily.com, I found an article posted February 2, 2003, stating that in the United Kingdom, the number of companies that are closing their DB schemes—as they're called there—to new employees has almost doubled from forty-six in 2001 to eighty-four in 2002. That means in two years, new employees of 130 U.K. companies will not be offered a pension.

Employee groups and unions are screaming, doing their best to protect employees' DB pension benefits. Scream and shout all they like, the hard, cold financial facts are that employee benefits are expensive. Investors know that employee benefits are an expense not only to the business, but also to the investor. So it is the investors that are often on the other side screaming to reduce the expense of employee benefits. The irony is that today employees are also investors. So who is taking the money? In many situations, it really is an example of Peter stealing from Paul. On one hand, the employee wants the benefits, but on the other hand, the employee who is also an investor wants the company's profits and share price to go up. If the company's profits do not go up, due to high pension expenses, their pensions go down. So who is taking the employees' money? Could it be the employees themselves? Could it be retired employees are working against new employees?

How Expensive Are DB Pensions?

The *Fortune* magazine article ends with this warning: "For the millions of baby-boomers lucky enough to still be counting on a lush pension in retirement, 'Don't take for granted what you have today.'"

Why should workers with DB pension plans be worried? The following is a list of the ten most under-funded DB pension plans in billions of dollars as of 2003:

1.	General Motors	−94.7
2.	Ford	−46.6
3.	IBM	−25.3
4.	SBC	−19.6
5.	Boeing	−17.7
6.	Exxon	−15.5
7.	DuPont	−13.0
8.	Verizon	−13.0
9.	Lucent	−11.9
10.	Delphi Auto	−11.7

Source: company 10K reports

When you look at the list, now you can understand why I chuckle when I hear someone say, "I only invest in blue-chip companies." When I look at blue-chip companies such as General Motors and Ford Motor Company, I wonder how many cars those two companies will have to sell in order to make up the $140 billion shortfall in their pensions?

How Much Retired Employees Cost

The "Bye-Bye, Pension" article in the March 17, 2003, issue of *Fortune* states that these blue-chip companies currently pay $111 billion each year to 21 million former employees who have already retired. Talk about an annual expense to the company for workers who are no longer working. I really do not know how these companies' share prices can keep going up if the numbers of these former employees continue to increase and the stock market stays flat.

A Worldwide Problem

It is obvious that many people will never be able to retire, having to work until they can work no longer. As the world's population ages, old-age security systems are in trouble worldwide. It is reported that in addition to Japan, France and Germany are in even worse shape than the U.S. and the U.K. when it comes to the challenge of how to afford the growing number of retirees. As I write, workers in France are in the streets, protesting the changes to the pension systems. How long will it be before the same protests take place in the U.S. and the U.K.? Will the baby boomers who protested the war in Vietnam in the 1960s be the ones protesting in the streets for pension reforms?

Winning the Game of Money

I mentioned the game of money in the introduction but I want to now share how I was introduced and learned about this game. My rich dad often said, "Life was a game of time and money." After I got in trouble financially, in my late twenties, he shared with me his financial game plan. He said, "For most people, our working years are often defined as the years between ages twenty-five and sixty-five. In other words, we work for approximately forty years. If you look at your working life as the game of money, then you can break your game into quarters, each ten years long. In other words, a professional football game is made up of four fifteen-minute quarters and your working life is four ten-year quarters." He then took his yellow legal pad and wrote:

The Game of Money

Age	Game Period
25 to 35	1st Quarter
35 to 45	2nd Quarter

———— **Halftime** ————

| 45 to 55 | 3rd Quarter |
| 55 to 65 | 4th Quarter |

Overtime

Out-of-Time

Rich dad was concerned because the first quarter of my life was a financial mess. Using his legal pad to illustrate his point, he wrote:

Ages 25-35 First Quarter

Income

Expense

Asset	Liability
None	$700,000

"You've lost the first quarter," he said. "If you don't shape up and learn from your mistakes, your whole life will be a financial mess."

What he said was true. In the first quarter of my financial life, I had lost my first business, was deeply in debt, disgraced, and was still a sloppy businessman. One of the reasons I decided to leave Hawaii around the age of thirty-five was because I knew I had to straighten my life out. Between the ages of twenty-five and thirty-five my life had been about having fun, surfing, playing rugby, chasing women, and trying to get rich quick. I knew I had to make some changes. In 1984, at the age of thirty-seven, I left Hawaii to start all over again. I left Hawaii to create a new me.

The book *Rich Dad's Retire Young Retire Rich* is about my life during the second quarter of my life. For those who have read the book, you may recall the decision we made on the ski slopes of Canada in December of 1984 to retire in less than ten years. In 1994, Kim and I retired. I was forty-seven years of age and she was thirty-seven. We had reached our goal to win the game of money by halftime for me, and by the end of the first quarter for Kim.

Winning the game of money is defined as money coming in from our assets, rather than from our labor, that is greater than our expenses. By 1994, Kim and I had approximately $10,000 a month coming in from our investments and $3,000 in expenses. While not rich, we were financially free. We no longer had to work anymore. We did not need a company or government pension. We had won the money game, barring any changes in our financial situation.

After winning the game by age forty-seven, I took the next two years off to contemplate life. During that period, I wrote the rough draft for *Rich Dad Poor Dad* and created the board game CASHFLOW 101. Also during this period, a group of us founded several oil and mining companies in different parts of the world. Some of those companies made it and others folded.

In May of 2000, Oprah Winfrey's show called and invited me to be a guest on her show and the rest is history. *Rich Dad Poor Dad* went worldwide and suddenly I was famous. The third quarter of my life, the years between forty-five and fifty-five, has been a life beyond my wildest dreams. Never would I have imagined that I would spend a hour with Oprah, as well as be on the *To-*

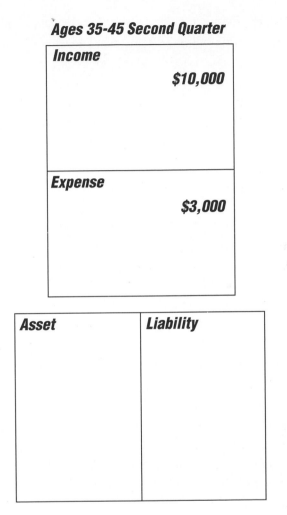

Ages 35-45 Second Quarter

Income	
	$10,000

Expense	
	$3,000

Asset	Liability

day show, CNBC, and TV and radio programs throughout the world, and have five books on *The New York Times* best-seller list. Although the first quarter of my financial life was a mess, the second and third quarters have been great.

As I now embark upon the fourth quarter of my money game, I am not doing anything different. I am still an entrepreneur, building businesses in the B quadrant and investing in real estate and other investments in the I quadrant. In other words, the game remains the same . . . I just continued to get better at the game one quarter at a time. My concern is that many baby boomers are waking up and realizing that they are short on time and short on money and do not know how to play the game. The second half of this book is about winning the game of money, even if you are short on time and money.

Although I was a loser at entrepreneurship and real estate in the first quarter of my life, life did change once I decided to take the game of money more seriously.

Why I Keep Going

One question I am often asked is, "If you can afford to retire, why do you keep working?" There are four answers to that question:

1. The first answer is because I love the game of building businesses and investing, especially in real estate. I'll probably continue to play those games for the rest of my life. When I retired at halftime, got out of the game, and started playing golf, I became very bored and felt I was wasting my life. For me, money was just the score of the game . . . and I missed the game. After taking two years off, I got back into the game.

2. The second answer is because I am concerned about the growing gap between the haves and have-nots in the world. I am also concerned about the number of people who will never be able to retire, simply because they lost the game of money, even though they worked all their lives. Many of my fellow baby boomers are at the beginning of the fourth quarter of the game and behind in points.

3. Answer number three is that the growing greed of the already rich disturbs me. Many of those who stole money from their corporations were already very rich. How someone who has already made over a hundred million dollars would want to steal more money from employees and investors is beyond me.

4. The fourth reason is that the financial ignorance in our academic institutions is damaging our country. It truly disturbs me that our school system continues to ignore the importance of financial education for all students. Regardless of whether a student is an A student or a failure, rich or poor after graduation, if they graduate, all of us will use money. Learning to

manage and invest our money is a life skill all of us need. Why we do not have an honest curriculum in schools about money is beyond me.

If I were to be put in charge of financial education for our schools, one of the first things I would teach kids is the tax code. I would explain to young people that most of the tax breaks go to business owners and very few tax breaks are allotted to employees. Maybe that fact would inspire more young people to be entrepreneurs, entrepreneurs who provide jobs and spur the global economy as Henry Ford, Anita Roddick, Bill Gates, Michael Dell, Rupert Murdoch, Akio Morita, and Richard Branson did.

You Can Lose After Winning

One reason why the game of money is so important is because you can lose after winning. For example, in a football game, let's say the score is 24–14 at halftime. Even if the losing team does not put another score on the board, at the end of the game the losing team will still have the 14 points they had at halftime . . . even if the final score is 48–14.

The game of money is different. Again using the game of football as an example, a person can have a score of 24–14 at the half, yet, unlike in football, at the end of the game have a score of 24–0. In other words, a person can be winning financially in the second quarter, having scores on the board, but lose it all in the fourth quarter of the game.

Prior to the stock market crash that began in March of 2000, many people were winning financially. Many were paper millionaires. A few even quit their jobs. After the crash, they found out the hard way that a winning score in one quarter can be taken away in another quarter.

Many of my fellow baby boomers are now entering the beginning of the fourth quarter of their lives with nothing to show for their years of work. Many are listening to their financial advisors saying to them, "Invest for the long term." The problem with that advice is that they are in the fourth quarter of their money game. What they used to have is gone. Many who were winning at halftime are losing in the fourth quarter . . . and Father Time is still marching on. I read a report the other day that said two thirds of people today live past the age of sixty-five. Life expectancies are dramatically longer than when Social Security was created, but the retirement age is still sixty-five to sixty-seven.

Pilots Are Losing

After graduation in 1969, rather than sail ships, I volunteered for the U.S. Marine Corps and went to flight school in Pensacola, Florida. Between 1969 and 1974, instead of being a ship's officer, I was a military pilot. Many of my fellow Marine Corps officers went on to become airline pilots, flying for United, American, Eastern, Western, Hawaiian, TWA, Northwest, and U.S. Air. Being a commercial airline pilot back in the 1970s was a glamorous, high-paying profession. But again, Father Time has moved on and things have changed. Today, as you may have noticed, some of the airlines listed are no longer in business or are in bankruptcy. Today, many of those pilots have no pensions or pensions that have been greatly decreased in value.

The July 1, 2003, edition of *The Wall Street Journal* ran a story with a headline that read: "Most Workers Are in Dark on Health of Their Pensions."

The article starts off with:

> For millions of American workers, few retirement issues are more vital than the health of their pension plans. But companies have waged a successful battle to keep crucial information about their plans a secret.
>
> The fight comes amid rising alarm about the fate of pensions. Some employers, notably steel makers, have killed decades-old pension plans. Many other companies have reduced pension benefits by restructuring their plans. And employers are now lobbying Congress for formula changes that would let them make smaller pension contributions and smaller payouts when people retire.
>
> Yet employees and retirees have almost no way to find out how financially sound their own pension plan currently is—in part because companies have long resisted attempts to let them have more up-to-date information. The result is that employees are hard-pressed to find out if their pensions are in any current danger.

The article goes on to explain that it used to be easier for employees to find out information on the health of their pensions. But in 1995, that all changed. In 1995, Congress began requiring companies to provide more details about the health of their pension plans to the PBGC. The PBGC is a quasi-public insurance agency that is supposedly there to insure the pensions of workers, which is why PBGC stands for Pension Benefit Guaranty Corporation. In exchange for providing this information to the government on the health of a company's pension, companies required the PBGC to not disclose to citizens any information it received. In other words, after 1995, employees could no longer find out how healthy their pension plan was.

Company Takes Pilots' Pension

The article also explains how pilots of U.S. Airways lost their pension because they could not find out any information on the health of their pension plan.

> On March 31, U.S. Airways Group extinguished the pension plan for 7,000 active and retired pilots.

That means 7,000 pilots suddenly lost their retirement and all the money they had in the plan. The company, U.S. Airways Group, pocketed $387 million . . . money from the pension fund that belonged to the pilots. This is not an isolated event. Many companies have used similar tactics to make the rich richer and the workers are out of work or out of their pension. So the question is, How safe is your pension fund? How can you find out if the PBGC is not required to tell you?

Father Time Waits for No One

The Wall Street Journal article describes how some retirees are coping with the loss of their pension plan:

> Disabled retirees will be among the hardest hit, because they've lost supplemental disability payments linked to their pensions. Hugh Greenwood, who retired in 1997, has lost a $2,000 monthly disability check that was supplementing the pension he took as a lump sum. Mr. Greenwood's wife has returned to work, and the former pilot, 67 years old, will likely do the same.

When you apply rich dad's measurement of the money game to Hugh Greenwood's life, in many ways he was winning the game at the end of the fourth quarter. Suddenly, due to a change in the world's economy, he is starting with virtually nothing . . . and short on time.

Will You Work Forever?

When I was struggling financially in the first quarter of my life, I asked rich dad what happened to people who did not have anything at the end of the fourth quarter. He quietly said, "They go into overtime." In other words, they may have to work for the rest of their lives, which may not be a bad thing as long as you are able to work. In fact, I believe working keeps us healthier and happier. I know because I retired at forty-seven and found it depressing . . . which is why I keep working, even though I do not have to.

Going into overtime after the fourth quarter is not bad as long as you enjoy what you are doing. One of the problem commercial pilots have is that they are required to stop flying at age sixty.

One of my recommendations to people is if you are faced with an *overtime* situation financially do something you enjoy and you can work at for as long as you want to work at it. In other words, don't be like some of my classmates who are old pilots without any other profession. And remember, even if you feel strong and healthy today, there will come a time when you will call an end to the working game and really want to retire and do nothing. Also remember that doing nothing can still be expensive.

Pay Attention to Father Time

As rich dad said, "Every investor must know when a flower is about to bloom . . . and how long that bloom will last."

That means every investor needs to pay attention to time. As my generation is finding out, what worked for our parents' generation may not work for many of us. That means an investor needs to pay attention to cycles. Millions of baby boomers lost trillions of dollars simply because they listened to salespeople and failed to watch the change in cycles.

Today, we all know that markets boom and markets bust, just as most of us know that spring follows winter and winter follows fall. Even living in Hawaii, where it is summer all year long, we as surfers were aware of the change of seasons. We knew that in summer the waves are big on the southern shores. In winter, the waves are big on the northern shores.

When *Rich Dad's Prophecy* was first released in the fall of 2002, many so-called financially astute journalists asked me how I could predict a stock market crash. My reply was, "Because every professional investor knows that all markets boom and all markets crash. Predicting a market crash is like predicting winter in Maine." As simple as that answer is, many financial journalists wanted to argue with me, attempting to deny any possibility that markets crash or that another crash was on the way. Rather than simply accept the natural cycle of markets, many repeated what they learned from their financial planner's sales pitch, saying, "History has shown that the stock market has gone up 9 percent per year on average."

Talk about a sales pitch to lure in the unsophisticated investor. A professional investor knows that markets boom and bust. My standard reply to that statement about averages is, "Only average investors invest on averages." Another answer I have used is, "The average annual temperature of Maine is 70 degrees. That doesn't mean you wear only a sweater in January." This second answer is usually too far over most of their heads.

Commodities

In 1996, as the stock market began to climb, I began to invest in commodities such as gold, silver, and gas. A banker friend of mine, who had suddenly found the new religion of mutual funds and the stock market, wondered why I was in commodities rather than equities. My reply was, "Because commodities operate in a twenty-year cycle. They fell out of favor in 1980. Now as we approach 2000, it's time to start buying them while prices are low." He scoffed at me and kept buying high-tech mutual funds well into 2002, trying to fight the trend, believing his stockbroker's advice of "buy the dips" and "dollar-cost averaging." It took him nearly losing everything to finally stop buying as the stock market dropped and realize he was fighting a change of cycles. I have already mentioned the 20-10-5-year cycle trends, but I will explain them more fully in the second half of this book.

Commodities are such things as gold, silver, pork bellies, corn, coffee, gasoline, heating oil, and other such tangible items. While a student on board the ships during my sea year, I began to study the relationship between the cycles of the stock market and the cycles of the commodities market. One of the things I learned was that when stocks are high, start moving out of the market and begin looking for the next market. That is investing with respect to the cycles of Father Time.

As I will get into later, markets seem to move in twenty-year cycles. In 1973, the stock market became a bear market. Bear markets seem to last about ten years. In 1983, just after the commodities market crashed, namely, gold and silver in 1980, the stock market began to move back up, hitting an all-time high in 2000. As the market climbed, many smart investors began to move into commodities. Why? Because that seems to be the cycle that Father Time has for the markets. So who took the mutual fund investors' money? Was it their stockbrokers or Father Time?

The Crystal Ball

If you want to look into a crystal ball, just study demographics. The baby-boom generation is one big bulge in population. In the 1970s, when they left school and entered the job market, they got married, started families, and began to buy homes. That led to the boom in housing prices in the 1970s. In the 1990s, as they entered their forties and fifties, they hit the stock market in force, causing one of the biggest market bubbles in history. In 2010, when they begin to retire, again this generation will cause a boom and bust in many markets. In 2010, the question will be: "What and where will this generation be going to?" Figure that out ahead of time and you will do well financially. In the year 2030, you can easily predict where most will be going. Again notice the twenty-year trend, this time caused by demographics. The good news is that we may all be living much longer, possibility well past 100. That will cause another boom.

If you want to become rich, figure out where the boom will be and avoid the busts. If you watch demographics, it is like looking into a crystal ball. When I wrote *Rich Dad's Prophecy,* I was primarily looking at the crystal ball known as demographics. The problem was, I had no idea how bad the problem is. Not only are many baby-boomer pension plans out of money, so are many corporations' pension plans out of money, and so is the federal government's treasury out of money, or more accurately deeply in debt.

Respect Father Time

To be a great investor, an investor must respect Father Time and the impact time has on a person's financial scorecard. Some of the cycles and trends a person must pay attention to are:

WINDOWS OF OPPORTUNITY

The other day, I was listening to a radio program, with the host interviewing two so-called investment experts. One expert said, "Warren Buffett is investing in junk bonds. That is why I am advising my clients to do the same."

The second advisor's response was, "Warren Buffett *was* investing in junk bonds—last year. He is out of them this year."

That is an example of a window of opportunity. During the stock market boom, many investors began quoting Warren Buffett and investing in stocks. As stated at the start of this book, Warren Buffett was out of the market just as millions of first-time investors came rushing in. As they say, *time waits for no one*. The same is true for opportunities.

LIFE CHANGES

One of the reasons why rich dad's concept of the four quarters of the money game is so important is because life does change. I have several friends who were flying high financially up until age forty-five. Then their midlife crisis hit them. Some quit their jobs, others should have quit but didn't. Some got divorced and lost everything. A few got divorced and lost everything more than once. One friend became disabled and had no disability insurance. Today, with companies downsizing, many people are starting over just at the time they should be finishing.

Today, a person's financial education is more important than ever before simply because things are changing faster than ever before. Years ago, rich dad drew the CASHFLOW Quadrant and asked me:

"At the end of your life, which quadrant do you want to be in?"

After studying the quadrant for a while, I replied, "Obviously, I want to be in the I quadrant."

He then said, "If you plan on ending up in the I quadrant, why not start there?" That is why he began teaching me to invest as a young boy, teaching me with the game of Monopoly. One of the reasons I was able to recover financially after a disastrous first quarter was because I had the skills of the I quadrant. In the second half of this book, I will share some ideas on how you can gain some of those investor skills without risking much money.

Today, I hear many politicians and journalists calling for more jobs. In my opinion, we need *more* than jobs . . . we need more financial education. As I have said in other books, a job is only a short-term solution to a long-term problem . . . the problem of how we survive financially, especially when we are not working; or are not able to work any longer, or lose everything and have to start all over again.

One big problem today is that our schools focus only on the E and S side of the quadrant and really do need to begin focusing much more on the I quadrant.

DO NOT EXPECT TO WIN EVERY TIME YOU THROW THE DICE

Many investors lost money because they were lucky at one time. During the stock market boom, many first-time investors got lucky, made some money, lost their money, and hoping to get lucky again invested more—only to lose the game.

One of the harder lessons I have had to learn is that just because I made money on one investment at one time does not mean I will make money again, even if I invest in the same type of investment.

The lesson is, markets move on as time marches on. Investing for the long term, buying, holding, and praying, is ridiculous advice when the market is changing directions or changing cycles such as the change of cycle from stocks to commodities.

JUST BECAUSE YOU ARE SMART TODAY DOES NOT MEAN YOU WILL BE SMART TOMORROW

At my company's meetings, I often look around the room at my staff, most of whom are in their twenties and thirties. My comment to them is, "If I were applying for a job today, I would not hire me." The big problem today is not age or race discrimination, the big problem today is technological discrimination. Simply put, I would not hire me because I am technologically obsolete. Thankfully I own the company.

THE DEPRESSION COMES AGAIN

Historically, if a person lives to be seventy-five years of age, he or she will go through one depression and two recessions. The last economic depression began in 1930. Since we have not had a depression for over seventy years, as I write, we can expect one. Back in the 1930s, the federal government tightened up on credit, a move that many economists say deepened the depression. Learning from that mistake, after 2001, the Treasury, rather than tighten up on credit, flooded the market with easy money and cheap credit. Today, we have an economy where people either have too much money or no money at all. Today, we have investors with millions to invest at the same time there are unemployed people lining up for food. If there is a new depression, which group do you want to be in . . . the group without money, or the group with money?

TIME AND MONEY

One of the reasons the rich are getting richer is because the wages of the workers have not kept up with Father Time. *The New York Times* ran an article that compared the increase in the average worker's salary to that of a CEO. It stated that while the average worker's salary went from $32,522 in 1970 to

$35,864 in 1999, about a 10 percent gain over twenty-nine years (adjusting for inflation and using 1998 dollars), the average real compensation of the top 100 CEOs (citing *Fortune* magazine) went from $1.3 million to $37.5 million during the same period.

In other words, in approximately thirty years, workers' pay went up 10 percent and CEOs' pay went up 2,800 percent. That is a very large difference in time and money.

Father Time Waits for No One

Like it or not, Father Time is moving on and changing. To ignore the changes and cycles of Father Time—to simply buy, hold, and pray—is financially very dangerous. It is obvious that many investors of the baby-boom generation will never be able to retire simply because they failed to see Father Time moving on. As rich dad said, "Every investor must know when a flower is about to bloom . . . and how long that bloom will last."

Part II of this book is about how to make up for lost time.

Sharon's Notes

We see stories all the time about the financial crisis of the aging population. A U.S. Bureau of the Census study entitled *65+ in the Untied States* showed clearly that the segment of the population over eighty-five is the fastest growing segment of the population.

The older population—persons sixty-five years or older—numbered 35.6 million in 2002 (the latest year for which data is available). They represented 12.3 percent of the U.S. population, about one in every eight Americans. But by 2030, there will be more than twice that many, or 20 percent of the population.

This shift in sheer numbers of the older population when taken into consideration with longer life expectancies and the crisis in the Social Security system in the U.S. is what *Rich Dad's Prophecy* is about. Robert talks about the 83 million baby boomers who are now turning fifty-five and will start retiring in a few years. If you assume a Social Security payment of $1,000 per month, that will be $83 billion per month that will need to be funded by the U.S. Social Security system.

This, combined with the shift to defined contribution plans, the financial woes of defined benefit plans, lower interest rates, falling stock prices, and fear of the markets in general, is creating a financial catastrophe. It is imperative that people take control of their financial lives and future and not rely on their companies or governments to take care of them.

Ask an Investor

QUESTION:
"Can you turn $10,000 into $10 million?"

ANSWER:
"Yes . . . more if you want."

Four Reasons Why

Can just anyone turn $10,000 into $10 million? Obviously the answer is no. But many more people could if they have the desire and have better advice. Part II of this book is the advice. But before going into the advice, there are four very subtle yet simple points that I need to make prior to sharing the advice. The four points are the four reasons why so many people do not become power investors.

The next chapter goes into the four reasons.

Chapter 10

Four Reasons Why Some People Can't Become Power Investors

Before getting into the formula I use for power investing, I feel it important to discuss the four reasons why some people do not become successful power investors. All four reasons are related.

REASON #1: THE POWER OF THE WORD CAN'T

After high school one day I said to my rich dad, "My science teacher told us today that by design, the bumblebee should not be able to fly."

"Well, let's hope that your science teacher doesn't tell the bumblebee."

"You Can't Do That Here"

In August of 2003, I was driving through the streets of Cape Town, South Africa, one of the most spectacular cities in the world. I was there to deliver a talk to one of the largest banks in Africa. Driving along the harbor front, my host, who was riding in the back seat with me, said, "Your books are good. I like the idea of investing in property and having passive income come in. It's a great idea for your country, but you can't do that here. Our interest rates are too high so you can't make any money the way you say to make money. Positive cash flow from passive income is impossible here."

The car was now winding around some of the most brilliantly designed mass-scale real estate projects I have ever seen. The commercial projects and residential projects are world-class in design, innovation, and land usage. Pausing for a moment to gather my thoughts, I took a deep breath and replied as politely as I could to my host, "You might not be able to make money in real estate here in Cape Town, but rest assured, someone is."

One of the reasons the bumblebee can fly is because it does not know it cannot fly. One of the reasons so many investors cannot find great investments that make them a lot of money is that they often say "You can't do that here." Or "I can't afford it." Or "Prices are too high." Or whatever people say to justify their inability to do what others are doing.

The Price of Saying "I Can't"

Henry Ford is quoted as saying, "If you think you can, you can. If you think you can't you can't. Either way you're right."

As I drove through the streets of Cape Town, my host continued on with his ideas on why my ideas would not work there. "Oh, the price of real estate has risen so much in the last three years. How can anyone afford to own a home, much less invest in rental property? That is why I say your ideas on investing will not work in this town."

Letting him drone on, I gazed out the car's window and could see that Cape Town was a world-class city and that there was a lot of money being made there. Sure Cape Town and South Africa had their problems that were keeping many timid investors away, yet it was obvious to me that investor dollars were pouring into this city. Many people were becoming very rich. My host, on the other hand, had let his poor attitude and limited reality defeat him. We were together for about five hours that day. During that period of time I heard him use the word "can't" many times . . . far too many times.

Talking Straight

After my graduation from the academy, rich dad began speaking more directly to me. He was less polite, less cautious. He wanted me to learn quickly, so he did not mince his words as he did when I was a kid. As my Cape Town host was speaking, telling me why it was hard to make money investing in real estate there, my mind drifted back to rich dad saying to me, "Poor people and lazy people use the word *can't* more often than successful people. They use the word *can't* because it's easier than saying *can*. If you say you can't do something, you don't have to do it . . . even if you can."

Glancing back at my host, who was gazing out the car window as he talked, I realized that he had missed out on becoming rich not because he was stupid or incompetent. He was missing out on becoming rich because he was lazy. It was much easier for him to say, "You can't do that here." Even though it was obvious that people were doing it right in front of his eyes.

Lazy People Work Hard

Rich dad often said, "It's easy to work hard and go nowhere. It's easy to stick to a job and blame your boss for not giving you a bigger raise. It's easy to say 'I can't afford it.' It's easy to say 'I can't do that.' It's easy to blame your husband, your wife, or your children for your financial problems." He also said, "There are many lazy people who work hard. They continue to work hard because it is easier to keep working hard than to change." When it came to investing, rich dad said, "Many people just turn their money over to total strangers and wonder why they get such poor returns. Or many people seem to think that it should be easy to find a great investment. They seem to think that great investments grow on trees or should be handed to them. The fact is, it's easy to find bad investments. The world is filled with people offering you bad investments to invest in. If you want your money to work hard for you, you cannot afford to be lazy. Lazy people invest in the investments that ambitious people reject."

Not to Be Cruel

Saying that hardworking people are lazy is not done to be cruel. I make that statement to pass on one of the most important lessons rich dad ever taught me—his lesson on the power found in the word *can't*. He said, "The word *can't* makes strong people weak, blinds people who can see, saddens happy people, turns brave people into cowards, robs a genius of their brilliance, causes rich people to think poorly, and limits the achievements of that great person living inside us all."

Millionaire Going Broke

Recently, I read an article about a woman who was struggling financially. The headline of the article read "Millionaire Going Broke." This woman was seventy years old, a graduate of an Ivy League law school, and a successful attorney. After she retired, she sold all her stocks and mutual funds and took a cash position. "After the market crash, I felt so smart because I did not lose money in the market as many of my friends did," she said. "Instead, I had over $1 million in certificates of deposit, earning almost 5 percent interest. That meant I had nearly $50,000 a year to live on, plus $22,000 from Social Security. I thought I was set. Eight years after retiring, those certificates of deposit are paying less than 1 percent interest, which means my $50,000 in interest has dropped to less than $10,000 in interest income. I'm having a tough time making ends meet right now, even though I'm technically a millionaire. If interest rates don't go up soon, I'll have to start drawing on my principal . . . and that might mean I could go broke if I am lucky to live a long life."

As expected, the reply from the financial expert was, "You've done the right thing but now is the time to get back into the market. If you invest wisely, with the proper allocation into a well-diversified portfolio, you should earn on average 5 percent per year."

While this is good advice for a person with her level of financial education, 5 percent per year from your investment is hardly a good return. With a little financial education and experience, she could easily be receiving a 15 percent return or even more. So why doesn't she receive these higher returns? The answer is, it is a matter of education and who the teacher is. In other words, many people are bumblebees who are being taught how *not* to fly by people who also think they cannot fly.

Four Green Houses . . . One Red Hotel

Starting when I was nine, rich dad began teaching me the principles of becoming rich. He started with simple lessons and then playing Monopoly with me for hours. He repeatedly said, "The formula for great wealth is found on this game board. The formula is four green houses, trade them in for one red hotel." He then completed my education by actually taking me to his rental properties that represented his green houses. While I was at the academy in

1967, rich dad actually traded in his four green houses and bought one of the biggest hotels on Waikiki Beach. While the hotel was not red in color, at the age of nineteen I knew why bumblebees could fly and why my rich dad had become so rich in ten years.

In July of 2003, I was in Waikiki, walking with Mike, rich dad's son, along the beachfront spot where rich dad's hotel once stood. The hotel has since been torn down, replaced by an even more massive beachfront hotel, owned by a large insurance company. While rich dad's family does not own the building, it does control the master ground leases under the new hotel. The rents they collect from that piece of land are staggering. Mike said, "This land is now virtually priceless. Dad started with nothing but he had a plan, a vision, and a dream. He started playing Monopoly as a kid and he never stopped playing. No one ever told him that he could not play the game of Monopoly in real life."

As Mike stopped to talk to one of the shop owners on his property, my mind drifted back and could hear my mom and dad telling me to "Put that silly Monopoly game away. Get back to your homework. If you don't get good grades, you won't get a high-paying job." As Mike and I continued our walk along the beachfront property, Mike said, "It was lucky for me that no one ever told my dad that Monopoly was only a game for kids."

Nodding, I silently said to myself, "Or tell bumblebees that they cannot fly."

REASON #2: THE POWER OF EASY

"The key to becoming rich is to make things easy," rich dad said one day while he was giving his son and me a lesson on business. "One of the reasons schoolteachers make less money than businesspeople is because the school system is designed to take the simple and make it complex." Not understanding what he meant, I asked for further clarification. Rich dad promptly replied with, "The school system takes 1 + 1, simple math, and turns it into calculus. That is what I mean by taking the simple and making it more complex."

School had always been a frightening place for me. I always seemed to be living in fear of the upcoming year, knowing that next year the studies would be harder than the current year. I remember being in elementary school and having people tell me that high school was going to be much harder. When I was in high school, I was then told that college was going to be even tougher. So it did seem to me that school was about making life harder. Not fully understanding the difference between the world of business and the school system, I asked rich dad, "Does that mean that business takes the complex and makes it simple?"

Nodding, rich dad replied, "That's correct. The purpose of a business is to make life simpler, not harder. The businesses that make life the easiest are the businesses that make the most money."

"Can you give me an example?" I asked.

"Sure," replied rich dad. "The reason the auto industry makes so much money is because a car makes getting from one point to another easier."

"Easier than walking. Is that what you mean?"

"Exactly. Because a car makes life easier, millions of us are willing to pay money for a car."

"The same is true for the airlines," I added, as I began to understand this lesson.

"And the telephone, the supermarket, the electric company. They all make money because they make life easier," said rich dad.

"And school makes life harder?" I asked.

"Yes," replied rich dad. "They take the simple and make it harder and harder. If you want to be rich, you should learn to take things that are difficult and make them simple. If you will focus on that, making life easier for people, you will become a very rich person. The more people you help in making life easier, the richer you will become."

Rich Dad's Rule

Rich dad's rule was, "Money flows to the person who makes life easy."

Investing Made Easy

One of the reasons the stock market does well is because it makes investing easy. The stock market takes a company and chops it into millions of shares, and makes it easy for people to buy these pieces of a company.

One of the reasons mutual funds attract so much money is because it makes deciding what stocks to buy easy. All you have to do is buy one mutual fund and hopefully the fund manager has chosen a group of stocks that will grow in value.

If you understand rich dad's lesson on making life easy, you will understand why the people who run stock markets or manage the mutual funds are the ones getting rich—not necessarily the person who is investing the money.

Investing Made Affordable

Not only does the stock market and a mutual fund make investing easy, it makes investing easy to afford. A person can elect to invest just $50 a month. That's all they have to do. They do not need to raise a massive down payment, prove they have good credit to arrange bank financing, as real estate or business loans often require. All they have to do is hand their money over. That is all they have to do.

Who Makes Money Even in a Crash

In a crash, a mutual fund still makes money, even if their investors are losing money. During the crash, as stock prices plummeted as did mutual fund values, the fund companies continued to collect management fees. Why? Because they made investing easy.

A Direct Relationship

All of the reasons are related. People who often say *can't* are often the people who seek the easy investing techniques.

During one of his lessons on investing, rich dad said, "Many people seem to think that great investments grow on trees. They think that investing should be easy. Many think that all they have to do is hand their money over to a magician and suddenly like magic they strike it rich. In reality, investing is a continual process of searching, negotiating, financing, and managing people and money. When it comes to investing, the people who take the hard road find life easy. People who take the easy road usually find life hard."

This leads to the third reason why few people become power investors.

REASON #3: THE RICH MAKE IT EASY TO BE POOR

Have you ever noticed how easy it is to get a credit card? Have you ever noticed how easy it is to get into *bad debt?*

When Kim and I were building our fortune, we ran into trouble with bankers because we had too many investment properties. Even though they were all positive-cash-flow investments, the bank wanted to call some of our loans because we had too much good debt. At the same time the bank was concerned about our multimillion-dollar investment portfolio, they were eager to give us a new credit card as well as give us a loan for a new car. In other words, our banker was concerned that we had too much good debt and at the same time wanted us to load up with more bad debt. Why is that?

Early in 2003, our mortgage broker called and asked if we wanted an additional $300,000 in cash from a home equity loan on our residence. Since interest rates had fallen so low, Kim and I could afford to take the money and still make the same mortgage payment each month.

When we wanted to refinance one of our apartment houses, pulling out $250,000 in equity, the same mortgage broker became hesitant. Although we got the money from another broker, I found it interesting that the first broker was eager to give us a loan for a liability, our house, but hesitant to loan us money for an asset. Why is that?

One other interesting point is that many personal finance money magazines recommend that a person buy a second vacation house, a second house that *costs* money, but not an investment property that *makes* money. Why is this? When we go into power investing in the next few chapters, this question will become even more curious because most rich people either made their money in real estate or hold their wealth in real estate. The real estate market is also a far bigger market than the stock market. So why do so many financial experts recommend against real estate and recommend easier investments such as stocks, bonds, and mutual funds?

REASON #4: INVESTING WITHOUT GUARANTEES

Why are so many millions of investors willing to pay a little money each month without any guarantees that the money will be there in the future? Why are so many millions of investors so willing to lose money each month rather than make money each month? While many average investors are willing to gamble on making money in the future, a power investor wants guarantees on their returns today.

In an upcoming chapter, I write about a woman who wanted to buy a stock for $55 a share because her stockbroker told her the price would soon be $75 a share. The question is, how can so many people be so gullible and invest in lies? The answer is found in reason number 4.

Reason number four why many people are not power investors is because they are gullible enough to invest in the promise of the future. Why so many investors are gullible enough to invest in promises is often because they cannot find an investment that pays them today. As stated earlier, all four reasons are related. It all begins when a person says "I can't afford it" or "I can't find a good investment." Once a person cannot find a good investment that pays them today, many look for an easy answer and are willing to wait to be paid tomorrow.

If you are going to be a power investor, you cannot afford to invest in lies. You must invest in guarantees. In the upcoming chapters you will find out how power investors invest with those guarantees.

Sharon's Notes

Review these four reasons that hold people back from becoming power investors.

Reason #1: The Power of the Word *Can't*
So you find yourself saying "It's easy for him to say! I can't do that!" In *Rich Dad Poor Dad* Robert shared how his poor dad would always say "I can't afford it!" His rich dad, on the other had, forbade him from saying "I can't afford it!" and challenged Robert to ask instead, "How can I afford it?" The word "can't" closes your mind, while the phrase "How can I?" opens your mind.

Reason #2: The Power of Easy
Rich dad said, "Money flows to the person who makes life easy."

However, creating an investment that makes life easy is not easy at first. But once created, the money starts flowing.

It may sound contradictory but remember, rich dad also said, "When it comes to investing, the people who take the hard road find life easy. People who take the easy road usually find life hard." If you take the time to create the investments today, your life will become much easier later.

Reason #3: The Rich Make It Easy to Be Poor
It is so much easier to get bad debt (personal debt like credit cards that you have to pay for from personal funds) than to get good debt (debt that is paid

for by the income from the underlying investment). Personal debt is at an all-time high.

Reason #4: Investing Without Guarantees
This comes back to investing for actual cash flow today versus the promise of capital gains tomorrow.

Can you see yourself controlling each of these reasons in your personal investing strategy so you can become a power investor?

Chapter 11

The Power of Power Investing

"What is power investing?" I asked rich dad.

"It is investing using all three asset classes, reinvesting cash flow, leveraged with OPM, other people's money, and accelerated by tax incentives," said rich dad.

"Sounds difficult," I replied.

"That's why so few investors use it and that is why so few investors achieve accelerated returns on their money."

The Three Asset Classes

As stated previously, the three major asset classes are:

1. Business
2. Real estate
3. Paper assets

One of the reasons so many people achieve poor investment results is because most people invest in only one asset class. Power investing requires that the investor invest in two, and preferably three, asset classes.

In the world today, other than a personal residence or a vacation home, most people invest primarily in paper assets such as stocks, bonds, mutual funds, or cash in certificates of deposit. Why? Again the answer goes back to the word *easy*. Paper assets are popular because they are easy to get into and easy to get out of. Also when compared to business or real estate investments, paper assets require very little management skills on the part of the investor.

A Loss of Control

When you drive a car, a car has a gas pedal, brakes, and a steering wheel to give the driver control. Investing in paper assets, the investor often gives up control over the investment and often turns control over to total strangers they hope are better drivers than they are. Giving up control is very risky, yet it is often best they give up control if they do not know how to drive.

For a professional investor, a major drawback of paper assets is that the investor, by not being active in management, gives up *business control* over the asset. For example, as a minor shareholder of Microsoft, it would be difficult for me to call Bill Gates up and tell him he is spending too much money or that I want a greater return on my investment. In my own businesses and in my real estate holdings, I can do that. I have control over how much money I can make, my expenses, taxes, and what to do with my earnings. I also have better control over less-than-honest activities that may be going on in the business. Another control given up with paper assets is that the investor has very limited tax advantages, if any. One of the best reasons to own a business or invest in real estate is because the tax department loves you.

In my opinion, a business and real estate are far better investments for people with the skills to manage them. Without management skills, again, control is difficult. Obviously, if a person lacks the skills to manage a business or real estate, these two investment classes can be nightmares. If you cannot drive, and do not know how to coordinate the gas, the brakes, and steering wheel of a car, driving a car can be dangerous to your health.

If businesses and real estate have far more advantages, why then do so many more people invest in paper assets and give up so much control? In my opinion, the answer is again found in the word *easy*. For millions of people, it is easier to turn over control of their money than to learn how to drive their money. That is why millions of investors have their portfolios filled with mutual funds without any idea who is driving the fund. For many busy people, investing in mutual funds is easier so they can keep working hard rather than to financially learn how to drive. For many people mutual funds are the meat and potatoes of their financial life.

Shopping for mutual funds is like going to the frozen dinner section of the supermarket. It's all prepared, prepackaged, and ready to go. All you have to do is pick up the dinner of your choice, pay for it, take it home, then heat and serve. While I do invest in stocks and mutual funds . . . I use them as dessert, not the main course. When I decide to use a paper asset, it is often because I need to get my money in and out quickly. I like paper assets primarily for their *liquidity,* as it is called, more than their long-term value.

The big disadvantage of real estate or a business is that the ins and outs are often very sticky, tedious, complicated, and involved. That is why I invest in them for their long-term value.

Buying Stocks Is Like Dating

Rich dad used to say, "Buying stocks is like dating. You go to a dinner and a movie, and if you do *not* get along, you shake hands at the door and you don't go out again. Buying real estate is like getting married. Before getting married, first there is generally a lot of dating . . . personally looking at as many properties as possible. Then after you find the property of your dreams, there is a big wedding ceremony at the bank, and then you settle down and see what happens. If you and your property do not get along, and the marriage becomes a nightmare, getting divorced can be a tedious and stressful transaction." When it comes to a business, rich dad said, "Building or owning a business is by far the most rewarding but also the most stressful of all the three assets. If investing in paper assets is like dating, and acquiring real estate is like getting married, then investing in a business is like being married with kids."

See the World Through the Eyes of a Business Owner

When I returned from Vietnam in 1973, rich dad insisted I learn how to sell, to build businesses, and learn to invest in real estate. He said, "If you want to be rich and be a great investor, you need to see the world through the eyes of a business owner and an investor, not as a worker who works for a business."

Not really understanding what he meant, I asked, "If I am investing in real estate, why would I need to see that investment through the eyes of a business owner?"

Smiling, he took out his legal pad and drew a rectangle, then said, "A farmer may be willing to pay $10,000 for this piece of land. If he pays more than that, his business will suffer because his vegetable business is not profitable enough to buy the land. In other words, if the farmer pays more than $10,000 for the land, the land may be more valuable than the business and the farmer's business could not afford to pay for the land."

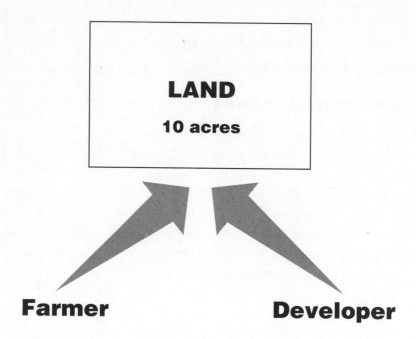

"But a real estate developer could afford to pay more for the same piece of land," I said, understanding where rich dad was going with this lesson. "Real estate is only as valuable as the business."

Rich dad continued with the lesson. "A real estate developer may be willing to pay $100,000 for the same piece of land that the farmer was only willing to pay $10,000 for. The land is more valuable because the business the developer is in is more profitable. The developer sees the same piece of real estate through a different set of eyes."

Marcel Proust, author and poet, said: "The only real voyage of discovery consists not in seeking new landscapes but in having new eyes."

Missed Opportunities

In an earlier chapter, I wrote about driving through the streets of Cape Town and having my host say that it was impossible to make money in real estate in that town, at least in the ways I described in my books. One reason he and I did not see the same opportunities is because we did not see the same real estate through the same set of eyes.

Blind to Opportunities

During the 1960s and 1970s, my rich dad could see the changes coming to the sleepy tropical islands of Hawaii. He knew he had to make his move or be left behind. My poor dad only saw that the price of his house was going up.

For years, Hawaii had been just a dream for many people. Traveling to Hawaii was only for the rich and travel was primarily by ships. It took five to six days to sail from California to Hawaii. Many people did not have the money or the time to afford two weeks of travel, round-trip. Rich dad saw the advent of jet travel bringing millions of tourists to Hawaii, making Hawaii not only closer but more affordable. He knew the new passenger jets would change everything.

Just as the farmer saw the land valued at $10,000 and the developer saw it worth $100,000, my poor dad saw the changes through the eyes of a schoolteacher and my rich dad saw the changes through the eyes of a businessman and an investor . . . a different set of eyes.

Ironically, during the 1960s and the 1970s, my poor dad earned more money than my rich dad. My poor dad had a high-paying government job. During the 1960s my rich dad was chronically short of cash. Every spare dollar went back into building his business and buying as much real estate as he could. My rich dad did not have a steady paycheck and there were many times he had no money at all, yet he kept going.

During this period, my poor dad was actually in a better position to afford the investments my rich dad was buying. Having a high-paying job, my poor dad would have had an easier time getting the bank to give him a loan to buy the properties before they skyrocketed in value. My rich dad had to go from banker to banker, investor to investor, to find the money. It was hard to get people to trust him because he did not have much money and he did not have a normal steady job.

Although my poor dad was in a better position to get rich during this era, he didn't. Instead he worked hard, stayed busy, played it safe, bought a house, saved money, and was excited that the equity in his home was going up as real estate values began to climb. Then suddenly, in 1967, it was rich dad who seemed to come out of nowhere when he purchased a major hotel on Waikiki Beach. All my poor dad said was, "How can he afford a hotel on Waikiki Beach? He doesn't even have a real job!"

Rich Dad's Power Investing: How to Afford Anything You Want

From 1970 on into the early 1990s, rich dad's personal wealth increased exponentially. But my poor dad got poorer during the same period of time. By the mid-1970s, rich dad was no longer scrimping, he was no longer strapped for cash. Cash was flowing in at high speed from all his investments. Besides owning a major hotel on Waikiki Beach, he was now purchasing other beachfront hotels and commercial properties with the cash flow from his big hotel. Instead of wasting his money, he continually reinvested it, which made him even more money. After 1970, it was my poor dad who did not have a job. After an unsuccessful bid for lieutenant governor, running against his boss the governor, my poor dad was blacklisted from jobs in state government.

In 1973, while still in the Marine Corps and stationed in Hawaii, I would often drive to Waikiki to have lunch with rich dad. I would sit and ask him for guidance, preparing for the day when I would leave the military. During that year, I often asked rich dad about how he did what he had done, starting with so little money. Although I had heard of his ideas on power investing many times before, I heard them as a kid. Older, wiser, and having two dads to compare one against the other, I now had greater respect for his plan. During one of these lunches, rich dad said, "As a young man, I knew that if I followed this power investing plan, I could someday afford anything . . . anything I wanted . . . if I was successful."

Being twenty-five years of age, I was now more interested in his plan, especially when I heard the words *I could afford anything I wanted*. Up until this point, I knew of rich dad's plan of power investing, but to me, it seemed like too much work. Now that I could actually see his major hotel on Waikiki Beach and all his other beachfront properties on other beaches on other islands, I was more interested in his plan. On top of that, it did seem to be better than the plan my poor dad was endorsing.

The First Quarter Begins

During the first quarter of my personal money game, the ages of twenty-five to thirty-five, I knew that my new job was to learn to build businesses, invest in real estate, and for dessert, invest in paper assets. Although I knew that I would probably earn less than my peers for the first and maybe the second quarter of my life, I knew that if I applied myself, I would be better off in the second half of my life, the second half that began at age forty-five.

Rich Dad's Plan for Power Investing

The following section of this chapter is the oversimplified overview of rich dad's plan for power investing. In later chapters, I will go into greater detail on a few points that help make this plan work. I wish I could say I could offer you every important point of this plan, but I am afraid that would take a library of books to accomplish. The way I learned how to drive rich dad's power investing plan was by understanding the concept and then going out and learning how to drive. At the age of twenty-five, I committed to learning how to build and drive a business, to invest in and drive real estate investments, and to identify and drive my investments in paper assets. In other words, I wanted to have control of my assets rather than just turn my career and my money over to strangers. I am certain that there is no way a person can learn to do this plan just by reading about it. It would be like learning to ride a bike by reading a book on bike riding. It is not possible. You still need a bike even though you read the book.

A Reminder

Before reading rich dad's power investing plan, I remind you of the previous chapter. As you read rich dad's plan, I recommend paying close attention to your internal dialogue, which is the conversation you have with yourself. Notice if you are saying *you can* or *you can't* and if you're saying that it sounds too hard and you want an easier answer. If you find yourself saying "I can't" too often and want easier investment answers, then mutual funds may be the answer for you.

Rich dad's power investing plan requires the ownership of a profitable business, investing in real estate that produces positive cash flow, and then investing in paper assets, paper assets that produce higher returns than a bank savings account with the same liquidity. While I have mentioned this plan in other books, in this book I go into more detail on the tax and leverage angles that actually give a substantial boost to the returns I receive.

Rich Dad's Power Investing

A plan for people who want to afford anything they want. This is the basic plan that the richest investors in the world follow. It was described in the table in the introduction and is shown again here for your reference. The B-I side of the chart is Rich Dad's Power Investing Plan: Start a business, invest the cash flow from the business into real estate, and then balance your asset classes with investing your excess cash flow in paper assets.

ASSET #1: BUSINESS

Your own personal business is by far your best asset because, if successful, you can generate the most income with less work and with the least *taxes*.

One of the reasons Warren Buffett turned Berkshire Hathaway into an insurance company rather than a garment manufacturing company was because the tax advantages of an insurance company are greater than those of a garment manufacturing company. In other words, the tax rules are different for different businesses. Also, by investing through different legal entities rather than investing personally, he again achieved higher investment yields because of tax law differences. *Always remember, taxes are your single largest expense.*

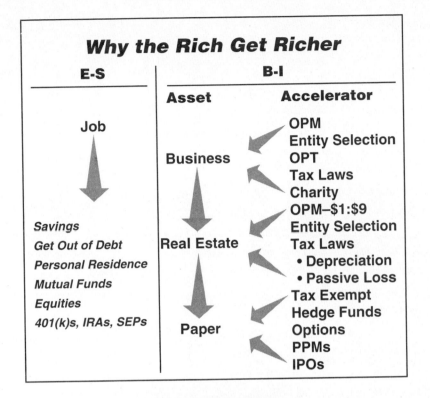

Why the Rich Get Richer

E-S

B-I

Asset   **Accelerator**

Job

Business
OPM
Entity Selection
OPT
Tax Laws
Charity

OPM–$1:$9
Entity Selection

Savings
Get Out of Debt

Real Estate
Tax Laws
• Depreciation
• Passive Loss

Personal Residence
Mutual Funds
Equities
401(k)s, IRAs, SEPs

Paper
Tax Exempt
Hedge Funds
Options
PPMs
IPOs

AUTHOR'S NOTE

Obviously, this subject of taxes, corporations, and different businesses is a very complex and involved subject . . . a subject far beyond the scope of this book and my writing ability. If you would like further information on this whole subject as well as the rest of rich dad's plan for power investing, go to our Web site, richdad.com.

We always recommend that any advice, especially advice on taxes, business, investments, and corporate entities, should be verified with a licensed CPA and attorney. Each situation is different and each situation should be checked with a licensed professional.

There are also the Rich Dad's Advisors series of books that are available to supplement this important subject. To find the topics covered by the Rich Dad's Advisors books, again, please go to our Web site for a complete listing of Rich Dad products.

The drawback: Of course, if you are not successful in building a profitable business, a business can be a very big liability and loss of money, which is why I so often recommend starting a part-time business before quitting your daytime job.

Accelerator #1: Other People's Money

The first accelerator in starting a business is to use other people's money. As you become a better businessperson, this will become easier because investors like winners.

Many people start their businesses using their own personal credit cards, loans from family members, or personal loans from banks. While this may be necessary if you are just starting out, remember that the quickest way to accelerate your business is by inviting investors to join you. However, a word of caution: Be careful whom you invite to participate. You may want to maintain control of the management of the company and limit the involvement of the investors.

Also be careful how much equity you give up because as your company grows and needs additional moneys to expand, you may need to look for a second and or third round of investment dollars. Have this factored in when you create your original business plan.

You may also be able to fund your growth through the excess cash flow from your business. The first two years of the Rich Dad company, Sharon, Kim, and I took no money out of the company but reinvested it into growing the business.

The next step we took was to look for strategic partners. By licensing certain rights to them, and sharing the profits with them, we were able to expand using our strategic partner's money and our strategic partner's distribution systems. We have used this strategic partner model many times in growing our business.

Accelerator #2: Entity Selection

Choosing the proper entity in which to hold your business is critical. You absolutely do NOT want to hold your business as a sole proprietorship or general partnership.

Review the various requirements and benefits of a C Corporation, S Corporation, Limited Liability Company (LLC), or Limited Partnership (LP) with your attorney and tax advisor to see which entity will provide the best protection for your business and result in the best tax advantages, thus maximizing your cash flow.

Accelerator #3: Other People's Time

If you are a good business owner, you have the *leverage* of other people and systems doing your work. In other words, if you are a good businessperson, it is the same as earning money for nothing, once the business is up and running. Most people will have to work for money for much of their lives because *they work for a business rather than work to build a business.*

Accelerator #4: Tax Laws

The tax man is on your side as a business owner. Review Chapter 5 on how the tax laws were written to benefit business owners and investors. By starting a business you may even be able to convert personal expenses into legitimate deductible business expenses.

Accelerator #5: Charity

My rich dad always reminded me of the saying "Give and you shall receive." Being generous and giving back to the community are essential elements in growing your business.

You may not know how the returns on your charitable giving will be realized, but they will be. The more people you serve, the richer you will become.

At our company, we regularly donate books and games to organizations. In addition we created the Foundation for Financial Literacy, which awards financial grants to organizations that create and support financial literacy programs, that support the Rich Dad mission statement, "To elevate the financial well-being of humanity."

In addition, we have reinvested part of our company's profits into developing the commercial-free Web site, www.richkidsmartkid.com, which has financial mini-games and curricula for children from kindergarten through high school. Schools from around the world may apply through this Web site and receive a free copy of our electronic game CASHFLOW for KIDS.

It is through the combination of all of these accelerators that you will be able to maximize the velocity of growing your business and your cash flow. You can then reinvest your cash flow into the business to continue its growth or invest it into new assets like real estate.

ASSET #2: REAL ESTATE

Accelerator #6: Other People's Money

My banker is on my side for investing in real estate. Let's say I buy a $100,000 property by using:

$10,000 of my own money

$90,000 of my bank's money

The banker allows the investor to also take the phantom cash flow as well as capital gains from their side of the investment. In other words, even if the bank technically owns 90 percent of the investment, the investor also gets the banker's share of the phantom cash flow as well as the banker's share of the capital gains. Think about that one. How many business partners will give you their share of the profits? In this case, your banker does. The banker has 90 percent of the risk but you receive their share of the profits. They get nothing but the interest, which is paid by your tenant. Ask your financial planner if your mutual fund will give you that great a deal. Will your mutual fund loan you 90 percent of the money, assume 90 percent of the risk, but take 0 percent of the profits? This is what rich dad called magic money.

Financial planners often say that employers often match their employees' contributions. That is at best a 1:1 ratio versus the 1:9 ratio in real estate.

Review Chapter 3, "Ask Your Banker," for the three types of leverage offered by the bank:

1. In securing the investment
2. Depreciation of entire asset
3. Ownership of appreciation

Accelerator #7: Entity Selection

Entity selection is again critical in understanding the secrets and strategies that the rich have used for generations to protect their real estate assets. Often you will want to have separate entities for each property so if one property is put at risk, your others are not.

Popular entities for holding real estate are limited liability companies (LLCs) and limited partnerships (LPs). You will want to get competent advice from your attorney and tax strategist, as the choice may also be important based on your state laws.

Accelerator #8: Tax Laws—Depreciation and Real Estate
Paper Losses

The tax man offers great accelerators in your real estate income and cash flow in the form of depreciation. This is also called *phantom cash flow,* which means more money into the investor's pocket *today*, not when they retire.

Why I invest in real estate secondarily is because the tax advantages for real estate, as explained in Chapter 5, "Ask the Tax Man" are different from the tax advantages in paper assets. If I invested in paper assets second, rather than real estate, I would not receive the greater leverage.

ASSET #3: PAPER ASSETS
Accelerator #9: Tax-Exempt

The tax man offers even greater leveraged advantages to investors who invest in projects the government needs financial assistance in. After my money passes through the leverage of real estate, it often goes into the stock market, especially in tax-free paper assets such as municipal mortgage REITs (real estate investment trusts) and other such paper investments. At this point I am usually receiving a 5 percent to 8 percent tax-free return on my extra money, often called savings. It is far better than the 1 percent taxable return I would receive from a bank certificate of deposit, which is often less liquid than my municipal mortgage REITs.

Accelerator #10: Hedge Funds

Hedge funds allow me to invest with insurance. They have the benefits offered by mutual funds in that they are "easy," but without the downside risk. A hedge fund is a fund that can take both long and short positions, use arbitrage, buy and sell undervalued securities, trade options or bonds, and invest in almost any opportunity in any market where it expects gains at reduced risk. There are many different hedge fund strategies but their primary goal is to reduce volatility and risk while preserving their investors' capital and delivering positive returns under all market conditions. Most of these funds hedge against downturns in the markets—which is especially important today with the volatility in the stock markets.

Accelerator #11: Options

Investing in stock options allows me to leverage my investments in paper assets. Instead of buying the stock I can still control it through the purchase of options for a fraction of the cost. Options give me the right to buy or sell a fixed amount of stock at a fixed price (called the "strike price") over a specific period of time. A contract allowing me to "buy" stock at the fixed strike price is called a "call option," which allows me to purchase, say, 100 shares of the underlying stock. People buy *calls* because they hope the stock price will go up, and they will make a profit, either by selling the calls at a higher price, or by exercising their option, which means buying the shares at the strike price at a point when the market price is higher.

On the other hand, a contract that lets me "sell" stock at a fixed price is called a "put option." People buy *puts* because they hope the stock price will go down, and they will make a profit, either by selling the puts at a higher price, or by exercising their option, which would force the seller of the put to buy the stock at the strike price at a time when the market price was lower.

Accelerator #12: PPMs (Private Placement Memorandums)

A private placement memorandum, however, is an offering of stock in a company that is exempt from federal registration. In March 1982, the SEC adopted Regulation D to coordinate the limited offering exemptions and to streamline the existing requirements applicable to private placements and sales of securities. Within this there are three different rules that can be followed:

Rule 504, which provides exemptions for nonreporting companies, stipulates that:

- The sale of up to $1 million of U.S. securities within twelve months is allowed.
- An unlimited number of investors may purchase the securities.
- Investors are not required to qualify.
- The stock can be sold on the public market one year after purchase.

Rule 505 allows for the sale of up to $5 million of U.S. securities, while Rule 506 allows for the sale of unlimited amounts of securities. However, both 505 and 506 require that the investors be accredited investors (you are allowed to have up to thirty-five unaccredited investors).

Investing in private placement memorandums is typically a capital gains strategy where you are expecting the value of the stock to increase over time and an exit plan for the founding shareholders.

Again, the documentation and legal requirements of this type of investment are critically important. You need competent securities legal advice as well as tax advice to select the funding tool appropriate for your situation.

Accelerator #13: IPOs (Initial Public Offerings)

An initial public offering (IPO) is a company's first sale of stock to the public. Typically, an IPO involves the stock from a young, new, and not usually well-known company. An IPO is highly regulated and costly to prepare, as it requires tremendous legal and accounting professional time. It also requires a great deal of the executive management team's time, which might take their focus off the core business. It, however, provides great leverage, since the hope is that the initial price will be low and the price of the stock once on the public exchange will increase. Once again this is usually a capital gains investment strategy and an exit strategy for the company's founders.

$105,000 into $30 Billion

Warren Buffett was able to turn $105,000 into $30 billion using a similar method of investing, although he did not use real estate as much as I do. The lesson to be learned is that power investing is based upon a synergy of investments and leveraged accelerators. This synergy between asset classes is what makes turning $10,000 into $10 million, on a regular basis, easy, once you learn how to do it and once your system is set up. It can be difficult at first, but once the system is working, the cash flows and flows in, rather than out.

$10,000 into $10 Million

So can a person turn $10,000 into $10 million with only one asset class? Yes, they can. In fact, most people start with only one asset class in the beginning. Can you successfully invest in all three asset classes? Only you can answer that question.

The Weakest Link

A very popular TV show is *The Weakest Link*. If a person just buys and sells a stock, bond, mutual fund, or a piece of property, they are often missing out on the hidden advantages of power investing, often taking greater risks, and paying too much in taxes—if they make money. By missing the invisible links, or accelerators, between asset classes, the investor becomes the *weak-*

est link. Their lack of education or desire to get rich quickly causes them to rob themselves of money they could be earning. As rich dad often said, "Our greatest expense is the money we are not earning."

=== **Sharon's Notes** ===

Taxation As an Accelerator

As one of the accelerators available to all three asset classes, taxation can also be the most complex to understand. We do not expect you to become a tax expert, but by becoming more aware of the tax laws and deductions available, you can maximize your income and minimize your taxes legally. It is very important to seek competent tax advisors to help you create the strategy that suits your investment needs and to know what questions to ask and to understand the impact taxes have on your cash flow.

As an employee, your taxes are withheld from your income, so your cash flow pattern is:

$$\text{EARN} \longrightarrow \text{PAY TAX} \longrightarrow \text{THEN SPEND}$$

As a business owner, your cash flow pattern is:

$$\text{EARN} \longrightarrow \text{SPEND} \longrightarrow \text{THEN PAY TAX}$$

This difference in cash flow and the tax benefits available to business owners is why rich dad and Robert recommend you start a part-time business. As a business owner you have the use of the money and can use it to reinvest in building your business, before you pay taxes, instead of the government taking its share even before you receive your income.

Increase Your Cash Flow Through Starting a Business and Deducting Legitimate Business Expenses

As a business owner you can take advantage of tax deductions that are not available to employees. With proper advice and documentation, you might even be able to convert some personal expenses into legitimate deductible business expenses. Of course, your business should have a legitimate money-making business purpose, other than just saving taxes. Here are just some of the business deductions you might be able to take advantage of:

- Home office expenses
- Business equipment (computers, cell phones)
- Office supplies
- Internet and telephone service
- Software and subscriptions
- Mileage and other auto expenses
- Travel, meals, entertainment
- Business gifts
- Medical insurance premiums
- Medical expenses
- Tuition and seminar educational expenses
- Child labor expenses
- Furniture

The Way Real Estate Depreciation Works

Robert describes the bonus of depreciation of real estate and how it increases your cash flow and provides a paper loss that can be offset against your other income.

Let's say we buy a building for $1 million. We determine that the building is worth $800,000 and the land is worth $200,000. The following chart shows the cash flow from the property. First, notice that we have been able to leverage our down payment of $100,000 with a bank loan of $900,000. So our $100,000 cash has allowed us to invest in a $1 million property. That is leverage of 9:1. (Remember that the banker told Robert he would NOT lend him money to purchase mutual funds, but he would consider lending him money to buy real estate or start a business.)

	CASH FLOW
Rental Income	$148,257
Less: Operating Expenses	– 67,497
Less: Debt Service (30-year loan @6.5%)	68,268
Cash Flow from Property	$12,492

This represents a 12 percent cash-on-cash return, ($12,492 net income on the initial investment of the $100,000 down-payment) BEFORE depreciation.

Now let's add the impact from the depreciation deduction allowed by the tax law. Let's assume that this property is a residential rental property, as the deductions allowed are based on the type of property. The tax law allows you to do a cost segregation between personal property and the building and then also allows you to depreciate the personal property more quickly than the building. This is where your tax advisor can assist you in getting the largest depreciation deduction possible. Let's see how the depreciation impacts our income from the $1 million property outlined above.

Cash Flow from Property	$12,492	
Less: Component Depreciation	$26,800	Phantom Deduction
Less: Building Depreciation	$21,746	Phantom Deduction
Net Taxable Loss from Property	$25,994	Paper Loss

This is where Robert's tax advisor Tom came in with his term *magic money*. This taxable loss, which is called a "paper loss," is created by the "phantom deduction" of depreciation. If you or your spouse qualifies as a real estate professional you can offset your other taxable income by this loss of $25,994.

Let's say your effective income tax rate (federal, state, and local) is 40 percent, your actual tax savings will be $10,398 from this paper loss offset. This brings your total cash return from the property to $22,890.

Cash Flow from Property	$ 12,492
Plus Tax Savings from Paper Loss	$ 10,398
Total Cash Return from Property	$ 22,890

Your cash-on-cash return is now 23 percent

Utilizing Real Estate Paper Losses

As described earlier, the Tax Reform Act of 1986 made changes related to the deductibility of passive losses for individuals. Rental income is treated as a passive activity, and under the tax code an individual may offset any other passive income with real estate paper losses and may qualify to use up to an additional $25,000 of these passive losses as an offset against income from nonpassive sources like dividends and wages each year. However, this $25,000 limit starts to phase out once the individual's adjusted gross income hits $100,000 and is completely phased out at $150,000.

So how does an individual benefit from paper losses from real estate? One answer lies in making real estate your, or your spouse's, business.

An individual, or his or her spouse, may qualify as a real estate professional, which would convert their rental income from passive income to active income. To qualify, one of them must meet *both* of the following requirements:

- more than one half of the individual's personal services are performed in real-estate-related activities (not as an employee unless he or she owns more than 5 percent in the employer); AND
- spend more than 750 hours in the business of real estate.

If you want to qualify as a real estate professional it is important to keep accurate records of your activities and to seek a competent tax advisor. As a real estate professional you may also qualify to utilize the business deductions outlined in the business section above.

Paper Assets

In analyzing paper assets for investment it is important to understand enough of the jargon used in the market to ask the right questions of your financial advisor. For instance, rich dad and Robert both talk about investing in tax-exempt securities, which increase your cash flow without increasing your income tax. While these securities may be exempt from federal income tax, they may be subject to state income tax.

EBITDA, P/E Ratio

Both acronyms have become part of everyday investment talk. But do we really understand what they mean?

EBITDA, which means earnings before interest, taxes, depreciation, and amortization, has become a popular term from the recent corporate scandals and investor mistrust. As it reads, it does NOT take into account interest expense and taxes, both of which are actual cash outflows. Depreciation and amortization, on the other had, reflect the gradual expensing of assets over time.

When WorldCom revealed that it inflated its EBITDA by classifying $3.8 billion in normal expenses as capital expenditures, it triggered a firestorm of questions about the accuracy of financial reporting. Warren Buffett summed it up best: "EBITDA is a meaningless financial indicator that seriously distorts and misrepresents a business's earnings."

EBITDA is not a good cash flow measure in valuing a business. It ignores working capital, capital expenditures, and debt, all significant factors critical to the long-term health of a business. For instance, if a company has a large amount of debt, EBITDA will not reveal the related interest expenses and you could be misled.

You might be much better off looking at a company's "free cash flow," which also backs out amortization and depreciation, but not interest expenses and taxes.

P/E ratio is shorthand for a company's individual share price compared to its per-share earnings. You divide the current market price of one share of a company's stock by the company's per-share earnings. It may be a popular indicator because it is easier to understand than many other indicators. For instance, if you purchase a share of stock in a company with a P/E ratio of 10, then it will take 10 years for the company's earnings to add up to your original purchase price of the stock.

While P/Es are usually computed based on a trailing earnings figure (calculated over earning from the previous twelve months), they can also be computed based on leading earnings (projected earnings for the next twelve-month period). It may be difficult to determine the actual method used to generate a particular P/E. You may want to compare the P/E ratio over time to the company's growth rate and to other companies within the same industry, to look for a trend.

In truly investigating a company's stock you may want to get the annual filings, which will include their entire financial statement package as well as information that the company is required to provide to the public. A publicly traded company will have a 10K and 10Qs that will be available. Pay careful attention to the "Statement of Cash Flows," as it may reveal changes in how the company is doing business. In fact, the "statement of cash flows" is often the last financial statement prepared by a company's accountants, but in my opinion is the most important part of the financial statements. It is often overlooked or even ignored by investors, when it may contain the very information the investor needs to know. As we hear more and more about the manipulation of financial statements, it is even more important to ask the right questions and to know the vocabulary used in investing.

Understanding the vocabulary of investing is essential. One of the advantages of our board game CASHFLOW 101 is that it teaches the vocabulary of money in a fun and nonintimidating format.

The Power of Accelerators

Power investing goes beyond just the three asset classes. One of the reasons there is so much power in power investing is due to the invisible accelerators between the assets, connections such as tax and banking leveraged advantages. The power is not found in the asset itself, the power is found in the invisible accelerators.

One more point I think important to state now is that this process probably cannot be done by one person. If you remember, the right side of the CASHFLOW Quadrant is a team sport. It is important to have a good team of advisors, including accountants, bankers, attorneys, insurance agents, tax advisors, and others. The good news is that if you have a good team behind you, this process of generating higher and higher returns gets easier and easier.

Rich dad said, "You don't have to know all the answers, you just need to know whom to call."

Chapter 12

Gambling Rather than Investing

"The biggest thief of all is hope."

— RICH DAD

Selling the Dream . . . Buying the Lie

During a luncheon presentation in 1999, near the peak of the stock market hysteria, a woman raised her hand and asked me, "I just purchased 500 shares of XYZ blue-chip corporation. What do you think of my investment?"

"Why did you purchase those shares?" I asked.

"Because my stockbroker said they were going up in price. I bought them at $55 a share and he says they are expected to go to at least $75 a share in six months. They've gone up a little so I'm thinking about buying another 1,000 shares before it's too late to get in. Do you think I should buy more than 1,000 shares?"

Ask for a Money-Back Guarantee

After a long thoughtful pause, I decided to say what I wanted to say, regardless of who was buying lunch for this group. My response to the woman client was, "The market is very high. It is at its riskiest point. Will the person who sold you those shares at $55 a share give you a money-back guarantee if the stock does not hit $75 a share? Will the firm give you your money back if the market crashes?"

"A money-back guarantee?" the woman asked sheepishly. "Do stockbrokers give money-back guarantees?"

Without answering her, I continued, "Well, most restaurants give money-back guarantees if a person is not happy with their food. Most department stores and many businesses offer a money-back guarantee if you are not satisfied with the products or services you buy. Why not your stockbroker?"

"Do stockbrokers offer money-back guarantees?" she asked again.

"Not that I know of," I said.

"So why did you ask me that question?"

"Because I was wondering why you were so willing to accept the crystal ball prediction of your stockbroker, the prediction that your stock may go from $55 to $75 a share. Are you buying the shares of stock just because you want them to go up in value? Or are you buying the stock because you truly want a share of that company's stock? And what if the stock price falls to $30 a share. Will you still want that stock? Will you be glad you purchased it?"

"I don't think so," she said. "I want the stock because I want it to go up in value . . . I want it only if it goes to $75 a share as he said it might."

"Then ask for a money-back guarantee. If his company is a reputable company, then he should give you your money back if you are not satisfied with the product they sell you. I went to a department store the other day, and they gave me my money back for a shirt that I was not satisfied with. That is why I like shopping there. They offer a money-back guarantee."

The Boss Steps In

The room was beginning to squirm. Finally, the district manager of the stock brokerage firm stood and did his best to save his client base. "It was one of my agents that made that recommendation," he said. "We as a company are very bullish on this stock and are recommending it. Obviously, as a company that deals in financial products we cannot make any guarantees. I do not know of any financial institution that does."

"I do," I replied.

The room went silent with my comment. At that moment I knew this company would never invite me back. "Well, who does offer a money-back guarantee?" asked the woman who had asked me the question.

"Your banker," I replied. "Or should I say, *you* offer your banker a money-back guarantee. You offer a money-back guarantee every time your banker lends you money. In fact, that is what a mortgage basically is—a money-back guarantee. If you do not give the bank their money back, you've agreed to let them come after you until you do."

"So if my stockbroker says a stock will go to $75 a share, I should ask for a money-back guarantee?"

"Maybe you should," I replied.

"But what if they won't give me a guarantee?"

"Then *you* should give yourself a money-back guarantee. That is what smart investors do."

"And what if I cannot give myself a money-back guarantee?" she asked.

"Then just say that you are gambling, rather than investing. True investors are not gamblers . . . yet the world is filled with gamblers who think they are investing."

What Are You Investing For?

In *Rich Dad Poor Dad*, the two most important words the book focused on were *assets* and *liabilities.* In this book, I would say the two most important words are:

CASH FLOW

VERSUS

CAPITAL GAINS

When a person says, "I bought this stock (or property) because I believe the price will go up," this person is most likely investing for *capital gains.* Rich dad used to say, "Capital gains is the dream of gamblers. A true investor first invests for cash flow, not capital gains." The woman who asked me about buying shares at $55 and hoping they would go up to $75 was investing for capital gains, which according to rich dad is gambling on the future—not investing.

Rich dad said, "When you invest for cash flow, you're investing in a money-back guarantee. If you invest for capital gains, you invest in hope. The biggest thief of all is hope."

Gamblers Who Think They Are Investors

A good question at this time is, Why do so many people invest for capital gains rather than cash flow? The answer is again found in the perils of allowing yourself to say "I can't afford it" or "You can't do that" or "It's too risky." You become vulnerable to financial predators. One of the tools of deception that financial predators use is the promise of a better future. They may say, "In three years the price of this property will double," or, "The stock market goes up 6 percent on average every year." Rich dad used to say, "People who cannot find an investment today gamble on the promise of tomorrow. They count on hope rather than intelligence. They have dreams, so they buy lies."

Investor Versus Gambler

In a previous book, I wrote about me showing rich dad a real estate investment that was going to lose money for me every month because the rental income was less than the mortgage and operating expenses of the property. It was *negative cash flow* rather than *positive cash flow*. Most retirement plans are based upon hope and promises for years. That makes very little sense to me, yet it seems to make a lot of sense to millions of investors who are hoping the money will be there after the fourth quarter of their money game.

Rich dad used to chuckle and say, "It does not take much financial intelligence to find an investment that loses you money. The market is filled with experts telling you how to do that. All you have to do is just give them your money." Rich dad also said, "Anyone can find an investment that loses money. Why people pay so-called financial experts to do that for them is beyond me."

The real question is, How can so many people be so gullible? While there are many answers, one answer is that because they cannot find cash flow today, they invest the hope of *capital gains* tomorrow. On top of that, they invest without a money-back guarantee.

A Massive Snow Job

The question is, How can so many millions of people be deluded into the idea that losing money every month, for years on end, without a money-back guarantee or insurance against catastrophic loss can be considered smart investing? It has to be one of the biggest mass sales jobs in the history of the world . . . a sales job that could only occur with a financially naive population. In fact, this is more than a sales job . . . it is a snow job. Today, the snow job goes on as schools begin to adopt financial literacy programs by teaching kids how to cut up credit cards, balance checkbooks, and pick stocks. The stock market industry is hard at work in our education system, teaching youngsters to be future clients, teaching them to be gamblers, betting on *capital gains,* rather than astute investors, investing for *cash flow.*

Why People Lose Money

In my opinion, one of the primary reasons people invest in tomorrow, rather than in today, is simply because *in their minds* they cannot find or afford an investment that pays them today. When a person cannot find an investment that pays them *today*, they often become believers in *tomorrow,* which makes them gamblers, betting on capital gains. That is why so many people lose money. They are willing to lose money, even if it is only a little every month, in the hope and promise that tomorrow their ship will come in. These people, people who do not know the difference between cash flow investing and capital gains investing, are the people who fall prey to financial predators.

What Do Investors Invest For?

Rich dad said, "An investment needs to make sense today *and* tomorrow." Rather than focusing on which investment is best, stocks, bonds, mutual funds, real estate, or a business, rich dad taught his son and me to invest for:

1. Cash flow
2. Tax advantages
3. Capital gains

If you want, you may want to look again at rich dad's formula for power investing. Rich dad's formula is difficult to have work without a steady stream of cash flow. Without cash flow, there are limited tax advantages, which is another form of cash flow. To rich dad, capital gains was not that important. His power investing formula worked with or without capital gains.

Rich dad made sure he had his money-back guarantees. To him, capital gains was just gravy. That is why it is listed in the third order of priority.

It is unfortunate that most of the investing public invests in this order of priority:

1. Capital Gains

They only know how to buy low and sell high. According to the U.S. tax code, people who buy and sell are classified as *dealers*, not *investors.* When you look at the CASHFLOW Quadrant,

. . . someone who buys and sells is in the S quadrant, not the I quadrant. In real estate, there are many people who do *flips, quick cash*, and *wraps* as real estate transactions. Their primary focus is on buying and selling for a higher price, which is investing for capital gains, rather than cash flow. In most cases these people risk being classified as *dealers*, not *investors,* according to the U.S. Internal Revenue Service and tax code, and may be subject to higher taxes than true investors are. Without the proper entity and tax planning in America, a person who buys and sells for capital gains could risk being taxed as a self-employed person and may be subject to self-employment tax as well as ordinary income tax rates. When I talk to many real estate flippers, they claim they are not subject to those taxes. That may be true as long as they stay small, but if they become big, successful, and make a lot of money at flipping, quick-cashing, and wrapping, they may find the government tax collector coming to make a house call. As always, check with a qualified accountant and attorney for a more accurate ruling because every situation is different.

What About Foreclosures?

During a talk to real estate investors, I brought up the points on the difference between dealers and investors. A young man in the room raised his hand and asked, "I buy foreclosures. Am I a dealer or an investor?" My reply was, "You're asking me about a financing process. What I am talking about is your exit or your use of the foreclosure. If you buy a foreclosure and use it as a rental unit and receive cash flow, then you are an investor. If you buy foreclosures to sell for the quick cash or to wrap it, which is to sell to someone else at a higher price, then you are investing for capital gains and that could put you in the S quadrant as a dealer."

Another hand went up and the person asked, "What about nothing-down investments? Are you an investor if you put nothing down to purchase the property?" Again, my answer was the same. "It is not the financing process that matters. It is the exit. Do you plan on flipping it for a higher price or do you plan on renting. Are you long-term or are you short-term. Those are the questions that matter."

There are many people who sit and watch the stock market go up and go down. They are happy when the Dow goes up and depressed when it goes down. These are people who generally invest for capital gains. They are often called momentum investors, buying when stocks move up and selling when stocks move down. It is this momentum investing philosophy that makes paper assets so volatile and risky for the little investor.

When I hear a person say, "My home has gone up in value. I made money because my home is worth $50,000 more than I paid for it," I know this too is a person who invests for capital gains. If you want to be a power investor, you need to look at investing through the eyes of a business owner regardless of what asset you invest in . . . because business owners know that *cash flow*, and *phantom cash flow from tax advantages,* are far more important than *capital gains.*

Who Are the Big Losers?

The point of this chapter is to illustrate why so many people think investing is risky and why millions of people lost trillions of dollars between 2000 and 2003. One reason, other than bad advice and a lack of basic financial education, is because most people invest for capital gains. This is also true for most professionally managed mutual funds. I find it ironic that so many mutual funds advise their clients to invest for the long term and yet most do exactly the opposite. Most mutual fund managers are under pressure to make a quick buck buying low and selling high. They are doing everything but investing for the long term . . . advice they give . . . but do not follow. Why? Because they invest for capital gains. A true investor invests for cash flow. Why? Because they do not believe in hope . . . they believe in the same thing your banker and tax department believe in . . . they believe in a money-back guarantee.

The Lesson

One of the reasons people invest in hope rather than guarantees is because they cannot find an investment that pays them money today. There are other reasons, some of which will be covered as this book comes to a conclusion.

The next chapter will go into some of the ways an investor finds investments that pay today, rather than tomorrow.

Before going into the next chapter, I would like to remind you that rich dad encouraged me to look at all investments as a business. Once you find a great business that pays you cash flow on a regular business, hold on to it. As Warren Buffett says, "We like to buy businesses. We don't like to sell, and we expect the relationships to last a lifetime."

An Extra Summary Bonus for You

Much of this method of investing was covered extremely simplistically in *Rich Dad Poor Dad.* The difference in this book is that I am doing my best to go into more detail without going into too much detail. As with all our books, we always recommend you first consult trained professionals such as an accountant and a lawyer to further clarify the points discussed.

As an extra bonus to you, the reader, Sharon and I have decided to include a further audio summary to better explain this method of investing. We decided to add this free audio piece rather than go into more written detail in this book. Sometimes it is easier to understand something if the explanation is via talking and listening rather than writing and reading.

This method of synergy investing—power investing—that we are describing here is very important for anyone who wants to achieve financial freedom in their lives. That is why we want to offer you an even more in-depth explanation, verbally, of this very important, yet often complex, subject. So go to *richdad.com* and learn more about this method of investing from Sharon and me in person.

A Reminder

But before going on, I want to remind you of the power of your mind and caution you about saying "I can't" or "You can't do that." It is the people who say such things to themselves who become the people that turn their money over to strangers and wonder why they do not achieve the great returns on their money that they expect. Always remember that the financial services industry does not offer a money-back guarantee. That is why *you* need to be the person who guarantees that your money does come back.

Sharon's Notes

Is Robert saying a saver is a gambler? The concept of saving for tomorrow when you don't know what is going to happen tomorrow and you have little control over what is going to happen tomorrow—that is what we call gambling without even having the education of a professional gambler.

While traditional thinking is that "investing is risky," our belief is that NOT investing is much riskier. To bet your future on your employer or government taking care of you is risky to us. To hand your money over to someone else to manage unless they are part of your investment strategy team is risky.

I refer to one of our most recent books, *Rich Dad's Success Stories*, where individuals took the steps to start taking control of their financial futures—during the same time period many of their friends were seeing their savings and 401(k)s wiped out. While their friends were losing at the gambling table (the market), the individuals in *Success Stories* were investing in and creating assets that generated positive cash flow for them. The first step is often the hardest. Our goal is that by reading their stories, others may find the courage or opportunity to take control of their own financial lives.

Chapter 13

How to Find Great Investments

"Opportunities repeat themselves because people repeat the same mistakes."

— RICH DAD

"Most people get interested in stocks when everyone else is. The time to get interested is when no one else is. You can't buy what is popular and do well."

— WARREN BUFFETT

The Life and Death of Lemmings

When I was in elementary school, my teacher showed the class a movie on the life cycle of lemmings. The class was excited to see a mother lemming give birth to tiny baby lemmings. We laughed and giggled as the movie showed the cute furry creatures playing, nursing, and growing. Suddenly, my young class-mates and I gasped as the movie showed thousands of these now grown-up, but still cute furry lemmings, en masse, jumping off a cliff into the ocean and swimming out to sea and to their deaths.

Between 1995 and 2003, millions of investors acted like lemmings. In-stead of losing their life, many lost their life's savings. Why does this happen? As always, there are many reasons. One reason is because investors blindly follow the pack, doing what is popular rather than what is profitable. In 1995, as the stock market started to really heat up, the lemmings began to poke their heads out of their burrows. Upon seeing their friends getting rich and not wanting to miss out on the action, many emerged from the safety of their burrows and were following the herd as they jumped off the cliff into the hottest stock market in recent history.

What Happened to the Lemmings That Did Not Jump?

Of course, not all lemmings jumped off the cliff and into the stock market ocean between 1995 and 2000. Many, upon realizing the market was going down, jumped into real estate and bonds as interest rates went down. Again, being lemmings, they followed the crowd.

As interest rates dropped between 2000 and 2003, millions of investors left the stock market in search of safety and began investing in real estate and bonds at the worst possible time. Why was it the worst possible time? It was the worst possible time because everyone else was now investing in them—which made them risky rather than the safe investments people were looking for. Investing in bonds was becoming riskier and riskier because interest rates were going down. Even though interest rates and yields from bonds were going down, investors continued to put their money in bonds. Buying bonds as interest rates are going down is much the same as buying a dot-com stock as prices are going up.

At the same time, as interest rates headed down, real estate prices went up. As real estate prices went up, more and more investors began investing in real estate, making real estate a risky investment.

The Worst Time to Invest

There is a lot of truth to the statement "When taxi drivers and shoeshine boys are investing, it is time to get out of the market." Rich dad used to say, "The worst time to invest is when the market is good."

Instead of teaching us to chase the next hot investment trend, rich dad taught his son and me to sell our bad investments when the market is high and buy value investments when the market is low. He said, "The best time to get rid of the nonperforming assets in your portfolio is when the market is good and amateurs are in the market buying." As interest rates dropped and the real estate market climbed between 2000 and 2003, Kim and I began selling off our marginal real estate investments to investors desperate to get out of the stock market and into the real estate market.

One property we sold, Kim and I had purchased for $55,000 in 1989 and we sold it for approximately $100,000 in 2003. We sold it because rents were not going up, expenses on the two-bedroom unit were increasing, and the unit did not seem to be appreciating in value, relative to the rest of our properties. On top of that, the property was tiny when compared to the rest of our investments. The property sold in less than two weeks.

Even though it was not a great investment, for fourteen years we did receive an average of a $1,000 a month in rent with very little vacancy. We had one tenant that stayed in the unit for over seven years. That equates to 12 months $\times$ 14 years = 168 months $\times$ $1,000 a month = $168,000 gross income over 14 years. We had no mortgage payment, since we paid cash for the property. Our expenses were minimal, but as I said, expenses were increasing. Even though it was not a great investment, it was approximately a 300 percent return of our money over fourteen years. Technically, the property was free to us after the fifth year, since we had paid back our initial $55,000 and that money was reinvested in other properties. After year five, it really was like getting money for nothing. While it is not big money, making a little money sure beats losing money.

Finding an Investment

The point of the above story is not to brag about a small investment. The point of this story is to illustrate why some investors find great investments and why many investors do not.

One of the main reasons why so many investors fail to find a great investment is due to what I call the *lemming factor*. The lemming factor occurs when investors buy because other investors are buying. In most financial publications, you will see adds that claim, "Voted the #1 Mutual Fund for 2002." Or, "A 36% Return for the Past 5 Years." Or, "5 Star Rating." It is ads like these that draw the lemmings in. Generally, if it is true, a mutual fund is number one or has delivered a 35 percent return for five years, that usually means the end is near. In real estate, the lemmings are drawn in when they know of a friend or office worker who bought a property for $125,000 and sold it three months later for $165,000. As rich dad often said, "Tales of success bring suckers to the market."

The Lessons Learned from Experience

As a young boy, there was one disturbing fact left with me from the movie on lemmings. The disturbing fact was that the lemmings would do the same thing again, and again, year after year. The same fact is true with investing. As rich dad said, "Opportunities repeat themselves because people repeat the same mistakes." He also said, "One of the ways to find great investments is to become an expert on the mistakes that other investors make." One of the most common mistakes is when people become lemmings after a market heats up. In other words, once a market is hot or famous, it is too late. So the words of wisdom are: When markets heat up, remember to not be a lemming. While that sounds easy and good common sense, when everyone is jumping off the cliff it's often difficult not to follow. The primary mistake people make is the mistake of investing in what is popular. Between 1995 and 2000, the most popular investments were mutual funds and stocks. Their manic popularity should have been a sign not to invest in them, yet people invested in them in droves. Repeating Warren Buffett's statement, "You can't buy what is popular and do well."

Seven Ways to Find a Great Investment

Rich dad taught his son and me to find great investments, simply by teaching us to read financial statements, understanding trends, having good advisors, and most importantly by not investing in what was popular. He said, "If you are going to be a successful investor, you need to be able to find great investments others miss." In my opinion, one of the reasons so many people turn their money over to strangers is because they do not know how to find a great investment. The following are seven ways to find great investments in good markets and in bad ones. Most of the seven ways are based upon not being a lemming.

THE #1 WAY TO FIND A GREAT INVESTMENT: REMEMBER THAT PEOPLE ARE LEMMINGS

One of the simplest and best ways to find investments is to wait for amateurs to get into the market. Amateurs always get in late . . . usually at the top of the market. Generally, because they are late, they come in droves, create a frenzy, prices go up, and then the amateurs pay too much for the investment. After the market crashes, which it always does, then the real investors go back in to find the best investments at the best prices. This is true for any asset class, be it paper assets, real estate, or businesses. This truth has been true throughout history and I will bet that it will remain true into the future.

A Day in the Life

I am often asked how I find investments. The following is a description of one day in September 2003. It is an example of how I keep my eyes and ears open to the market and find investments. Every day, regardless if the markets are good or bad, I spend some time talking to amateur investors and professional investors, which is my way of keeping my pulse on the market.

On this particular day in September 2003, a friend's daughter came to me and said she was making a fortune in real estate. She had bought three small properties and flipped them for a combined profit of $9,000. She was all excited and wanted to quit her job to go into flipping real estate full-time. Talking to her confirmed that the real estate bubble was reaching its breaking point, and I needed to be extra cautious. When markets are moving up quickly, and profits can be made quickly by amateurs, to me, it means a market top is near. When amateurs begin quitting their jobs, it means the market top is imminent. As Hunter S. Thompson once wrote, "When the going gets weird, the weird turn pro."

Later in the morning of that same day, a friend called with a diamond for sale. He said, "I'm having trouble with my business. Sales are off and I have bills to pay. Are you interested in my diamond? If you give me the money for the diamond I'll be able to hang on for a few more months until Christmas. After Christmas, I'll even buy my diamond back for 25 percent more than you pay for it." Since I would not know a diamond from a piece of glass, I passed on this opportunity.

After lunch, a friend from Singapore e-mailed me and asked if I wanted to buy some of his property in New Zealand. He wrote, "I've overextended myself a bit on my last real estate investment. I started remodeling, but the cost of remodeling is more than I anticipated. I am out of money and I have the mortgage to pay. The bank is applying a lot of pressure. I need $100,000 quickly so

I can finish the project and sell it. I have three lots in New Zealand I will sell to you for their appraised value, if you would wire me the $100,000 immediately."

"What are the three lots worth, where are they, and what will you sell them for?" I wrote back.

He never did get back to me. I assume the pressure from the bank got hotter.

After dinner, my wife, Kim, received a phone call from one of our real estate partners. His message was, "The buyer fell out. The last bank turned him down."

"So after waiting nine months, the property is finally ours?" asked Kim.

"That's right—at a better price than we originally offered."

"Good," smiled Kim. "Tie it up and let's begin our due diligence process."

Eleven months prior to this phone call, our group had the same property tied up with a letter of intent. Instead of selling it to us, the seller sold it to the buyer, who paid much more than we offered. Now the buyer who paid too much was in financial trouble and needed to get out quickly. He was losing a lot of money every month because he was not taking care of his tenants and they were moving out in a hurry. So, not only was he losing money on his loan, he was losing rental income as tenants moved out. He called us five months later and offered it to us, but at a higher price. We refused to pay, so the new seller sold it to a new buyer he thought would save him from his mistakes. When his new "white knight" buyer fell out because he could not find the money, the buyer who beat us initially then called our group. He was willing to sell at a loss and at a price lower than we had originally offered. He had had enough. He thought real estate would be easy, but for him it wasn't. He was losing money rapidly and he just wanted out. He did not have the time to wait for a new buyer to make up their mind. After a long, patient wait, the property was now ours.

This Happens Every Day

"Opportunities repeat themselves," said rich dad. "You can count on people to make the same mistakes over and over again. The people may change but the mistakes remain the same. Become an expert on certain mistakes and you will become rich. When people make mistakes, the market offers you some of the best investments in the world."

Warren Buffett says, "I only go to the market to see if someone is about to do something silly."

The Greater Fool

In the world of investing, people who play the game of *capital gains* rather than *cash flow* are often playing the game of the *greater fool.* For example, a greater fool exists whenever someone says "I bought this stock for $25 and I will sell it when it hits $35." Or, "I bought my house for $250,000 and my broker says it will be worth $350,000 in five years." Those are the words of greater fools investing on the premise that a fool greater than themselves exists—and they usually do exist. In fact, I would say most of the investment markets are based upon the idea of the greater fool. When any market runs out of greater fools, the market turns down. The market turns down when the last fool turns and finds the fool that sold him the stock, business, mutual fund, or real estate is gone and no longer wants the asset back. When fools begin to run, the best bargains begin to appear. As Warren Buffett says, "Be fearful when others are greedy and be greedy when others are fearful."

The Best Time to Find Great Investments

The number one way to find an investment is when the lemmings are running for the cliff and greed is multiplied with even more greed. Rich dad liked to say "Greed + Stupidity = Opportunity."

So remember these five lessons from the first way to find investments, simply by remembering that *when it comes to investing, most people are lemmings.*

1. Lemmings are late and investors are early . . . and that applies to both buying and selling.
2. It is easier to find great deals in a bad market than in a good market.
3. When markets are bad, lemmings return to hiding in their dirt burrows. When markets are bad, investors are out and about getting rich.
4. You can still make money during a good market. You just have to be a much smarter investor in a good market. When markets are hot, markets are at their riskiest, so be extra careful.
5. When markets are good, the hardest thing to do is not be a lemming. When markets are bad, the hardest thing to do is be an investor.

THE #2 WAY TO FIND A GREAT INVESTMENT: PERSONAL TRAGEDY OR CALAMITY

The second way great investments are found is via personal tragedy and calamity. I do not enjoy finding great investments in this way, yet I have.

Many years ago, I found a property that was up for sale by a man who had just lost his job. He was two weeks away from foreclosure by the bank. "Just pay what I owe the bank and you can have the house," he said.

"I don't want to do that," I replied.

"Look. You'll be helping me and my family out," he said.

"How will I be doing that?"

"I won't have a black mark on my credit rating if you pay what I owe and keep the house. When I get back on my feet again, I'll be better able to buy a house for my family. If I have a foreclosure on my record, buying a house will be more difficult and I'll pay a higher interest rate."

Although I did not feel good about buying the house from this person, I knew he was asking me to help him, not exploit him during this period of personal tragedy.

The point is, when personal tragedy hits, many people are desperate to sell. While this is a good time to invest, I suggest you let your conscience be your guide.

THE #3 WAY TO FIND A GREAT INVESTMENT: A RECESSION

A recession is simply a contraction of the economy. They occur on a regular basis . . . again making the point that buying opportunities *repeat.* Obviously a recession brings on commercial as well as personal calamities. During a recession, many businesses are selling the business and its equipment for pennies on the dollar. Personal residences fall in value, and personal toys like cars, lake houses, and boats are also sold for pennies on the dollar. Individuals may find themselves asset (or toy) rich but cash poor.

A great example of this is a founder of a dot-com company who while his stock was flying high bought new cars, a big house, and lots of toys (we call them doodads in the CASHFLOW game). After the dot-com crash this very same individual had to sell his cars, house, and toys as quickly as possible to raise enough cash just to live on. This massive sell-off of possessions was a great opportunity for people looking for doodads with the cash to buy them at the fire sale prices. The seller was happy to find a willing buyer and the buyer was happy to buy their doodads at less than their retail value.

At the same time, the dot-com company's assets such as its furniture and computer equipment were also available for purchase at very reduced prices. The company was able to raise cash through the sale of its assets and the buyers were able to purchase barely used furniture and computers at great prices.

Again, I do not like trading on personal tragedy, yet sometimes you can actually help someone out, even if you are giving them only pennies on the dollar. Let your conscience be your guide. It's *you* that looks back at *you* in the mirror in the morning.

THE #4 WAY TO FIND A GREAT INVESTMENT: A TECHNICAL, POLITICAL, OR CULTURAL CHANGE

In 1986, the government changed the tax law in America. The 1986 Tax Reform Act made it difficult for highly paid individuals such as professionals like doctors, lawyers, accountants, architects, and others (in the S quadrant) to have the same tax advantages that nonlicensed businesspeople had. That change contributed to the stock market crash of 1987 and also the real estate crash that followed a few years later.

"Destroying Real Estate Through the Tax Code. (Tax Reform Act of 1986)"

by Roy E. Cordato, *The CPA Journal Online,* June 1991

The Tax Reform Act of 1986

"There is no sound economic reason for making a distinction between 'passive' and 'active' income. The division is completely arbitrary. It promotes the fallacy that income that isn't obtained through physical labor is somehow 'unearned.' And consequently should be more heavily taxed than labor compensation. In fact, such 'passive' investments are one of the fundamental engines of economic growth. Their primary function is to provide the capital by which other nonpassive activities grow. This was clearly the case in real estate. These investments helped significantly to increase the stock of housing and other structures. The fact that the investors hired others to manage the operations was simply the result of an efficient division of labor within the market. To penalize this efficiency is absurd. The adverse effects of the 1986 tax changes on real property were a major contributing factor in the collapse of many savings and loan institutions."

Suddenly, doctors, lawyers, and accountants and syndications of these groups were literally selling great pieces of real estate for pennies on the dollar, just because the tax law had changed. Value of property dropped because the tax benefits were taken away. Prices of real estate dropped so far that the U.S. government had to intervene and the Resolution Trust Corporation was formed in order to find ways of selling billions of dollars of property for pennies on the dollar.

During this period, fear was everywhere. Many people buried themselves back in their holes, rather than go out and invest. During this same period, Kim and I worked much harder to earn more money through our business so we could buy as many of these pennies-on-the-dollar real estate deals from the government. This one simple change in the tax law allowed Kim and me to become financially free.

Changes Are Daily

Today, there are more structural, technical, political, and cultural changes going on than ever before. Each change offers new opportunities to invest as well as lose money. Some of the changes I am watching are:

1. Terrorism: Terrorism is cheap and it can occur anywhere. Terrorism decreases a sense of safety. If safety is threatened, money tends to remain hidden rather than aggressively reinvested.

2. Jobs leaving the country: A few years ago, people were concerned about blue-collar jobs leaving for countries such as Mexico. Today, white-collar jobs are also leaving. Between 2000 and 2003, 50,000 jobs left Wall Street and went to countries such as India. Why? Because it is far cheaper to pay an Indian MBA $30,000 a year than an American MBA $300,000. This ability to have employees operating remotely at lower costs is a trend that will only increase. Today, even our directory assistance operators live in countries such as the Philippines, Malaysia, and India.

3. China may very well dominate the world financially one day: Anything that can be manufactured in the West can be manufactured in China for less. This change is one to watch carefully.

4. Aging populations: The West has a population that is aging rapidly and approaching retirement. Today, in many European capitals, protests are

already occurring because governments are strapped for cash and may not be able to continue to pay retiree benefits and still meet budget guidelines.

5. Increasing populations: In 2000, according to the U.S. census, America had a population of 281 million people. In the next twenty-five years, that population is projected to increase to between 350 and 400 million. California, already very crowded, is expected to have a population increase of 18 percent over the next two decades. While I do not know what China and terrorism mean for the stock market, I do know that such increases in populations in America will be great for real estate. Often I say to people who complain about real estate being too expensive, "If you think real estate is expensive today, just wait ten more years." I also say, "Don't you wish you had bought more real estate twenty years ago, even if it was expensive back then." Although real estate tends to go up an average of 6 percent per year, that is not an excuse to buy any old piece of real estate.

6. War: War is horrible, yet it often means a great change is at hand. England, France, Germany, and Japan were all at one time or another enemies of America. Today they are our strongest allies. (Even if Germany and France did not support us in Iraq, they are still strong allies in other ways.) Sometimes we have to fight before we become friends. Hopefully Iran, Iraq, Palestine, Russia, some African nations, and other areas of conflict will soon become friends and trading partners. The point is, sometimes war is a good time to buy because prices are low.

During World War II, the Japanese took over the Philippines and many of the businesses there. One of the businesses was a gold mining company listed on the New York Stock Exchange. The day Japan took the country and the mine, the stock of that mining company plunged to nearly zero. But there were some who jumped in at that very low price and made a fortune once the war came to an end and the mining company got back on its feet.

7. Age is a liability: When I was a kid, age was an asset. My parents knew that the older they got the more valuable they became as workers. In today's world, the older you get, the more obsolete you become, due to technology changes. When I talk to people today, I often say that they need to think like professional athletes . . . athletes like basketball players who are stars at twenty-five and physically obsolete by thirty-five.

One of the reasons I started being an entrepreneur and an investor early was because I had a lifetime to learn to get better in the B and I quadrants, rather than the E and S quadrants. I knew that if I owned my own companies and invested for myself, I did not have to worry about someone else having control over my life, how much I made, when I could go on vacation, and when I could retire. Although I was a failure in the first quarter of my life, from ages twenty-five to thirty-five, the next quarters I got better and better at business and investing. In the second quarter, the ages thirty-five to forty-five, Kim and I were able to become financially free, living just off of our investments.

Forbes *Magazine on Slow Learners*

Eighty years ago, the October 1, 1921, issue of *Forbes* magazine ran an article that headlined:

"F-Student A-List"

Thomas Edison was thrown out of school because he was "too stupid to learn." Teachers called George Westinghouse a dunce. Frank W. Woolworth probably would have failed to pass a grammar school graduation test. James B. Duke, "the tobacco king," was woefully uneducated. George F. Baker, the dean of American bankers, is said to have been a night watchman as a young man. Not one in twenty of our foremost men of affairs had risen to anything of prominence at thirty-five or forty. Almost all of them went through grueling experiences before they reached the summits of success.

Desire Versus Logic

When I was starting out on my journey at the age of twenty-five, both my rich dad and my poor dad knew that I was not an academically bright person. My poor dad, an academic star, said to me, "You will always be a slow learner." Since I was not a quick learner, my rich dad said, "You need to dedicate yourself to learning slowly and learn forever. That is your best chance of winning." He also said, "Desire can take you places where logic cannot." I did not write an international best-selling book until I was fifty. Having failed in high school twice because I was a poor writer, my having five *New York Times* best-sellers today is not logical.

Right after college, most of my classmates made more money than I did. Today, I make far more money than most of my peers who did well in school and got the high-paying jobs. Because I was slow coming out of the gates, I became financially successful late in life. Because I am a slow learner, it took me longer to get started and get the education and experience I needed. But I found what I needed to know by just plodding along and never giving up, even though many times I wanted to. So keep learning about investing no matter how old you are or how much money you have . . . or do not have. Every day that you learn something new, you get better at the game.

THE #5 WAY TO FIND A GREAT INVESTMENT: THE 20-10-5 CYCLE

Rich dad said, "The stock market dominates the investment market for a pe riod of twenty years. As the twentieth year approaches, the possibility of a market crash increases. After the crash, the stock market tends to stay down for ten years. During the ten years the stock market is down, commodities such as gold, silver, oil, and property dominate the investment world. And every five years, there is some kind of major disaster."

Early in my life, I did not really appreciate rich dad's lesson on the 20-10-5 cycle. Nonetheless I did follow his advice. Between 1973 and 1980, I was investing in real estate and gold . . . often categorized as hard assets or commodities. Some of you may recall the Hunt brothers taking silver all the way up to nearly $50 an ounce, and gold nearly hit $800 an ounce. Just prior to 1980, the commodities markets crashed. As predicted, from 1980 to 2000, the stock market dominated the world of investing. The disaster every five years seemed to be true also. Events such as stock market crashes, the savings and loan fiasco, real estate crashes, and tragic events such as September 11, 2001, seem to occur every five years. If the 5-year disaster theory is true, the next disaster should hit in 2006.

Not About Having a Crystal Ball

The reason rich dad told me about the 20-10-5 cycle was not to make me a fortune-teller with a crystal ball. The reason he told me of this cycle was because he wanted me to be aware of change. One of the reasons so many baby boomers are in trouble financially with their retirement is because their investments are still in the stock market and the market has just ended a twenty-year cycle. If they had followed the 20-10-5 cycle, they would have gotten out of equities and into commodities around 1996. Warren Buffett sold a lot of his stocks in 1996 and took large positions in silver prior to 2000. I do not know if he follows the 20-10-5 cycle, but his investing patterns seem to validate it.

If this 20-10-5 cycle holds true, then many baby boomers will not be able to retire because they will be in the stock or equities market during the commodity cycle, waiting for the price of their stocks to come back up, which may not happen till 2008 to 2010.

The way I learned to use the 20-10-5 cycle is not as a crystal ball but as a reminder to look into the future. For example, in 1996, when gold was at an all-time low, trading at around $275 an ounce, I began investing in gold mines. While I was laughed at by some of my friends who are in banking and the stock market, today they are not laughing as gold has hit $375 an ounce. In fact one of the companies in which I invested in 1996, where I am a director and the second-largest shareholder, just went public in November 2003.

In other words, as the twenty-year equity cycle was coming to an end, I began moving out of equities and began looking for opportunities in commodities such as gold, silver, oil, and other metals. When September 11, 2001, hit, even though stock prices were really low, I continued to stay out of the equities market just because I knew that equities had run their twenty-year cycle. Instead of stocks, I looked for more real estate opportunities after 9/11, even though real estate prices were high.

Don't Take This to the Bank

This 20-10-5 cycle is not something I would bet my financial future on. As I said, it is primarily a reminder that markets move in cycles. However, by knowing this, I tend to not get caught in the wrong cycle. One of the best ways to find good investments is to find investments that are out of favor but are soon due to come back into favor. This 20-10-5 cycle lets me know that stocks will probably be coming back in favor around 2008 and I will remind myself to consider selling my gold shares at about that time.

Since I love real estate, and I trust the demographic trend of America's ever increasing population growth, I will continue to invest in real estate. In Japan, where birth rates are down, I would be hesitant to invest in real estate. Real estate property values only go up if there are people who want to rent them.

In *Rich Dad's Prophecy*, I wrote about the possibility of a massive stock market crash between 2012 and 2020. The reason for this crash is not due to the 20-10-5 cycle but more to the demographics of the Western world's population. At year 2016, the first baby boomers turn seventy and a half years of age and, at that age, the law that created the 401(k) retirement plan in America requires that the baby boomers start to withdraw from their plans, which will result in the sale of their equities in order to fund the withdrawals and they will have to pay the deferred taxes on their accounts. So the reminder is, even if the market is really hot around 2016 and has not crashed, remember the more of all three asset classes you have the more secure your financial house will be no matter what happens to the equities market.

THE #6 WAY TO FIND A GREAT INVESTMENT: HAVE A FRIEND IN THE BUSINESS

Most of us are mature enough to know that the best investments are often never advertised for sale. In most cases, the best investments are legally and illegally sold to insiders at the best prices. Often, by the time the little investor hears about a great investment, the prices for that investment are too high, which makes it a bad investment for the little investor.

One of the best ways to find great investments is to have business partners who are in the market every day. Kim and I find great investments because we pay our brokers more than other investors do. For example, while many investors are trying to ask their broker to lower their commissions, we give some of our brokers their full commission as well as 10 percent of the profits from the investment. For some reason, because we are generous, we tend to get the first shot at the best investments. We have purchased several properties before they hit the market by having friends in the business and making them partners in the investment.

THE #7 WAY TO FIND A GREAT INVESTMENT: PAY MORE MONEY

In early 2003, a real estate broker came to Kim and me and asked us if we were interested in selling one of our properties. My reply was, "While we are not really interested in selling, everything we own does have a price."

"How much do you want?" asked the broker.

After thinking about it for a day or two, Kim and I said, "If you give us $2.5 million we will sell."

"That's way too much," said the broker. "How about $1.9 million?"

At that, we discontinued talking to him. Negotiations were over.

No One Likes Cheap People

Rich dad often said, "No one likes cheap people. Yet for some reason, more people try to get rich by being cheap." The same holds true in investing. Personally, I find it distasteful when people attempt to offer me less than what I want . . . for what I have . . . that they want.

Change the Business

Earlier in this book, I stated that rich dad recommended that his son and I understand business so we could become better investors. One reason for this is due to the fact that an investment, real estate included, is only as valuable as the business behind the investment. Earlier I used the example of a ten-acre piece of land.

10 acres

To a farmer, this piece of land may be worth $10,000.

To a real estate developer, this same land may be worth $100,000.

Why the difference in value? The answer is because *they are in different businesses.*

An Insult

One of the reasons I asked $2.5 million for a property that cost me less than $700,000 is not because I am greedy. The reason I asked for the higher price is because that is what that property is worth to me today. When the broker immediately asked for a lower price, I took it as an insult. Let me explain.

When Kim and I purchased that property, it was a motel that was in financial trouble due to high vacancies and low rent. The reason it was in financial trouble is because newer motels were being built all around it. When Kim and I purchased it, we planned to change the business model. Instead of a motel, we changed it into an apartment house, a business we knew well. In other words, it was not worth $700,000 as a motel but it was worth $700,000 as an apartment house, since it is in a great location. Today, eight years after converting it to an apartment house, it is worth even more money because in five years our plan is to tear down the old building and put up high-end condominiums and sell them. Our plans show that we can build twelve three-bedroom, two-bath condominiums with garages, and sell them for at least $350,000 each, a gross value of $4.2 million. That is why the property is worth at least $2.5 million to us today. It is worth that much because we are going to change the business that is currently on that property and we expect to make that much from the sale of the new buildings. If the broker knew our plans, he would have seen that we were asking a price for what the property was worth to us. If his buyer could look into the future and also see a potential change in business, he might have found a way to offer us what we wanted and still made what he wanted to make. Instead he went cheap and we never talked to them again.

My Favorite Way to Get Rich

All too often, people try and buy a good investment by being cheap and then lose the investment. It takes no intelligence to ask for a lower price to make a lowball offer. It takes creative intelligence to spot opportunities that others do not see. So before you insult someone by asking for a lower price for an asset you want, see if you can see potential value they cannot see. In my opinion, this is the best way to get rich. I have used this method of finding a great deal many times. I simply look for value or opportunities others do not see and pay the asking price . . . which makes both parties happy. It is my favorite way to get rich.

There Is More Than One Way to Find a Great Investment

As you can see, there is more than one way to find a great investment. The seven methods listed offer you some flexibility as to what method you choose depending upon the market situations of the day. The four basic points are:

1. Know your numbers—don't be a guessing gambler
2. Know the mistakes that lemmings make
3. Be generous
4. Be creative

If you keep these basic points in mind, your chances of finding better investments will improve.

Sharon's Notes

Let's try to put it all together. Robert has shared many of his strategies in locating, selecting, and purchasing investments. The overall process is summarized here:

The seven ways to find investments:

1. Remember, people are lemmings—look for what's not popular.
2. Personal tragedy or calamity—your good investment may reduce someone else's tragedy or calamity, benefiting you both.
3. A recession—great time to invest.
4. Technical, political, or cultural changes—create opportunities.
5. 20-10-5-year cycles—these are investment cycles that are good indicators.
6. Have a friend in the business—it is a "who you know" world sometimes. Be the first person they call with a new deal.
7. Pay more money. This allows you to tie up the deal (with contingencies and then analyze). Don't haggle.

The next four steps are to analyze the investment found:

1. Know your numbers . . . don't be a guessing gambler . . . do the due diligence.
2. Know the mistakes that lemmings make . . . don't follow the crowd.
3. Be generous . . . rather than greedy.
4. Be creative . . . there are many ways to make a deal.

Then remember the five considerations for each investment and how the investment fits into your overall investing strategy:

1. Earn/create—how will it generate cash flow for you?
2. Manage—how will you manage this investment?
3. Leverage—how much leverage will the investment provide, or can you get?
4. Protect—how should you hold the investment, maximize its profitability, and protect it from potential creditors?
5. Exit—how will you get your original investment moneys back?

Purchase the investment using rich dad's velocity of money investing plan:

1. Invest money into an asset using accelerators.
2. Get the original investment money back (exit strategy).
3. Keep control of the original asset.
4. Move the money into a new asset.
5. Get the investment money back.
6. Repeat the process.

It is the combination of all of these steps that generates true wealth and provides financial control over one's future. For reference, I am also including the chart "Why the Rich Get Richer," which brings it all together.

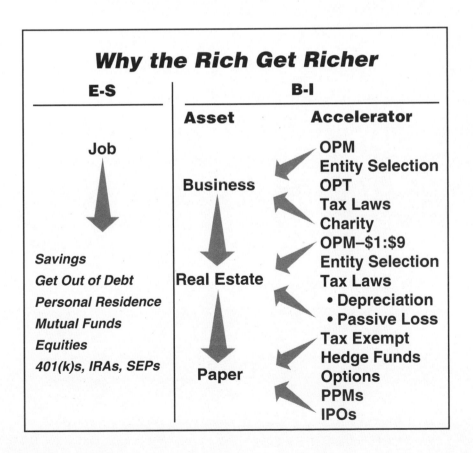

Chapter 14

How to Be a Great Investor

"You need two professions. One for you and one for your money."

—RICH DAD

Finding a Job for Your Money

As we come to the end of this book, you may have picked up my sense of frustration . . . the frustration of repeatedly being asked such questions as,

1. "If you had $10,000, what would you invest it in?"
2. "You recommend real estate, don't you?"
3. "What is the best investment for me?"
4. "How do I get started?"

When I hear such questions, I know these people are actually looking for a place for their money to go to work. That is what investors do.

Out of Work in Three Months

While I was in Washington, D.C., on a book tour, an older man approached me in the parking lot and rather rudely said, "You're the guy that tells peo ple to put their money in real estate, aren't you?"

Being as polite as possible, I replied, "No, I don't tell people where to put their money."

"But you're in real estate, aren't you?" he demanded, tapping my chest with his pencil.

Pushing his pencil away, I replied, "I teach people about investing in businesses, real estate, and paper assets. I invest in all three asset classes. What asset class the people invest in is up to them."

"Look," said the stranger, "I'm retiring in three months and I need to know where to put my money. I don't have any retirement income. I was told you could help me."

"I can help you if you're willing to learn to be an investor," I replied quietly.

"How much will it cost me to become an investor?" he asked.

"That depends on you," I replied. "How much do you have to invest?"

"About $18,000 in the bank and I own a small house and my car. I have no debt," he replied. "That's all I have. My wife left me years ago and she was the one with the steady government job and benefits. I work as an engineer for a small company but the company is not doing well. I like working for the company, but the pay is low and there are no real benefits or guarantees."

Nodding silently, I truly could feel the pain coming from behind his words. His pain reminded me of my poor dad's pain when he continued to look for work, even though past the retirement age. Finally I said, "Well, maybe you shouldn't retire. Why not put that money in the bank and keep working, doing something you enjoy doing."

"I know better," he said. "I've known for years that I need to invest. I can't keep pretending that I can work forever. I know there will come a day when I have to stop working. It frightens me to think of myself, a well-educated man, someday becoming a burden to society because I cannot work and cannot afford to take care of myself. I've always been a hardworking man, but I know my working days will someday come to an end."

There was a long pause between the two of us. As stated earlier in this book, I do get tired of being asked the same questions over and over again. I get tired because I do not have an easy answer that will magically make things better again. Money, investing, and long-term financial security are not subjects with simple answers.

"Can you tell me anything that can help me be a better investor?" asked the man seeking quick answers to his retirement problem.

Thinking for a moment, I asked him, "What is your profession?"

"I am a plant engineer," he replied proudly. "I have twenty-five workers who report to me every day."

"Good," I replied. "What profession is your money in?"

"My . . . money's profession?" he stammered. "I don't know. I just keep my money in the bank."

"Good," I smiled. "So your money's profession is banking."

"I don't understand. What do you mean my money's profession is banking?"

"Because that is where your money is working for you," I replied. "You see, my rich dad taught me to look at my money as my employees. My job as an investor was to find work for my employees. So your 18,000 employees are working for you in the bank. That means they are professional bankers."

"My money is in the banking business?"

"That's correct," I said, nodding. "Their profession is banking because a bank is paying them to work there."

"I never looked at it that way," he replied.

"And how well is the bank treating your employees? Is the bank paying them well?"

"Not well," said the engineer.

"So the bank doesn't pay them well?" I asked with a grin, knowing that he was beginning to catch on to my message.

"No," smiled the engineer, his rough exterior changing. "In fact, the bank used to pay 5 percent and now it pays my 18,000 employees less than 1 percent per year."

"That's not much," I replied. "And what about the benefits?"

"Benefits? What benefits?" he asked.

"Benefits like capital gains, tax benefits, tax-free loans, nontaxable income. Do your employees get benefits like that from your bank?"

"No. The interest I receive is taxed. I don't receive any tax-free benefits," he said, a little puzzled. "Do your employees get those kinds of benefits?"

"Absolutely," I said. "That is why many of my employees work in the business of real estate. The real estate industry treats their employees very well and there are lots of extra benefits."

"What kind of benefits?"

"Benefits like tax-free money to invest with, tax-favored capital gains, phantom cash flow for depreciation, lower taxes due to expenses, insurance against losses, protection from financial predators, and much more. I do have some money in the bank, but not much. Like you, my bank does not treat my employees well."

"And the stock market?" asked the engineer. "How does the stock market treat its employees?"

"The same way most big corporations treat their employees. That is why employees of big corporations often form unions to protect the workers' interests from owners and management. Instead of joining unions, many financial employees belong to mutual funds. Different name, same idea. In either case there is always the struggle between workers and management; pay and benefits. In fact, the corporate management always gets paid but the workers may not get paid if management does not do a good job."

Standing silently for a moment, the engineer was beginning to understand what an investor's job was. "So my job is to find a profession for my money. That is what an investor does. I need to find places were my money is safe, paid well, receives great benefits, and [is] free from abuse and corruption."

A Good Investor Cares

I nodded and smiled. "Just as a parent cares for their children, an investor cares about how well their money and their financial employees are being treated. Most people blindly turn their money over to total strangers who work for big corporations, and have no idea about how their workers are being treated. They park their money. That is why so few people do well as investors. They often let their money be abused, mistreated, and poorly paid. Your job as an investor is to find the right profession for your money . . . *your* employees. Educate yourself, so you can treat your workers with respect, find them great places to work, protect them, make sure they are paid well, and your workers will multiply and work hard for you."

Working for Strangers

It was time for me to go. I had a talk to give and the gentleman in front of me seemed to have his answer. At least he seemed to have a better understanding about what investing is all about. He smiled, extended his hand, and said, "Thank you." Shaking his hand I said, "My rich dad said, 'Give your money to strangers and your money will work for the strangers—before your money works for you.' So be smart, find the best profession for your money, and your money will take care of you. That is what investing is about."

What a Good Investor Cares About

Earlier in this book I wrote that an investor does five things. They are:

5. Exit
4. Protect
3. Leverage
2. Manage
1. Earn/Create

The reason a professional investor does these five steps in planning their investments is because they care about their money—their employees. In professional investing terms, these five steps are similar to a *due diligence* checklist.

When I was training to be a pilot, we were taught the importance of always following checklists. For example, before starting engines we ran through a written checklist. Before landing, we also ran through a written checklist. The same is true for professional investors. For example, before we purchase a new building we always go through a due diligence checklist. The process of going through this checklist has served us well and made us a lot of money over the years. If you are interested in seeing or using the same checklists we use, these can be found in our real estate investor products such as *6 Steps to Becoming a Successful Real Estate Investor* and *How to Increase the Income from Your Real Estate Investments,* which is an in-depth guide to being better at property management, one of the most crucial aspects of real estate investing. You can find out more about these products from our Web site at richdad.com.

What Is Wrong with a Job and a 401(k)?

In my previous books, I have often pointed out the limitations of a job and 401(k). By simply using the five-point checklist it is easy to see why.

1. Earn/Create: Earning income from a job, personal labor, is the highest-taxed way to earn money. As many of you already know, there are three types of income: earned, portfolio, and passive. A professional investor is generally investing for portfolio and passive income, which in most cases is income that is *created,* rather than worked for.

2. Manage: Having a job gives you little to no management control over taxes. Also, workers whose 401(k) invests in stocks or mutual funds have no control over the expenses of these organizations. A professional investor wants to manage taxes and expenses because taxes and expenses affect the return to the investor.

3. Leverage: Investing in a 401(k) offers very little leverage. At most, employees get a 1:1 matching contribution from their employer. A professional investor wants to use OPM, other people's money, rather than their own money.

4. Protect: A 401(k) has very little protection against market losses. At best you can diversify as recommended within the plan. Also, most workers tend to own everything in their own name, which keeps them wide open to personal lawsuits. Professional investors keep much of what they own in the name of a corporate entity, not their own name. They utilize insurance to protect as many of their asset positions as possible.

5. Exit: When a person retires, income from a 401(k) will be taxed at the highest rates possible because income from a 401(k) is classified as earned income. That means that even the capital gains and dividends that would now be taxed at the highest rate of 15 percent, could be taxed at the highest-earned income rate of the individual, now up to 35 percent. This whole structure was based on people being in a lower income tax bracket when they retire. I, for one, expect my income to continue to increase as I build and buy more assets to work for me. A professional investor expects his or her income to continue to grow, even after retirement.

A Warning from a Checklist

A checklist will often warn you if something is wrong with an investment. When people tell me they like their job security and their 401(k) retirement plan filled with mutual funds, I know they have not gone through this simple five-step checklist. Not only are they being financially abused by the tax system and the companies they invest in, their money is not leveraged, not safe, and when they retire, if they have been financially successful, their exit will be abused again by the tax system.

What Investors Do

Regardless of what I invest in, be it a company, real estate, or a paper asset, before I invest, I run through the five-step checklist. For example, before investing in a piece of real estate, I run through the same checklist:

1. Earn/Create: I do not want *earned* income. If I choose a property correctly, it will create *passive* income, plus *phantom* income, which are the lowest-taxed incomes.

2. Manage: I work to reduce my expenses, increase my income, choose when I pay my taxes, and reduce my taxable income. If there are losses, I can use those losses to my advantage.

3. Leverage: Real estate is the easiest of all investments to leverage. Leverage of 80 percent to 90 percent is not uncommon. The tax department offers additional leverage through tax incentives, which are numerous.

4. Protect: I protect my property with different types of insurance. I also protect my property with different corporate entities. I protect my ideas with copyrights, trademarks, and patents. I also protect my property with nonrecourse financing, if I feel the need to be extra cautious. I can also add another layer of protection by setting up a sinking fund, which accumulates extra cash for emergencies.

5. Exit: Rather than sell my property, which would trigger a taxable event, I often exchange my property without paying taxes or I can borrow out the equity tax-free and invest my tax-free borrowed money in whatever I want . . . a new investment property or a boat.

Oversimplified

I realize that this has been an oversimplified example of how this five-step checklist is used. In real life, when following the checklist, there is far more detail with each step. In many ways, though, this five-step checklist could be used as a rough guide for a business plan for any investment. Nothing ever goes exactly as planned, yet this five-step checklist can assist you in quickly evaluating the pros and cons of any investment you may want to put your money, i.e., your *employees*, to work in.

Even though oversimplified, the two checklists outlined here are useful in comparing the pros and cons of a person with a job and 401(k) against a professional investor investing as a business owner in real estate. The lesson is, checklists are used by professional investors, and unfortunately most amateur investors do not use them.

The Best Way to Get Rich

Many people seem to think that investing is simply throwing money at some hot deal and hoping to strike it rich. Or just turning it over to a total stranger and hoping that stranger or that company returns your money to you someday. Obviously that is not investing—it is gambling. But worse than gambling, it demonstrates a lack of respect for something most people have given a part of their life, their sweat, blood, and time for.

Most people do not like working for abusive and cheap people or abusive and cheap companies. Yet when it comes to the money they invest, many people turn their money over to people and companies that seem to care more about their own self-interest than the investors' interests.

Warren Buffett said, "The best way to get rich is to not lose money." One of the best ways to not lose money is to invest a little time making sure the money you invest . . . your personal employees . . . are working in a financially intelligent, high-integrity, well-managed, financially responsible, and safe environment. That is what an investor does. That is what investors such as Warren Buffett do. Warren Buffett treats money, the businesses he invests in, his workers, and his investors with a high degree of personal intelligence, integrity, and respect. That is why his company is so successful. Rich dad said, "People who do not respect money, or abuse the money they earn, are themselves often not respected and [are] financially abused."

Regardless of whether if you invest in businesses, real estate, or paper assets, treat those assets and your money with the same respect you want for yourself. If you will do that, your money and those assets will grow and make your life easier and more abundant. Take care of your money and your assets and they will take care of you.

Sharon's Notes

The accounting profession has identified the following changes in the tax law that must be reviewed to decide if and how you should adjust your overall investment strategy.

In a December 2003 feature article in the AICPA (American Institute of Certified Public Accountants) *Journal of Accountancy*, a CPE (continuing professional education) leader for the accounting profession discussed the impact of the new tax laws on investors with CPA David Lewittes. In their discussion they highlighted several issues:

- About half of the investments in stocks are in retirement accounts.
- Retirement accounts do *not* get the benefit of the reduction in dividend income or capital gains tax rates because any distributions from the retirement accounts will be taxed as ordinary income.
- As such you may want to change your mix of assets in tax-deferred accounts to bonds and short-term capital gains stocks while holding stocks with high-paying dividends and long-term appreciation in the taxable accounts to take advantage of the reduced dividend and capital gains tax rates.
- Because of the reduction in the income tax rates to individuals there is also a reduction in the tax savings of contributions to retirement accounts such as IRAs and 401(k)s.
- Investment leverage through debt may be more attractive.

Investment Plan

You must create the investment plan that is right for you. The following oversimplified review of the three asset classes highlights the pros and cons for your consideration:

1. Business
Pro: Business is the asset that offers the highest of all returns on investment. A business made Bill Gates the richest man in the world.
       The tax laws were written to benefit business owners.
Con: Business is the hardest of all asset classes to own, build, and control.

2. Real Estate

Pro: Real estate is the easiest of all assets to leverage. It is easier to borrow
       money for real estate than for a business or paper assets.
       The tax laws favor real estate investments.

Con: For the little investor, real estate is far more capital-intensive than
       paper assets.
       Real estate is far more management-intensive for the small investor.

3. Paper Assets

Pro: Easiest of all asset classes to get into and out of.

Con: Least financial controls.
       Fewer tax advantages.
       High volatility.

Synergy Versus Diversification

Many people believe diversification is smart. Yet many people are not really diversifying, since they invest only in one asset class. For example, many people think they are diversifying but all of their money is in mutual funds.

Rather than diversifying, rich dad taught us the synergy of our investments by using a combination of asset classes. Through synergy of the asset classes, you can obtain much higher returns on your investments. It is the synergy between a business and real estate that makes Donald Trump so rich. It is the synergy between business and paper assets that makes Warren Buffett so rich.

Chapter 15

Conclusion: Winner or Loser?

When rich dad first showed me the four quarters of the game of money, I was just starting the first quarter and did not have much respect for it. I was twenty-five years old and all I thought about was winning even though I was not certain I could.

25–35	1st Quarter
35–45	2nd Quarter

Halftime

45–55	3rd Quarter
55–65	4th Quarter

Overtime

The Game Goes On

Although I technically won my money game at the end of the second quarter, and Kim won by the end of her first quarter, we both know the game is not over. We all know of people who were winners in one quarter of the game and wound up losers later in the game.

One of the best things to happen to me was to be a loser in the first quarter of my game. The international success of my nylon and Velcro wallet business went straight to my head . . . and success soon turned into arrogance and cockiness. By the time I was thirty, I had achieved financial success and had also lost it all. Being a financial loser early in life taught me a deep respect not just for money but also for the game of money.

The Scores at the End of Three Quarters

Today, as I begin the fourth quarter of my money game, I look back at the first three quarters and my scores look like this:

25–35	Investment income—$0 per month (massive debt)
35–45	Investment income—$10,000 per month

Halftime (took two years off)

45–55	Investment income—$100,000+ per month
55–65	Investment income—(?) (to be determined)

Overtime (?) (to be determined)

The reason I remain cautious, even though I am financially ahead today, is because I know the score of the game can change at any time. That is why I am glad I lost so badly in the first quarter. Losing not only taught me how to win, losing also taught me a deep respect for money and the game of money. I am very aware that just because I am winning today . . . tomorrow, the game can take it all away.

A Personal Concern

My personal concern is that there are millions of people today who are working hard but losing the game. One reason they are losing the game is because many people are simply *avoiding* the game. And if they are in the game, investing their retirement plans, many are not achieving high returns because they are diversified in one asset class, primarily paper assets, which means they lack the synergy between asset classes. Add to that, too many people turn their hard-earned money over to the government in the form of excessive taxes or to total strangers who pay themselves first, and may or may not return their money to them when they need it.

Again, as I do in all my books, I say I think it is time our educational system begin teaching people basic money management including the true differences between *assets* and *liabilities.* Schools should also teach different investment strategies, the different asset classes, and the difference between investing for *cash flow* versus *capital gains.* And last but not least, a strong financial education should teach the basics of the effect of taxes upon earnings. If people knew how much employees pay in taxes and how favorable the tax laws are to business owners, we might have more people starting a business upon leaving school rather than looking for a high-paying job. That is true financial education. Today, schools along with Wall Street are claiming to be teaching kids financial literacy by teaching them to pick stocks. Having Wall Street teaching kids to pick stocks is the same as racetrack owners teaching kids to pick the ponies. Rather than teach kids to be gamblers, it is about time we teach young people about the real game of money, long before they wind up in the fourth quarter of their lives, expecting their families or the government to take care of them.

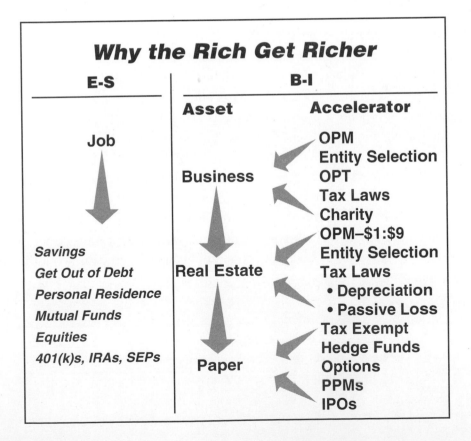

Why the Rich Get Richer

E-S

B-I

Asset   Accelerator

Job

OPM
Entity Selection
OPT

Business

Tax Laws
Charity
OPM–$1:$9
Entity Selection

Savings
Get Out of Debt
Personal Residence
Mutual Funds
Equities
401(k)s, IRAs, SEPs

Real Estate

Tax Laws
• Depreciation
• Passive Loss
Tax Exempt
Hedge Funds
Options
PPMs
IPOs

Paper

Once again, review the preceding chart, which compares the investing strategies of parking versus accelerating your money. Are you ready to take control of your financial future and to start accelerating your money instead of parking it?

The Best Part of Playing the Game

Before ending this book, I want to pass on one bit of wisdom gained from *playing the game* rather than *playing it safe*. The best part of playing the game of money, regardless of whether I was winning or losing, is that I got better at the game. As you can see by the scores from the first three quarters, even though my score was zero at the end of the first quarter, my scores improved after that.

Unfortunately, too many people will ultimately lose the game of money simply because they have spent their lives avoiding losing. Instead of playing to win, too many people have played the game of *playing not to lose.* Again, this is partly caused by an educational system that is not teaching subjects required for survival in the real world.

As I begin the fourth quarter of my money game, rather than being fearful of losing, or having nothing, or expecting the government to take care of me, as many people in the fourth quarter are . . . I am confident—not cocky and excited, but not fearful of the game. As I enter the fourth quarter, I know the game of money is a game I will play for the rest of my life, regardless of the score.

It is not that I cannot lose in the future, because I know that winning and losing are a part of any game. The difference for me as I enter the fourth quarter is that I have learned to enjoy the game. So for those of you who are contemplating taking control of your money and investing it yourself, rather than turning it over to strangers, these are the important points about the game. Remember that:

1. Losing is part of winning.
2. The more you play the better you get.
3. The better you get the better your team gets.
4. The better your team gets the more you enjoy the game.

5. The more you enjoy the game, the better your chances of improving your score.

As rich dad said, "The game of money is not really about money. It is about how well you play the game."

Thank you for reading this book.

Robert T. Kiyosaki
Sharon L. Lechter

About the Authors

Robert Kiyosaki

Born and raised in Hawaii, Robert Kiyosaki is a fourth-generation Japanese-American. After graduating from college in New York, Robert joined the Marine Corps and served in Vietnam as an officer and helicopter gunship pilot. Following the war, Robert worked for the Xerox Corporation in sales. In 1977, he started a company that brought the first nylon Velcro 'surfer wallets' to market. And in 1985 he founded an international education company that taught business and investing to tens of thousands of students throughout the world.

In 1994, Robert sold his business and retired at the age of 47.

During his short-lived retirement, Robert, in collaboration with co-author Sharon Lechter, CPA and business partner, wrote the book *Rich Dad Poor Dad*. Soon after, he wrote *Rich Dad's CASHFLOW Quadrant, Rich Dad's Guide to Investing, Rich Kid Smart Kid, Retire Young Retire Rich, Rich Dad's Prophecy, Rich Dad's Success Stories, Rich Dad's Guide to Becoming Rich Without Cutting Up Your Credit Cards* – all of which earned spots on the bestseller lists of the *Wall Street Journal, Business Week, New York Times,* E-Trade.com, Amazon.com and others.

Prior to becoming a best-selling author, Robert created an educational board game – CASHFLOW 101 – to teach individuals the financial strategies that his Rich Dad spent years teaching him. It was those financial strategies that allowed Robert to retire at the age of 47. The launch of CASHFLOW 101-The E game in the fall of 2003 united the Rich Dad community around the world with an on-line/multi-player game and serves as the foundation for the 2004 introduction of the electronic version CASHFLOW 202.

Complementing the books in the Rich Dad series are books by Rich Dad's Business Team on subjects ranging from corporate entities and sales skills to protecting intellectual property.

In Robert's words: "We go to school to learn to work hard for money. I write books and create products that teach people how to have money work hard for them. Then they can enjoy the luxuries of this great world we live in."

Sharon Lechter

CPA, co-author of the Rich Dad series of books and CEO of the Rich Dad Organization, Sharon Lechter has dedicated her professional efforts to the field of education. She graduated with honors from Florida State University with a degree in accounting, then joined the ranks of Coopers & Lybrand, a Big Eight accounting firm. Sharon held various management positions with computer, insurance, and publishing companies while maintaining her professional credentials as a CPA.

Sharon and husband, Michael Lechter, have been married for over twenty years and are parents to three children, Phillip, Shelly and William. As her children grew, she became actively involved in their education and served in leadership positions in their schools. She became a vocal activist in the areas of mathematics, computers, reading, and writing education.

In 1989, she joined forces with the inventor of the first electronic "talking book" and helped him expand the electronic book industry to a multimillion dollar international market.

Today she remains a pioneer in developing new technologies to bring education into children's lives in ways that are innovative, challenging, and fun. As co-author of the Rich Dad books and CEO of that company, she focuses her efforts in the arena of financial education.

"Our current educational system has not been able to keep pace with the global and technological changes in the world today," Sharon states. "We must teach our young people the skills – both scholastic and financial – that they need to not only survive but to flourish in the world."

A committed philanthropist, Sharon "gives back" to the world communities as both a volunteer and a benefactor. She directs the Foundation for Financial Literacy and is a strong advocate of education and the need for improved financial literacy.

Sharon and Michael were honored by Childhelp USA, a national organization founded to eradicate child abuse in the United States, as recipients of the 2002 "Spirit of the Children" Award. And, in May of 2002, Sharon was named chairman of the board for the Phoenix chapter of Childhelp USA.

As an active member of Women's Presidents Organization, she enjoys networking with other professional women across the country.

Robert Kiyosaki, her business partner and friend, says "Sharon is one of the few natural entrepreneurs I have ever met. My respect for her continues to grow every day that we work together."

Rich Dad's Organization is the collaborative effort of Robert and Kim Kiyosaki and Sharon Lechter, who, in 1996, embarked on a journey that would afford them the opportunity to impact the financial literacy of people everywhere and carry the Rich Dad mission to every corner of the world.

**Robert Kiyosaki's Edumercial
An Educational Commercial**

The Three Incomes

In the world of accounting, there are three different types of income: earned, passive and portfolio. When my real dad said to me, "Go to school, get good grades and find a safe secure job," he was recommending I work for earned income. When my rich dad said, "The rich don't work for money, they have their money work for them," he was talking about passive income and portfolio income. Passive income, in most cases, is derived from real estate investments. Portfolio income is income derived from paper assets, such as stocks, bonds, and mutual funds.

Rich dad used to say, "The key to becoming wealthy is the ability to convert earned income into passive income and/or portfolio income as quickly as possible." He would say, "The taxes are highest on earned income. The least taxed income is passive income. That is another reason why you want your money working hard for you. The government taxes the income you work hard for more than the income your money works hard for."

The Key to Financial Freedom

The key to financial freedom and great wealth is a person's ability or skill to convert earned income into passive income and/or portfolio income. That is the skill that my rich dad spent a lot of time teaching Mike and me. Having that skill is the reason my wife Kim and I are financially free, never needing to work again. We continue to work because we choose to. Today we own a real estate investment company for passive income and participate in private placements and initial public offerings of stock for portfolio income.

Investing to become rich requires a different set of personal skills – skills essential for financial success as well as low-risk and high-investment returns. In other words, knowing how to create assets that buy other assets. The problem is that gaining the basic education and experience required is often time consuming, frightening, and expensive, especially when you make mistakes with your own money. That is why I created the patented education board games trademarked as CASHFLOW®.

Rich Dad Poor Dad

What the rich teach their kids about money that the poor and middle class do not. Learn how to have your money work for you and why you don't need to earn a high income to be rich.

The book that "rocked" the financial world.

J.P. Morgan declares "Rich Dad Poor Dad a must-read for Millionaires."
The Wall Street Journal

"A starting point for anyone looking to gain control of their financial future."
USA Today

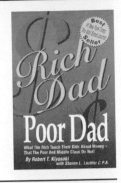

Rich Dad's CASHFLOW Quadrant

Rich Dad's guide to financial freedom. Learn about the four CASHFLOW Quadrants and you will understand the most important keys to creating wealth.

The sequel to Rich Dad Poor Dad, Rich Dad's CASHFLOW Quadrant describes the four types of people who make up the world of business and the core value differences between them. It discusses the tools an individual needs to become a successful business owner and investor.

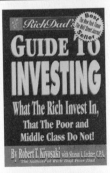

Rich Dad's Guide to Investing

What the rich invest in that the poor and middle class do not. Learn how you can apply the techniques of the rich to create your own wealth and have it grow.

This is the third book in the Rich Dad Series. Rich Dad's Guide to Investing discusses what the rich invest in that the poor and middle class do not. Robert provides an insider's look into the world of investing, how the rich find the best investments, and how you can apply the techniques of the rich to create your own wealth.

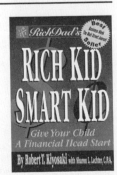

Rich Dad's Rich Kid Smart Kid

Give your child a financial headstart. Awaken your child's love of learning how to be financially free. Imagine the results you'll see when they start early!

This book is written for parents who value education, want to give their child a financial and academic headstart in life, and are willing to take an active role to make it happen. Rich Kid Smart Kid is designed to help you give your child the same inspiring and practical financial knowledge that Robert's rich dad gave him. Learn how to awaken your child's love of learning.

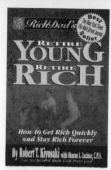

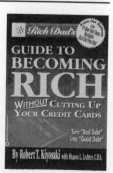

Rich Dad's Who Toook My Money?

Are you tired of the same old advice of "save money, invest for the long term and diversify?" Do you want to learn how and why professional investors increase the speed of their money, rather than park it? With job security at an all time low, it's never been more important to take control of your financial life. Conventional financial wisdom recommends you save money and invest for the long term. In other words, park your money. That was not the advice of rich dad. His advice was to increase the velocity of your money... not park your money. We all know that markets go up and markets go down. So, before the next crash comes along and takes your money again, find out how you can keep your money moving rather than parked in someone else's account.

Apply Your Knowledge with the CASHFLOW® Series of Games

CASHFLOW® 101

CASHFLOW 101 is an educational program that teaches accounting, finance, and investing at the same time...and makes learning fun.

Learn how to get out of the rat race and onto the fast track where your money works for you instead of you working hard for your money. The educational program, CASHFLOW 101, includes three audiocassettes which reveal distinctions on CASHFLOW 101 as well as valuable investment information and a video titled "The Secrets of the Rich."

CASHFLOW 101 is recommended for adults and children age 10 and older.

CASHFLOW® 202

CASHFLOW 202 teaches you the advanced business and investing techniques used by technical investors by adding volatility to the game. It teaches the advanced investment techniques of "short-selling stock," "put-options," "call-options," "straddles" and real estate exchanges.

You must have CASHFLOW 101 in order to play CASHFLOW 202. This package contains new game sheets, new playing cards, and four audiocassettes.

CASHFLOW for KIDS®

Give your children the financial headstart necessary to thrive in today's fast-paced and changing world. Schools teach children how to work for money. CASHFLOW for Kids teaches children how to have money work for them.

CASHFLOW for Kids is a complete educational package which includes the book and audiocassette titled "Rich Dad's Guide to Raising Your Child's Financial I.Q."

CASHFLOW for Kids is recommended for children ages 6 and older.

Please Help Make A Difference

Money is a life skill---but we don't teach our children about money in school. I am asking for your help in getting financial education into the hands of interested teachers and school administrators.

RichKidSmartKid.com was created as an innovative and interactive web site designed to convey key concepts about money and finance in ways that are fun and challenging...and educational for young people in grades K through 12. It contains 4 mini-games that teach:

    Assets vs. Liabilities
    Good debt vs. Bad Debt
    Importance of Charity
    Passive Income vs. Earned Income

AND, schools may also register at www.richkidsmartkid.com to receive a FREE download of our electronic version of CASHFLOW for Kids at School.

How You Can Make a Difference

Play CASHFLOW for KIDs and CASHFLOW 101 with family and friends and share the richkidsmartkid.com web site with your local teachers and school administrators.

Join me now in taking financial education to our schools and e-mail me of your interest at Iwill@richdad.com. Together we can better prepare our children for the financial world they will face.

Thank you!

Sharon L. Lechter

Rich Dad's You Can Choose To Be Rich

This powerful home study course will teach you the three-step plan to riches — Think It. Learn It. Do It. The program contains a Home Study Course Binder, 12 CDs or cassettes with specialized lessons from Robert's personal team of experts, one video that will show you how to stop living from paycheck to paycheck and enjoy the power of having money work for you, one bonus audio tape that reveals the six simple obstacles people face on their path to wealth, and a debt eliminator — a practical tool to help you eliminate bad debt and build a strong foundation.

Rich Dad's 6 Steps to Becoming a Successful Real Estate Investor

This product will show you how to use other people's money to build secure passive income while you build a huge net worth. You'll find that anyone can be a real estate investor — young or old, man or woman, rich or poor. Learn the secrets now from Robert and Kim Kiyosaki in Rich Dad's 6 Steps to Becoming a Successful Real Estate Investor. This program contains a 104-page workbook, five audio-cassettes or compact discs, or two videocassettes or one DVD, and more!

How To Increase The Income from Your Real Estate Investments — The Secrets of Professional Property Managers

Learn the hands-on trade secrets to successfully managing any type of investment property. There are many simple and effective tips and techniques you can begin using today with How To Increase The Income from Your Real Estate Investments. Whether you're just starting out or have years of experience — the information on this program will save you hundreds or thousands of dollars. This program includes four CDs or four cassettes, a workbook with sample documents and forms to assist you in day-to-day management of your properties.

What Others Are Saying About Rich Dad...

"Because of Rich Dad, I've learned that wealth is all around us. It's accessible and attainable. You can read books, you can seek advice…but playing the CASHFLOW game put things into perspective for me. It awakened the concept of becoming wealthy, of how rich people think, and what they do. This makes me want to continue my financial education to make a better life for my family."

— Roshiem A., Arizona

"Our children, Madeline (4 years old) and Makenzie (3 years old), absolutely love the interactive programs from Rich Dad. Madeline is already gaining real knowledge regarding investment and money matters through "Rich Kid, Smart Kid," which I find to be amazing at her age. It also provides a forum for me, as a parent, to begin discussing and teaching some of these concepts to my small children – something I probably would not do at this stage if it were not for your program."

— Jon F., Arizona

"The concepts taught by Robert Kiyosaki and the Rich Dad Team have had a major impact on our lives and our business. As tax and business consultants, the ways we serve our clients have changed and improved considerably. Everyone in our office now thinks in terms of "doodads" and cash flow and getting out of the Rat Race on a daily basis."

"One of the greatest impacts on our clients has been the CASHFLOW 101 game. For years, we have been looking for ways to instruct clients on accounting principals and tax strategies. CASHFLOW 101 is a terrific instructional tool for these concepts, as well as general investing and financial management. We play CASHFLOW 101 with clients and friends of the firm every month. These game nights give our clients the opportunity to broaden their perspective on money and investing, while allowing us to help them understand basic accounting principals, money management, and tax strategies."

"Thank you for creating a marvelous teaching tool in CASHFLOW 101 and helping us change the way we look at finances for ourselves and for our clients."

— Tom W. and Ann M., Arizona

"I was a project manager/engineer and had worked my way up the corporate ladder for 20 years. I was finally making good money only to find that I was getting killed on taxes. On top of that, I could not picture myself working 9-to-5 for another 30 years."

"After reading Rich Dad's Guide to Investing, it dawned on me that I was directing an engineering team at work. So why not orchestrate my own real estate investment team? My team of advisors now consists of two lawyers, an accountant, two real estate brokers, an insurance agent, three mortgage brokers, a home inspector and – one of the strongest players on the team – my wife and partner, Connie. Life's too short to shortchange yourself."

— Larry N., Mass.

What Others Are Saying About Rich Dad...

"A friend of mine introduced me to the Rich Dad books a few years ago, and I introduced them to my Dad, a farmer who was just beginning to invest in real estate. My Dad and I then gave books and tapes to my sisters...and the family was hooked!"

"We recently closed on four townhouses (a "deal" my Dad found by being open to opportunities...) and know we never would have been thinking about cash flow and passive income if we hadn't read the Rich Dad books. We all financed our properties differently and our returns on investment vary – but we're all moving in the right direction."

"It is so exciting to constantly stretch and change the way we think about money."

– Sally D., California

"Thanks to Rich Dad I have the courage and confidence to tackle life's Big Deal cards – and create true financial freedom."

– Cindy O., Texas

"We were realtors focused only on earning our commissions. And when we first heard of the book Rich Dad Poor Dad – from a "recommended reading" list given to us by our business coach – we realized that we were SELLING all the best deals...instead of capturing them for ourselves!"

"Thanks to Rich Dad we began to focus on the cash flow of our properties (instead of commissions) and ways in which we could leverage those properties to acquire more. Traveling the road to financial freedom has been an enlightening ride!"

– Curtis and Diana O., California

"A year ago I was drowning in bad debt and considering bankruptcy. I was frustrated and angry. My financial state of affairs — my financial ignorance — nearly cost me my family, my business, and my self respect."

"Rich Dad Poor Dad had such a powerful impact on me that I've bought a dozen copies and gave them to my staff, my friends, and my college-age children. As a business owner, Rich Dad's Cashflow Quadrant helped me understand the BI Triangle and taught me to create and implement systems that strengthen my business."

"My Money IQ is rising everyday and I can say, honestly, that the Rich Dad messages have saved me from financial ruin."

– Dr. Randy R., Ohio

What Others Are Saying About Rich Dad...

"My daughter, age 12, has been keenly interested in our pursuit of financial education as we read the Rich Dad series and play CASHFLOW 101. (She has played CASHFLOW with us and read Rich Kid Smart Kid.)"

"She often tells us of her future plans and one day we were outside gardening when she told me that when she owns investment properties she will also own a landscaping business so that she can care for the exteriors of her properties in a more cost efficient way! Her plan for the future now is to have her money work for her – through proper investing. We don't doubt it for a minute!"

– Kris P., Pennsylvania

"Three of my brothers – like me – are on fire with the Rich Dad materials! We have digested the messages and are moving full speed ahead with our lives with a deeply-renewed hope and passion! My brother (Joe) now calls himself 'Joe Freedom!'"

– Dan M.

"Robert Kiyosaki is blowing my mind away! I'm half way through the Cashflow Quadrant. I can't read enough! I have a whole new attitude – toward everything."

"I've been aware for a while that I knew damn little about money. I have been making myself read the business section of the Sunday paper for about a year and getting nowhere. I read Robert Kiyosaki's book in three days and I can see land! I love the direction and the hopeful feeling I am experiencing."

– Joe Freedom , (aka Joe M...brother of Dan M)

"I did everything my parents told me to do: get good grades, get a scholarship to pay for college, get a good job and be stable, stay at the same job…"

"My husband and I are now in our early forties, and more in debt and struggling financially than when we were in our twenties. Our eldest son is now a senior in high school, getting ready to go to college, and I don't want him to go down the same path that his parents did. My heart is heavy because I want the best for my family."

"I'm ready for another way, another path, another voice to guide me. My Rich Dad, Robert Kiyosaki, is that voice. I want to thank my Rich Dad for being there on that shelf, for lifting me out of the hopelessness I didn't realize I was living in, and for shining light on a better path for others, like me, to follow."

– Tia L., Hawaii

What Others Are Saying About Rich Dad...

"A huge thanks to Robert for helping me shift my context. It has made a huge change in how I view the world. I have been reading your materials, listening to audios, and playing your CASHFLOW games for over a year now. It has helped me grow my financial literacy so much that my husband and I have begun investing in real estate. We just purchased our first property!"

– Valerie P., Canada

"The Rich Dad books have been a life-changing experience for me. Robert has given me the faith and courage to follow my convictions and prepare my plan for financial freedom. The Rich Dad books have given me the courage to take the steps to financial freedom."

"I have purchased two properties apart from my residence and while it's tempting to repay my mortgages, I intend to leverage the equity from these properties to invest in others."

– Kay G., United Kingdom

"Thanks to inspiration from Robert and Sharon, our lives will be different from 99% of the population."

"You have been our guiding light in our quest for financial freedom. Playing the CASHFLOW game has taught me more about business than business school did! You are making a huge difference in this world of financial illiteracy and chaos."

– Merced, Jon, and Jeff H., Utah

What Students and Teachers Are Saying About CASHFLOW for Kids

"They can learn more in an hour of playing Cashflow for Kids than 10 hours of homework."

– Pam L. - Principal, Oklahoma

"I feel sorry for my mom, because (credit card debt) is hard to get out of and easy to get in."

– Carrie S. – 6th grader, Oklahoma

"One teacher asked the kids, 'If money was no object, what would you buy?' At the beginning of the day they wanted a car and by the end of the day they wanted a candy bar factory or other things to make money with."

– Michelle H., Scottsdale